1 & 2 THESSALONIANS

BELIEF

*A Theological Commentary
on the Bible*

GENERAL EDITORS

*Amy Plantinga Pauw
William C. Placher†*

1 & 2
THESSALONIANS

MOLLY T. MARSHALL

WJK WESTMINSTER
JOHN KNOX PRESS
LOUISVILLE • KENTUCKY

First edition
Published by Westminster John Knox Press
Louisville, Kentucky

22 23 24 25 26 27 28 29 30 31—10 9 8 7 6 5 4 3 2 1

Book design by Drew Stevens
Cover design by Lisa Buckley
Cover art: © David Chapman/Design Pics/Corbis

Library of Congress Cataloging-in-Publication Data
Names: Marshall, Molly Truman, author.
Title: 1 & 2 Thessalonians / Molly T. Marshall.
Other titles: 1 and 2 Thessalonians | First and Second Thessalonians
Description: First edition. | Louisville, Kentucky : Westminster John Knox Press, 2022. | Series: Belief: a theological commentary on the Bible | Includes bibliographical references and index.
Identifiers: LCCN 2022021727 (print) | LCCN 2022021726 (ebook) | ISBN 9780664232603 | ISBN 9781646982578 (ebook) | ISBN 9781646982578q(ebook)
Subjects: LCSH: Bible. Thessalonians--Commentaries.
Classification: LCC BS2725.53 .M37 2022 (ebook) | LCC BS2725.53 (print) | DDC 227/.8107 23/eng/20220--dc15
LC record available at https://loc.gov/2022021727
LC ebook record available at https://loc.gov/2022021726

Most Westminster John Knox Press books are available at special quantity discounts when purchased in bulk by corporations, organizations, and special-interest groups. For more information, please e-mail SpecialSales@wjkbooks.com.

Contents

Publisher's Note

William C. Placher worked with Amy Plantinga Pauw as a general editor for this series until his untimely death in November 2008. Bill brought great energy and vision to the series and was instrumental in defining and articulating its distinctive approach and in securing theologians to write for it. Bill's own commentary for the series was the last thing he wrote, and Westminster John Knox Press dedicates the entire series to his memory with affection and gratitude.

William C. Placher, LaFollette Distinguished Professor in Humanities at Wabash College, spent thirty-four years as one of Wabash College's most popular teachers. A summa cum laude graduate of Wabash in 1970, he earned his master's degree in philosophy in 1974 and his PhD in 1975, both from Yale University. In 2002 the American Academy of Religion honored him with the Excellence in Teaching Award. Placher was also the author of thirteen books, including *A History of Christian Theology*, *The Triune God*, *The Domestication of Transcendence*, *Jesus the Savior*, *Narratives of a Vulnerable God*, and *Unapologetic Theology*. He also edited the volume *Essentials of Christian Theology*, which was named as one of 2004's most outstanding books by both *The Christian Century* and *Christianity Today* magazines.

Series Introduction

Belief: A Theological Commentary on the Bible is a series from Westminster John Knox Press featuring biblical commentaries written by theologians. The writers of this series share Karl Barth's concern that, insofar as their usefulness to pastors goes, most modern commentaries are "no commentary at all, but merely the first step toward a commentary." Historical-critical approaches to Scripture rule out some readings and commend others, but such methods only begin to help theological reflection and the preaching of the Word. By themselves, they do not convey the powerful sense of God's merciful presence that calls Christians to repentance and praise; they do not bring the church fully forward in the life of discipleship. It is to such tasks that theologians are called.

For several generations, however, professional theologians in North America and Europe have not been writing commentaries on the Christian Scriptures. The specialization of professional disciplines and the expectations of theological academies about the kind of writing that theologians should do, as well as many of the directions in which contemporary theology itself has gone, have contributed to this dearth of theological commentaries. This is a relatively new phenomenon; until the last century or two, the church's great theologians also routinely saw themselves as biblical interpreters. The gap between the fields is a loss for both the church and the discipline of theology itself. By inviting forty contemporary theologians to wrestle deeply with particular texts of Scripture, the editors of this series hope not only to provide new theological resources for the church, but also to encourage all theologians to pay more attention to Scripture and the life of the church in their writings.

We are grateful to the Louisville Institute, which provided funding for a consultation in June 2007. We invited theologians, pastors, and biblical scholars to join us in a conversation about what this series could contribute to the life of the church. The time was provocative and the results were rich. Much of the series' shape owes to the insights of these skilled and faithful interpreters, who sought to describe a way to write a commentary that served the theological needs of the church and its pastors with relevance, historical accuracy, and theological depth. The passion of these participants guided us in creating this series and lives on in the volumes.

As theologians, the authors will be interested much less in the matters of form, authorship, historical setting, social context, and philology—the very issues that are often of primary concern to critical biblical scholars. Instead, this series' authors will seek to explain the theological importance of the texts for the church today, using biblical scholarship as needed for such explication but without any attempt to cover all of the topics of the usual modern biblical commentary. This thirty-six-volume series will provide passage-by-passage commentary on all the books of the Protestant biblical canon, with more extensive attention given to passages of particular theological significance.

The authors' chief dialogue will be with the church's creeds, practices, and hymns; with the history of faithful interpretation and use of the Scriptures; with the categories and concepts of theology; and with contemporary culture in both "high" and popular forms. Each volume will begin with a discussion of *why* the church needs this book and why we need it *now*, in order to ground all of the commentary in contemporary relevance. Throughout each volume, text boxes will highlight the voices of ancient and modern interpreters from the global communities of faith, and occasional essays will allow deeper reflection on the key theological concepts of these biblical books.

The authors of this commentary series are theologians of the church who embrace a variety of confessional and theological perspectives. The group of authors assembled for this series represents more diversity of race, ethnicity, and gender than any other commentary series. They approach the larger Christian tradition with a critical respect, seeking to reclaim its riches and at the same time to acknowledge its shortcomings. The authors also aim to make available to readers a wide range of contemporary theological voices from many parts of the world. While it does recover an older genre of writing, this series is not an attempt to retrieve some idealized past. These commentaries have learned from tradition, but they are most importantly commentaries for today. The authors share the conviction that their work will be more contemporary, more faithful, and more radical, to the extent that it is more biblical, honestly wrestling with the texts of the Scriptures.

William C. Placher
Amy Plantinga Pauw

Preface

While writing is a solitary process, it involves many conversation partners to prompt deeper reflection. Other commentary writers have served as helpful interlocutors, as their prior studies offer insight and fruitful scholarly pathways. While I trust that my own voice will sound through, I have consulted with New Testament specialists to enrich my theological insight. I have depended primarily on the thoughtful works of Linda McKinnish Bridges, F. F. Bruce, Gordon Fee, Cain Hope Felder, Andy Johnson, Abraham Malherbe, I. Howard Marshall, Beverly Roberts Gaventa, and Ben Witherington III. While some of these are more given to exegesis, sociocultural issues, and rhetorical criticism than my theologically focused contribution, each has informed my treatment of the Thessalonian correspondence. I am grateful for their attention to these early Christian epistles; their scholarship has inspired my own addition to the conversation.

Inspiration has also come from other writers in the Belief series. It is good to see a major project that is once again trusting theologians with the Bible, and the editors have gathered quite the array of authors. The volumes written by distinguished and diverse scholars who work in doctrinal, historical, biblical, systematic, constructive, practical, liturgical, and moral theology—to name a few of the specializations that fall under the aegis of theology—serve both academy and church through their theological commentary. Each volume in some way moves beyond the strict boundary of the assigned text and engages larger questions of value at the intersection of biblical and theological studies. It is because of gender, ethnic, and denominational diversity that this creative undertaking can offer new perceptions of historic creeds, earlier classics, catechetical processes, and the worship life of the church. The background or experience of these writers gives voice to minority perspectives and makes for a larger conversation, a sorely needed corrective.

One cannot do theological work without extended engagement with Holy Scripture; it is a privilege, indeed a responsibility, for a theologian of the church to offer theological commentary on Scripture. Cultivating a disposition that allows both a "hermeneutics of suspicion" and a "hermeneutics of consent" creates the proper tension for a contemporary interpreter to work with an ancient text. Such a process both vexes and promotes the task of coherent interpretation. The "surplus of meaning" (*sensus plenior*) the Bible extends to its reader awakens imagination for relevant application in a far different context than the original recipients. The Christian canon continues to guide faith and practice, for which we remain grateful. Even when its worldview seems off-putting, as it does in the Thessalonian correspondence, the church remains committed to listening to its perspective on the ways of God.

As I sat at my desk each morning to begin the writing for the day, I asked the Holy Spirit for the inspiration to understand what prompted the writing of 1 and 2 Thessalonians in the first place, believing that the Spirit who inspired these texts might inspire this author to study them well. I have been inspired anew by the early apostolic witness amid the welter of first-century challenges. Adversaries to the proclamation of the risen Christ seemed only to assure those of the Pauline tradition that they were actually on the right track as they engaged their context with wisdom. Their relentless travel, proclamation, church planting, and tending of fledgling communities provide a template for how the gospel can take root in a culture. I have not treated Paul or his colleagues as solitary figures; they were as dependent on communities of faith as we are today to sustain faithful commitment.

The Bible does not narrate the lives of perfect persons; rather, it reveals the grace of God who in humility deigns to work through such flawed human instruments. As one reads the Word of God that comes to us through Scripture, we realize the gap between what we profess and what we live. The call to live more faithfully resounds through the early Christian witness inscribed in texts and speaks in our time. Writing a theological commentary is an exercise in spiritual formation, which always calls to repentance and renewal. As we admire and give thanks for our forebears in faith, we are reminded that future generations depend on our own pursuit of fidelity as stewards of the mysteries (1 Cor. 4:1).

I am grateful to Central Baptist Theological Seminary for this sabbatical season in which to write after completing my service as president and professor of theology and spiritual formation in the spring of 2020. The Shumaker Library has provided useful resources to assist in this work, for which I am indebted. Both the librarian, Vance Thomas, and circulation assistant, Linda Kiesling, have been supportive, especially by letting me check out books for very long periods of time and renewing them over and over. Hopefully no one else in the seminary community was working on the Thessalonian epistles during this time of my research and writing.

Patient colleagues have listened to my shifting opinions about these letters, and their questions have sharpened my writing. I am particularly grateful for early conversations with Linda McKinnish Bridges and Phil Love, good feedback from editors Amy Plantinga Pauw and Don McKim, thoughtful early reading by Mark Medley and especially Clarissa Strickland (who has also provided significant editorial and formatting assistance), and the ongoing conversation with my inner circle whose names are known to God and to each other. One of them, a retired professor, has suggested that she will organize a *viva*, an oral exam customarily conducted at the end of doctoral studies, that will call me to account for my theological conclusions. Knowing her, it will be thorough. These friends have sustained me in this time of monastic solitude to bring this commentary to completion. They have valued this labor of love on my part and continue to show interest (without too much eye-rolling) in what I have been discovering about the Thessalonian Epistles. I also want to thank the WiTS (Women in Theological Schools), a colloquy of colleagues and friends, Cynthia Briggs Kittredge, Carol Lytch, Dena Pence, Lallene Rector, and Melissa Wiginton, who have walked with me as I pursued this writing but more importantly who have infused my life with encouragement and love for over a decade. This living cloud of witnesses has accompanied this project from beginning to end, and I could not have accomplished it alone.

This commentary is dedicated to generations of colleagues and students with whom I have shared a theological journey in faith, hope, and love. My own teachers have left their graceful imprint on my life; my pastors over the years have affirmed my vocation as a teacher for the church; international colleagues have interrogated my North American myopia; and my students, often my best teachers, have questioned how I have dealt with Christian traditions, challenging me with their global and liberatory insights. It has been a joyful task to journey with them toward their vocational horizons over these forty years in theological education.

I am grateful to be a part of the Belief series. Some of the theological minds I most admire have already written their volumes. It is good to be in their company.

Introduction
Why Thessalonians? Why Now?

Does the world really need another commentary on Thessalonians? What do these ancient texts have to offer now? Those questions have been an ongoing consideration as I undertake this task. Commentaries are written in specific seasons, and even if the author is not explicit about her context and epoch, somehow the reader understands for whom it is written and the season it engages. Ours is a season of liminality, and I will examine these early Christian documents in light of today's groaning challenges.

The brief letters to the Thessalonians are fraught with tension. Why should we work hard if Jesus is coming back any day now and the world is about to end? Tension surrounds the delay of the Parousia and the question of how to live in the meantime. Is it really worth alienating my family and community of origin, not to mention regnant powers of the empire, to be a part of the Jesus movement? Tension about belonging abounds. Can we really trust the apostolic witness when so much chaos accompanies their proclamation? Tension arises as Paul and Silas (Silvanus) and Timothy do their evangelistic work in Thessalonica.

The apostle Paul had a daunting task: to integrate his learning and practice as an observant Jew with the life-altering encounter with the risen Christ. Already zealous for the traditions of the law, his new commission required reorientation of his theological vision, extensive travel, hermeneutical agility, cross-cultural communication, and the sheer stamina of making a living as a tentmaker while giving himself to preaching and teaching the gospel in widely scattered cities in the first-century Mediterranean world. And on the move he was!

In light of the resurrection of Christ, Paul set about to form communities that would live according to the patterns revealed in the way of Jesus, by the power of the Spirit. God had reset the hopes of all people through overcoming death through Jesus' self-giving life. Paul's great mission was to invite both Jews and Gentiles to adopt a new self-understanding characterized by faith, love, and hope. This order of key Pauline virtues is unique in this earliest extant correspondence, as the apostles knew the need to accent hope. That they might become a unified expression of Christ's body was a consuming claim on Paul's life, as the chief New Testament architect of both the Jesus movement and the ongoing relevance of his Jewish kin. We cannot imagine the sustaining of Christianity through the centuries without this visionary theologian and missionary.

Luke's writing gives a sense of the geographical scope of Paul's ministry, and the Epistles give specificity to the particular theological issues he was engaging in varied communities. While Paul is the key figure in Acts from chapter 9 on, he was not the solitary figure who pursued his mission alone. The apostolic witness is much wider than what is chronicled in the Epistles and Acts, as churches were strategically planted in key cities in scattered Roman provinces, from which the knowledge of Christ might emanate. Without companions the evangelization of the Roman Empire would have foundered.[1] Ministry is not about heroic individuals but about forming thick bonds of love and friendship that can sustain gospel work. Like these early Christian communities, it is the only way congregations can make their way forward today as they become the gospel together.[2] In a time when faithful Christian witness is ever harder to demonstrate, we need friends to walk the pathway with us. We cannot be countercultural without a sustaining community.

---

1. See E. Glenn Hinson, *The Evangelization of the Roman Empire: Identity and Adaptability* (Macon, GA: Mercer University Press, 1981). Hinson stresses how Paul recognized the "operation of the Spirit through *many* persons . . ." (35).
2. See Michael J. Gorman, *Becoming the Gospel: Paul, Participation, and Mission* (Grand Rapids: Eerdmans, 2015), 75.

The Mission to the Thessalonians

Acts 17 provides the main source for a chronology of the apostolic mission to the Thessalonians; the information in the Epistles themselves is rather spare and retrospective. Caution is in order when making Acts the primary interpretive lens for the Epistles.[3] Traveling a major trade route from Philippi in the west, which took them through Amphipolis and Apollonia to Thessalonica (approximately one hundred miles), Paul and Silas began a ministry by preaching at the local synagogue in a significant "free city" (self-governed) of the Roman Empire.

Actually, the language denotes that he "argued with them from the scriptures, explaining and proving that it was necessary for the Christ to suffer and to rise from the dead"(17:2–3). Although Acts recounts that they were there for three Sabbaths, that is most likely not the extent of their time in Thessalonica, as the strength of the community formed there suggests a longer sojourn. When we get into the commentary proper, we will see the depth of friendship that was even construed as familial ties forged by Paul, Silas, and Timothy.[4]

It was customary for these messengers to begin with Sabbath participation if possible; but their preaching was not confined to an established synagogue. Acts narrates many other places of Pauline witness: varied Gentile settings (14:27; 15:12); a place of prayer by the river (Acts 16:13); the marketplace (*agora*) (17:17); the Areopagus, center of Athenian worship (17:22); the Sanhedrin, the Jewish council (23:1); Roman appellate court (21:33); aboard ship (27:23); to name only a few.

Paul and Silas came to Thessalonica after a brutal time in Philippi, the first Christian incursion into Europe. You recall Paul's vision of the Macedonian imploring him and his companions, "Come over to Macedonia and help us" (Acts 16:9). What began as a generative mission with Lydia (Acts 16:13–15)—perhaps the figure in

3. So argues Earl Richard, "Early Pauline Thought: An Analysis of 1 Thessalonians," in *Pauline Theology, Volume I: Thessalonians, Philippians, Galatians, Philemon*, ed. Jouette M. Bassler (Minneapolis: Fortress, 1991), 40.

4. Bruce J. Malina and John J. Pilch refer to this language as "fictive kin Jesus groups" in *Social Science Commentary on the Letters of Paul* (Minneapolis: Fortress, 2006), 9.

Paul's vision of Macedonia was after all a woman—and her band of devout God-fearers became a public outcry against the apostles' witness when they exorcized the slave girl with a spirit of divinization (16:16–18). Because she was a source of money to those who controlled her, the authorities, following the bidding of her owners, subjected Paul and Silas to public humiliation by stripping them of their clothing, beating them, and then casting them into prison.[5]

Praying and singing hymns at midnight, an earthquake, doors and shackles thrown open, the conversion of the jailer and his household were events surrounding the story of the apostolic prison break that are well-known. The prisoners did not flee, however. Paul and Silas invoked their Roman citizenship, demanding that their release be a public apology by the officials, who then escorted them from jail personally. Departing jail, they headed to the new community of believers housed in Lydia's home. Lydia was brave enough to harbor the so-called felons after the magistrates, who were now firmly convinced that messing with these messengers was unwise, had released them.[6] They were only too glad to see them on their way out of Philippi!

Paul and Silas then made the journey to Thessalonica. This visit also created quite a stir, no doubt because of the startling message about Jesus as the Messiah. Some believed, among them devout Greeks "and not a few of the leading women" (17:4b). This may reflect Luke's own class bias about who really belonged in the new faith community. It also reminds us of the significant role women played in early Christianity, a fact too often ignored in commentaries and histories. Only recently has this oversight begun to be remediated, primarily through the work of women scholars. Luke recounts the response of jealous Jews who kindled mob violence, which triggered a "city in an uproar" (17:5b). This would not be the only time Paul's life was in danger because of his determination to make the gospel known throughout the empire.

5. See Willie James Jennings's insightful reflection on the prison sequence in his volume in this series, *Acts*, Belief: A Theological Commentary on the Bible (Louisville, KY: Westminster John Knox Press, 2017), 164.

6. The pattern of house churches headed by women is prominent in Philippi. Not only does Lydia have a founding role in her city, we read later of Euodia and Syntyche, also leaders of house churches among the Philippian Christians (Phil. 4:2).

Jason, a leader in the Jesus movement in his city, had been host-ing the apostolic vanguard; so he and other believers were dragged before the "politarchs," a Macedonian title for city authorities.[7] His Christian hospitality was repaid with allegations of fomenting dis-sension against the monarchal claim of the emperor to be the only king. Like a faithful disciple, he took his share of suffering. The proc-lamation of Paul and his companions stressed that Jesus was the true ruler, God's approved sovereign authority. The contest between the risen Christ and Caesar will unfold throughout the early centuries of Christianity.[8] It will be the source of much suffering and persecu-tion, and Christ's challenge to the empire was virulent. The visita-tion to Thessalonica ended with these words: "The people and the city officials were disturbed when they heard this, and after they had taken bail from Jason and the others, they let them go. That very night the believers sent Paul and Silas off to Beroea . . ." (Acts 17:8–10 NRSV). Clearly, the townspeople and the apostolic team under-stood afresh how destabilizing their message of a new reign could be.

After this visit of perhaps a few months to Thessalonica, Paul became anxious about how the gathering of Jesus followers was far-ing, and consequently he sent Timothy, most likely from Athens, to visit and bring a report about how the fledgling Christian com-munity was managing in its hostile context. It was after the positive word from his ministry colleague that Paul wrote the novice believ-ers there to encourage their perseverance. Remembering his own difficulties in the city, he wanted to reassure those who were remain-ing steadfast in their faith, albeit with many adversaries. The loving regard he showered on the Thessalonians is unparalleled in his other correspondence. As the initial recorded congregation, first fruit of the apostolic mission, they held a position of high regard, especially as a test case for Paul's strategy of cultivating differentiated Christian communities.

---

7. At this time in the first century, Thessalonica is a part of Macedonia.
8. There is a profound tension in how to interpret Acts: Is Luke narrating a collision with Greco-Roman culture, or is he minimizing the threat of direct competition with the Roman government? See C. Kavin Rowe, *World Upside Down: Reading Acts in the Graeco-Roman Age* (Oxford: Oxford University Press, 2009) for a highly nuanced assessment of this nexus.

Who Received This Letter?

A letter held a prominent place in the first century. It stood in the place of the actual presence of its author, and it had a significant rhetorical and instructional role for the receivers. The author meant for it to be read aloud and even performed, as the community gathered, because some would be illiterate. The repetition of phrases would make committing much of it to memory possible. While not yet given canonical status, these epistles to the Thessalonian congregation would circulate among the believers and reinforce earlier proclamation from the apostles. Its early provenance, arguably the first letters of Paul, offered a portal for understanding the contextual challenges of bearing witness to Jesus Christ, who threatened the structures of the Roman Empire.[9] Crucified at the hands of the empire, he now reigns with God and empowers followers to turn the world upside down.

Letters could be of varied genres.[10] In the Thessalonian correspondence, two primary literary conventions are on display. The hortatory approach seeks to persuade the recipients to continue to live a certain way; this is also called *paraenesis*, encouragement toward an ethical lifestyle. The second approach, called *protrepsis*, urges "the addressee to change . . . life-orientation."[11] Encouragement and affirmation are the primary themes; these precede further instruction about how to live in a liminal time. More simply, some suggest that these are letters of friendship.

My professor friend, E. Frank Tupper of blessed memory, said his method of teaching was a "hermeneutic of friendship." His care for students allowed them to hear his theological wisdom in a context of mutual regard. Such is the case with this communication from those who planted the church in Thessalonica; and the loving words from

---

9. I will argue later that 2 Thessalonians most likely comes from the hand of a pseudonymous author, as the language and theological vision are markedly different than the first epistle.

10. Paul's letters reflect the rhetorical conventions of his day. For an overview of the varied approaches, see Abraham J. Malherbe, *Ancient Epistolary Theorists* (Atlanta: Scholars Press, 1988).

11. Mark Harding, *Early Christian Life and Thought in Social Context: A Reader* (London: T&T Clark International, 2003), 114.

Paul, the primary author, elucidate what bonds the apostolic team sought to create.

The Significance of Thessalonica

Thessalonica was the home of diasporic Jews, Gentile artisans and commercial entrepreneurs, learned philosophers and sophists, devotees of the imperial cult, and a considerable number of enslaved people. As a port city on a major Roman highway, it was a cosmopolitan place and a strategic location for birthing a Christian community.

Founded early fourth century BCE, Thessalonica was both a significant Roman city, capital of Macedonia, as well as a thoroughly Hellenized cosmopolitan center. According to the Greek historian Strabo, Cassander, king of Macedon, named the city after his wife Thessalonice, the half-sister of Alexander the Great.[12] Thessalonica was a major crossroads, which contributed to its commercial success. The Egnatian Way, the main thoroughfare between East and West, came through the city, linking Byzantium to the east with the western Adriatic ports. Because it was a free city rather than a Roman colony, certain pursuits were permissible. Thessalonica was where the ambitious came and where, with some success, they would remain for its many emerging opportunities.

Boasting one of the finest harbors in the Aegean, it teemed with sailors, artisans, traders, educated orators, and philosophers, both Jew and Gentile, who were mobile in their pursuits. The testimony of Acts 17 suggests a Jewish presence as early as the first century, which is not surprising given the widespread dispersal, even prior to the Diaspora, following the destruction of the temple in 70 CE.

Religious affections went beyond the imperial cult, as many other deities of Egyptian, Greek, and Phrygian origin were venerated. Like many swarming multicultural cities today, Thessalonica provided a context for lively competition among religious adherents. The close alignment between state and cult meant that some

---

12. See Gordon D. Fee, *The First and Second Letters to the Thessalonians* (Grand Rapids: Eerdmans, 2009), 5, and Abraham J. Malherbe, *The Letters to the Thessalonians,* Anchor Bible (New York: Doubleday, 2000), 14, for this background information.

options were more dangerous to pursue, and the weightiest theological question: Who is God? was contested, as two "lords" were on the scene now that Jesus is proclaimed as the risen Christ. We will engage this question at length, especially as "two comings" will arise in 2 Thessalonians.

Because of his own suffering for bearing witness to the grace he had come to know through Christ Jesus, Paul and his companions rightly assumed that the Thessalonians would also face persecution. To become followers of Jesus, they would have to renounce their affiliation with the imperial cult, which would put them at odds with the larger ethos. Although he never explicitly names the imperial cult, it suffused the varied contexts Paul sought to evangelize. Around 49–51 CE Paul wrote to offer encouragement and clarification of earlier instruction. His fear that they might abandon the gospel was allayed by Timothy's good report of their perseverance in faith (*pistis*), which entailed ethical probity and the pursuit of righteousness.

> **The Thessalonians were hardly impoverished when it came to religious options.**
>
> Beverly Roberts Gaventa, *First and Second Thessalonians*, Interpretation: A Bible Commentary for Teaching and Preaching (Louisville, KY: John Knox, 1998), 3.

The supply of the Spirit, the transforming indwelling presence of God, was doing its work among them. While there might be ongoing concerns about ethical expectations and eschatological hopes, the new converts had managed to create a community that expressed tangibly the body of Christ as a demonstration of resurrection life. They were living in a commendable way that put them at odds with the major sacramentals of their culture. And they had given up much to do so. The apostolic team assured them that it would be worth it when Christ was fully revealed.

Significance of Thessalonians for Today

Because believers today face many of the same challenges to coherent faith, the Thessalonian epistles still provide grist for Christian communities. While these early letters do not have the theological heft of other undisputed Pauline writings such as Galatians or Corinthians, and especially Romans, they supply wise guidance on how to trust the truth of the gospel by faith, how to live peaceably together in love, and how to look to the future in hope. Indeed, this triad of faith, love, and hope (so ordered in 1 Thessalonians) is the interpretive framework for these letters.

Why would believers today find this apostolic guidance persuasive? Removed by centuries and geography, current Christian communities face similar seductions and self-preserving temptations. The surrounding culture always seeks to bend all to its outlook and practice, and most of us succumb in compromising ways to the pressure to conform. Many in our time do not distinguish being a follower of Jesus from being a good citizen; and clearly, American identity and its absorption with market economy is its own form of idolatry. When all human meaning is boiled down to economic fortunes, we have lost our souls.

There is also cultural idolatry in our time: the preservation of white supremacy. The Black Lives Matter movement has exposed to a new level the latent racism that perdures in the white population, while government strategies to reduce immigration display similar colorized preferences. Many have described 2020 as a year of "racial reckoning." The many Black persons killed by police forces, mass incarceration, and health care disparities are glaring reminders that the original sin of America—chattel slavery—still lingers.[13] America has yet to repent fully for this egregious subjugation of fellow humans, in addition to the earlier displacement of Native Americans from their land, another form of original sin.

The long reach of patriarchy, with its presumption of noblesse oblige, continues to disfigure key markers of race, gender, sexual, and religious minorities with its concomitant claim of being the measure of otherness. Sexism is regnant, especially in churches, as complementarians continue to summon Paul's writings to support subordination of women to male jurisdiction. We also witness daily

---

13. See Jim Wallis, *American's Original Sin: Racism, White Privilege, and the Bridge to a New America* (Grand Rapids: Brazos, 2016). He asks a critical question: "What would it mean for us to die to whiteness?" (73).

the assaults on the character of women who dare defy a patriarchal hegemony.

An additional urgent concern is the growing climate crisis. Just as Paul longed for the Christians of his day to live in an ecosystem of mutual interdependence, we must expand our vision to include nature. More than ever before, common survival depends on cultivating interdependence with all creation. Those concerned with twin issues of justice and sustainability, according to Sallie McFague, must collaborate to overcome the dystopian reality of global warming.[14] The Thessalonian correspondence helps us think about the desired future with God and can offer reassurance for our living. The hint that the return of Christ to this world is for its renewal rather than a rapture that abandons it prompts constructive thinking about God's ultimate purpose for our earthly environs.

Pioneering ecological theologian Joseph Sittler places care of the creation at the center of faithful discipleship. He insists that the christological work we need to be doing includes nature. It does not view this world as simply an expendable backdrop, a theater of redemption that involves only humanity. He reads the Pauline letters, especially Romans 8, as a call to expand the cosmic dimensions of our view of Christ. As I consider the summing up of human history, I do so with a view to the freeing of creation from its subjection to futility, its plaintive groaning.[15] As the planet warms, we cannot read Scripture without full recognition that eschatological thinking is not about removing humans from the context without which we cannot be human. All of this earth provides home to those who bear God's image; Christ's lordship will be manifest in all that God declared good.

Two decades into the twenty-first century, North America displays great anxiety politically, socially, economically, and personally. Differentiation from dominant culture requires a sense of the futility of placing all confidence in the machinations of governing structures and corporate partners with their corrupting patterns. Those who

---

14. Sallie McFague, *A New Climate for Theology: God, the World, and Global Warming* (Minneapolis: Fortress, 2008), 2.
15. See the collection of Sittler's writings, *Evocations of Grace: Writings on Ecology, Theology, and Ethics,* ed. Steven Bouma-Prediger and Peter Bakken (Grand Rapids: Eerdmans, 2000).

chart a pathway that follows the itinerant Jesus will not be able to secure their future by relying on the normative interpretive framework of our epoch. This places us in close connection with these early believers.

Simply put, Paul wanted this bounded community of new converts to bear witness to God's redemptive work in the world. Only as the gospel is embodied is it compelling and accessible. Only as persons form a supportive community that is clear about its identity would its witness be sustainable, then as now. The Thessalonian community offers a helpful archetype of Christian living under duress, with lessons we can learn from its perseverance in a hostile context.

Commonality of Christian Challenges

The struggles of these early Christians remain in our time: how to determine the true and living God amid competing "gods;" how to maintain sexual ethics characterized by discipline and mutuality; how to make work an expression of faithful service; and how to live in the hope that Jesus will put the world to rights, as promised, overcoming death forever. The apostle engaged these in a forthright manner, and his wisdom is still relevant. Indeed, without this grounding early testimony, we would have no rudder for navigating our own challenges as "resident aliens," language popularized by Will Willimon and Stanley Hauerwas.

In many respects, 1 and 2 Thessalonians have a contemporary appeal because of their emphasis on Christian practice more so than on doctrine. The Practicing Our Faith project, guided by Craig Dykstra and Dorothy Bass, has demonstrated that persons are more drawn to concrete practices that introduce them to a distinctive way of life rather than learning catechetical nuances they struggle to apply.[16] In a sense, doctrine follows practice. We remember that early Spirit-infused Christian practices of baptism, eucharist, hospitality,

---

16. See the first volume in the series, Dorothy C. Bass, ed., *Practicing Our Faith: A Way of Life for a Searching People* (San Francisco: Jossey-Bass Publishers, 1997), where the project is illuminated in the first chapter. Many significant volumes follow.

the transgressing of ethnic boundaries, and preaching and teaching shaped the texts that sustain Christian identity. Continually refining their practices allowed their theological imagination to develop.

While Paul did not advocate a complete withdrawal from a pagan culture, what some today call a Benedict option,[17] he nevertheless offered direction for how to live as a faithful minority. This may be hard for North Americans to fathom as the Christian majority perdures in culture, congress, and communities, often displaying arrogance toward the religious "other," especially Muslims.[18] Yet restive changes are stirring, and the growth of nonaffiliated persons as well as venerable global religions now challenges the hegemony of the WASP (White Anglo-Saxon Protestants) profile that has long prevailed with its many discriminatory practices.

My work in theological education has taken me to Myanmar frequently over the past decade. My former seminary has a partnership with Myanmar Institute of Theology, a leading educational institution of Christian religious studies for undergraduate and graduate students. There, I have learned much from fellow Christians about what it means to live as a religious minority in a primarily Buddhist nation. The clear acknowledgment that their context is religiously plural gives them a respect for the lived religion of others even when that respect is rarely reciprocated. As six to seven percent of the population of Myanmar, Christians there suffer for their expressions of religious liberty. They cannot build churches or institutions without government permits that require an arduous process to procure. They are constantly under surveillance by powers of the state, and the Preservation of Race and Religion Laws, enacted in 2015, clearly favor Buddhism at every turn. Thus, they find themselves clearly at odds with the prevailing culture and thereby hone a persistent form of faith that I find instructive for what passes as Christianity in the United States in its truncated expression. Especially today, white evangelicals have sidled up to a form of governance that uses

---

17. See the interesting proposal offered by Rod Dreher, *The Benedict Option: A Strategy for Christians in a Post-Christian Nation* (New York: Sentinel, 2017).
18. See the important work of Martha C. Nussbaum, *The New Religious Intolerance: Overcoming the Politics of Fear in an Anxious Age* (Cambridge, MA: Belknap, 2012).

Christianity as a prop for political expediency and have lost much credibility about the contours of their faith by doing so.

My Reflection on Writing This Commentary

Writers of commentaries invariably begin with a sense of trepidation because much has already been written on their particular texts. Generations of scholars have devoted linguistic, exegetical, social scientific, rhetorical, and theological research to the discrete portion of Scripture they are engaging afresh. They also know that it is an encompassing task to understand the original claim on the readers and hearers of the text and the present claim on contemporary congregations. Scripture continues to shape Christian imagination and performance, and the ongoing conversation with it fosters what is essential to our practice. Stephen Fowl puts it succinctly: "Christians must read scripture in the light of their ends as Christians— ever deeper communion with the triune God and with each other."[19] This has been my purpose.

Writing a theological commentary places one squarely at the intersection of Scripture and theology.[20] Systematic theology and biblical scholarship have followed divergent pathways for over two centuries, diminishing both church and academy. Recovering and crafting new forms of theological hermeneutics are refreshing the church's preaching, the character of theologians, and communion with God, which are ultimately the goals of biblical interpretation.[21]

Approaching the Thessalonian correspondence has an exacting dimension because it is the earliest of the Pauline writings.

---

19. Stephen E. Fowl, *Engaging Scripture* (Oxford: Blackwell, 1998), vii.
20. Too often the Bible has simply been used as a source book for theology; its content has been subordinated to doctrinal claims as Peter the Lombard's *Sentences* illustrates. Telford Work offers a creative approach in *Living and Active: Scripture in the Economy of Salvation* (Grand Rapids: Eerdmans, 2002) by using systematic theology to construct a new doctrine of Scripture as revelatory of the Triune God's redemptive purpose in the world. R. S. Sugirtharajah, *Postcolonial Reconfigurations: An Alternative Way of Reading the Bible and Doing Theology* (St. Louis: Chalice Press, 2003), argues that biblical studies and systematic theologies "need each other for survival and credibility" (4).
21. I have been aided in thinking about the relational aspect of theological hermeneutics by Jens Zimmermann in his dense but helpful study *Recovering Theological Hermeneutics: An Incarnational-Trinitarian Theory of Interpretation* (Grand Rapids: Baker Academic, 2004).

An interpreter desires to set the stage for additional reflection on the formative texts of the New Testament that ground the nascent expressions of Christianity. Learning the semantic emphases and theological perspective offered in these slight epistles holds promise for interpreting the further apostolic corpus.

A theological commentary pursues a different goal than does an exegetical or expositional study: it seeks to provide a consideration of the vision of God, the redemptive project through Jesus Christ and the Spirit, and the effects in the establishment of Christian communities. It follows the Trinitarian history of God as it unfolds with humanity. It is less interested in the nuances of the writing's original language, the shape of rhetoric, the precision of geographical and historical anchoring, and a specialized understanding of the first century Mediterranean world. Although these contextual matters are of concern, the primary strategy of this commentary to is bridge the theological understanding of Paul's early proclamation with the needs of Christian believers in our time.

Scripture forms believers, ancient and current, with careful interpretation affording continuing generations a sense of the founding and sustaining of their faith. Additional sources such as early creeds, commentaries from early Christian interpreters, and the larger intellectual tradition of Christianity—both East and West—factored into this writing. No one person can fully grasp the power and beauty of these enduring texts, yet every epoch requires faithful listening and interrogation of these literary treasures.[22]

Writing this commentary during the 2020 COVID-19 pandemic adds another layer of perspective. Since January of 2020 to the time of this writing, over one million (and counting) Americans have died from the deadly virus, and the tally is still mounting around the world, well into the millions. It has been over a century since this kind of health challenge swept across the globe, and some speak in apocalyptic terms about its significance. As refrigerator trucks pull up behind hospitals to serve as temporary morgues for bodies yet to be cremated or buried, there is a palpable sense that death is winning

---

22. A helpful resource is John W. Miller's *How the Bible Came to Be: Exploring the Narrative and Message* (New York: Paulist, 2004), especially the chapter "First Steps toward Understanding the Bible as a Theological Unity," 77.

over life. More than ever, one's belief that history is in God's hands matters.

Some in our time liken the pandemic to the bubonic plague that struck Europe in the fourteenth century, "not in the number of dead but in terms of shaking up the way people think," according to medical historian Gianna Pomata.[23] She reflects on how some in that earlier epoch saw the disease as sent by God to chastise the unrighteous, as do some today. She is more interested in how minds shift as new empirical evidence comes to the fore and is valued. She believes that now "something as dramatic is going to happen, not so much in medicine, but in economy and culture. Because of danger, there's this wonderful human response, which is to think in a new way."[24] It is my hope that this commentary will help us think in new ways in apocalyptic times. While accenting this present COVID-19 disruption may render some of the observations irrelevant in the not-too-distant future, nevertheless I contend that there are far-reaching implications for all aspects of life that arise from the global pandemic.

In a recent op-ed column, conservative writer Ross Douthat suggests that it is important for persons of faith to try to make sense of our disorienting epoch. The "aspects of our circumstances that seem ridiculously scripted to the atheist are, for religion believers, a reason to meditate on what is be revealed, how we're being tested, and what lessons and examples we can draw from watching tragedies unfold."[25] This commentary invites a theological assessment of our circumstances.

I am drawn to W. B. Yeats's poem "Second Coming," which he wrote during the twin horrors of World War I and the 1918 influenza pandemic. Also apt for our time, Yeats's poetry speaks of the chaotic machinations humans can wreak on one another, on the whole order of creation. In addition to the pandemic, racial reckoning, climate crisis that spawns fires and evermore terrifying storms,

---

23. Lawrence Wright, "Annals of History: A Scholar of the Plague Thinks That Pandemics Wreak Havoc—and Open Minds," *New Yorker*, July 20, 2020, 18.

24. Wright quoting Pomata, in "Annals of History," 19.

25. Ross Douthat, "The Tragedy of Donald Trump," *New York Times*, October 4, 2020, 9.

continuing sexism and marginalization of sexual minorities, we have a fractured political system.

The 2020 presidential election in the United States had the possibility of derailing the very democracy we enjoy, and the continuing repercussions mount. When an incumbent president threatens the orderly transfer of power if he or she does not agree with the outcome, the anarchy about which Yeats writes may not be out of reach. Even now, the former president continues to make claims that the election was fraudulent, even though no courts have upheld his challenges. Hopefully by the time this commentary is in print, most of the repercussions of this turbulent election will have subsided. When foreign powers use social media to interfere with the freedom of the electorate, "the ceremony of innocence is drowned." When the Supreme Court is politicized for partisan purposes, "things fall apart." In the aftermath of the election, we witnessed what demagogic rhetoric can foment as loyalists to a defeated president stormed the nation's capitol. Tantamount to a coup, these acts of violence have deeply shaken our country.

> Turning and turning in the
>   widening gyre
> The falcon cannot hear the
>   falconer;
> Things fall apart; the centre
>   cannot hold;
> Mere anarchy is loosed upon
>   the world,
> The blood-dimmed tide is
>   loosed, and everywhere
> The ceremony of innocence is
>   drowned;
> The best lack all conviction,
>   while the worst
> Are full of passionate intensity.
>
> W. B. Yeats, "Second Coming,"
> Poets.org, https://poets.org/poem
> /second-coming.

Scripture gives voice to God's future, even in a time of conflict and threat. Thoughtful guidance for living in the present catastrophes is present in this literary deposit from early Christianity. It moves beyond quietism and calls for public witness, offering a theology and commendable culture for the common good of fellow citizens.

Just as many in the early Christian community of Thessalonica were anxiously awaiting the end of time and the return of Jesus Christ, there are those today who wonder if "end times" are on us as life has little normalcy and economic pressures for the great majority are mounting. With escalating global cataclysms of war, displaced persons, poverty, and racial tensions, persons who look to the Bible for guidance can find very practical instruction about how to live with forbearance with others through reliance on the strengthening of the Holy Spirit. The pandemic has exposed fissures in the social landscape, and we have the opportunity to mend these with faith and grit. And we have wise forebears in faith that instruct us. In 1527, Luther wrote instructively about his own encounter with cataclysmic illness in his time and the claim the suffering of others had on him to minister through his committed presence. Luther offered a better approach than expecting to be rescued/ raptured, escaping it all; that sense of Christian exceptionalism— as if we are not a part of the common travail of humanity—ignores God's concern for the exigencies all humans face in a groaning creation. It also reinforces the notion that this world is not truly our home and that one must flee it in order to be near God.

> With God's permission the enemy has sent poison and deadly dung among us, and so I will pray to God that he may be gracious and preserve us. Then I will fumigate to purify the air, give and take medicine, and avoid places and persons where I am not needed in order that I may not abuse myself and that through me others may not be infected and inflamed with the result that I become the cause of their death through my negligence. If God wishes to take me, he will be able to find me. At least I have done what he gave me to do and am responsible neither for my own death or for the death of others. But if my neighbor needs me, I shall avoid neither the person or the place but feel free to visit and help him.[26]

In this commentary we will explore the significance of the Parousia, the appearing or return of Christ, and seek to interface that expectation with the fears and concerns of faithful persons today. The Thessalonian correspondence is perhaps best known for its eschatological emphasis, so a constructive engagement in our time will prove fruitful. We will seek to understand why the apocalyptic fireworks are part of the rhetoric and how to think about them

---

26. Martin Luther, *Letters of Spiritual Counsel,* ed. T. G. Tappert (London: SCM Press, 1955), 242.

this many years removed. We will see that our different context requires a different accent. The emphasis on community will prompt renewed interrogation of the plague of isolation in our time.

Writers in our time speak of the loneliness that stalks so many, and the required self-quarantining during 2020, and beyond, exacerbates the sense of absence many inhabit. Even those who feel called to being solitary ultimately realize that they are best in community and that being a hermit has its limits.

> "You can kill a person with an apartment as well as with a machine gun. It only takes a little longer."
>
> Martin E. Marty, *Friendship* (Allen, TX: Argus, 1980), 11.

I recently officiated at the graveside service of a treasured friend. Only about forty-five of us were able to gather outside, at a distance from one another; in regular times, hundreds would have attended to honor this one beloved to so many. Because we were made for one another, as N.T. Wright puts it in *Simply Christian*, we live with a sense of incompleteness when we cannot gather fully. [27] The incarnational impress of the Jesus story remains core; as embodiments of God's presence, as was Jesus, we long to express our common humanity through graceful touch and close presence. It may be a while before this can occur.

As people connect with a few family members or carefully screened friends who are free of infection, there are demands for heightened attentiveness to courtesy and grace as the recurring rhythms of life involved these few. The pandemic has required an almost monastic sequestering over these months of writing this commentary, which most likely has been a boon for this extrovert. My actual location has been in my study at home; my social location is that I write as a privileged white theological educator, a Baptist Christian, and one who has faced significant challenges vocationally because of my unwavering advocacy for the propriety of women in all forms of ministry. I have not had the challenge of trying to work while educating children at home; nor have I experienced the

27. N. T. Wright, *Simply Christian: Why Christianity Makes Sense* (New York: HarperCollins, 2006), 30.

extreme economic challenge so many are facing. Yet, day-by-day dystopian news and alarmist opinions occupy my waking hours and disturb my sleep. Spending time with these early writings has given perspective. I trust it will for you also, even as we begin to regain our social footing because of vaccinations.

As we engage these Epistles, let us imagine ourselves at the beginning of faith and envision essential practices for following the risen One. It will kindle new faithfulness.

1 THESSALONIANS

1 Thessalonians 1:1–2:20

Encouraging a Fledgling Congregation

1:1

Apostolic Greeting

Many, many letters have crossed my desk over the years as pastor, professor, and president in theological education. I could almost tell by seeing the envelope which ones were trouble, as they often posted "CONFIDENTIAL" prominently or attached some end-time sticker. Some letters upbraided me about my theological aberrance, usually related to my being a woman theologian; others wanted to make some theological point that we were surely not attending to in our curriculum, often with the offer to teach such a course. One letter demanded that I submit every professor's syllabi so that the writer could assess doctrinal fidelity that matched his particular stripe. That one was signed, and I responded that the best way to know what professors were teaching was to enroll in their courses. My suggestion was not met with enthusiasm. It was a joy to receive a letter that simply began with identifying the author and clarifying the purpose for writing in a gentle manner. This is the approach of the founders of the church in Thessalonica.

First Thessalonians begins with identifying the authors: Paul, Silvanus, and Timothy, although most agree that Paul is the principal writer. Similarities in rhetorical style to other epistles suggest this is the case. Addressed to "the church of Thessalonians" gives concrete evidence of a sustainable community, and those who receive the letter must have felt satisfaction that they could be affirmed as such. Posting a letter was no small achievement in the first century, and receiving one was a special treasure for an individual or group. One can only imagine the excitement of gathering to hear it read in the community.

The apostolic greeting includes the chief marker of the congregation: It is "in God the Father and the Lord Jesus Christ."[1] This is a unique demarcation in the Pauline correspondence, and it is a strong reassurance of participation in the divine life.[2] For the new believers (*pisteuontes*) their spiritual location in the dynamism of God's own self-giving in Christ would secure Christian distinctiveness in their beleaguered context. Finding one's true home in God is the goal of Christian identity. The new believers will learn that it is by the power of the Holy Spirit that they are granted participation in God's own life, and the apostle will offer further teaching on the Spirit in the letter. We will see a nascent Trinitarian theology unfolding.

I remember a beloved seminary president who faced a serious heart surgery, the outcome of which was not assured. He said what kept him confident as he prepared for the operation was the simple verse in Colossians: "Your life is hid with Christ in God" (3:3). The reader gets the same sense of inhabiting the holy relationship within God in this opening greeting; it is a secure dwelling, much as the psalmist spoke of dwelling in the shelter of the Most High (91:1). Rather than a solitary individual spiritual practice, the whole community dwells within God's expansive presence and care.

The Thessalonian correspondence is embryonic in its Trinitarian construction, and the nuances of the mutual indwelling of the three expressions of divine identity (*perichoresis*) have hardly been worked out at this point. Whereas other Pauline texts will name God in the threefold cadence of triune relationship, this early letter speaks of each without clarifying how unified Trinitarian action effects redemption and consummation. Yet there is an emerging sense that the dynamic relationship between Abba, Son, and Spirit

---

1. While I will use inclusive language for God and humanity in this commentary, I will not change the original nomenclature that the first century author employed. It was his worldview and sense of the Divine; actually, it is more about his understanding of the filial intimacy between Jesus and God that drives his usage. So, when Paul calls God "Father," I will follow suit, although I am always conscious that this masculine language must not ascribe literal gender to God.
2. Michael J. Gorman, *Becoming the Gospel: Paul, Participation, and Mission* (Grand Rapids: Eerdmans, 2015), 76.

sets the framework for the congregation and its mission. I will address this in further reflections at the end of the chapter.

At the very outset the apostle makes clear that grace and peace will suffuse the letter. Favorite topics of Paul, grace and peace speak of a new world order where retributive justice, an eye for an eye, is surpassed as the grace of forgiveness prevails. The peace that Christ offers is not the *pax Romana* that comes from violent suppression of any insurrection. Rather, it is peace between God and humanity that leads to a renewed belief that persons can live without retaliation or rancor. It will require constant vigilance to allow these expressions of the Spirit to configure the community after the likeness of Christ, full of grace, full of peaceful truth. In a context fraught with competing religious claims, this peace will be hard won.

1:2–3

Apostolic Thanksgiving for These Believers

It is a prayerful remembrance that prompts the apostolic team to intercede on behalf of the Thessalonians. I remember a wise pastor saying that there was no more important work than modeling prayer for the congregation and that in praying for them, the pastor was doing the faithful task of holding them before God. Thanking God for their work of faith, labor of love, and steadfastness of hope in the Lord Jesus Christ, Paul lavishes on them the encouragement that the good news is taking root in them, and they are displaying what God wants from those who follow in the way of the beloved Son. One can imagine how welcome these words were for a congregation seeking to mature in righteousness. Basically, the apostle is saying, "I can't stop thinking about you!" Since he is not with them, the best thing to do for them is to pray.

The triad of faith, love, and hope will recur in this epistle as well as the larger Pauline corpus. This different ordering is where Paul wants to put emphasis with the Thessalonians; by placing hope last, the apostle is speaking to their deepest longing—for hope in a fearful time—and is a summation of how to respond to great mercy from the One who loves with fierce concern for human flourishing.

Work (*ergon*), labor (*kopos*), and steadfastness or perseverance (*hypomones*) are the engines that make these spiritual virtues thrum in the community, and Paul is decidedly not in favor of flaccid faith. His desire for these new Christians is a robust manifestation of grace and peace that will compel others to believe, which is what is happening as the Thessalonians stand firm in their commitment to confessing a new Lord. Paul is frankly astonished at the progress they are making. Evidently others are taking notice also.

1:4–10

Thessalonian Response to the Gospel

Paul launches further into thanksgiving for these beloved ones, loved by God and loved by those who labored among them. That he addresses the community as brethren is thought by some to mean strictly men, members of an artisan community that provided a context for him to work alongside them in his own craft of leather works.[3] Others say it is simply the conventional means of address, which subsumes women and children under the aegis of male domination.[4] I do not believe that the question of whether it was a strictly male community or mixed community is determinative for the whole hermeneutical arc of the epistle. So I proceed assuming that both women and men are a part of the emerging Christian community.

Paul calls them not only beloved but chosen (*ekloge*). This has great resonance within his own Jewish tradition as he remembers God's covenantal history with Israel, with its rites of circumcision, special food laws, rituals such as Passover, and holy places from tabernacle to temple. To include Gentile believers among the elect is

---

3. This is the thesis that Linda McKinnish Bridges artfully argues in her fine commentary, *1 & 2 Thessalonians* (Macon, GA: Smyth & Helwys, 2008). The chief importance of her work is that it offers a different social location for a congregation; rather than a house church, it is a marketplace shop where fellow workers would share not only livelihood, but times of community meals and worship. Lone Fatum also writes from this perspective in her chapter on 1 Thessalonians in *Searching the Scriptures*, volume 2, *A Feminist Commentary*, ed. Elisabeth Schüssler Fiorenza (New York: Crossroad, 1994), 250, and believes that the presumption of a male only audience makes a significant interpretive difference.

4. The NRSV always includes sisters alongside brothers as a recognition of their presence.

the supreme goal of his mission. God desires to make one people out of a formerly bitterly divided reality, Jew versus Gentile, the chosen and the nations (*ta ethne*) who do not know the true God as they are not a part of the founding covenantal relationship. To this union of formerly separated peoples, Paul has committed his life, and he has suffered at the hands of his own kinspeople for this effort.

He radically alters the meaning of being "chosen," however. Christ is God's Elect One, and those who make their life in his body receive this new identity of inclusion. This is an ever-widening election; indeed, in Christ God has elected all of humanity for redemption. I will give further attention to this idea in 2 Thessalonians, especially the doctrinal development related to election.

> **The concept of election has been christologically reconfigured.**
>
> Andy Johnson, *1 and 2 Thessalonians,* The Two Horizons New Testament Commentary (Grand Rapids: Eerdmans, 2016), 42.

Paul captures the original intent of chosenness. It was never about a simple favoritism; rather, God chose and continues to choose to include humanity in the redemptive process, of which Israel was a chosen instrument. Through Israel's special relationship with God, all would be blessed (Gen. 12:3; 22:18). Yet many have opposed this divine decision, finding the story of Israel's election an affront.

The persecution of Jews throughout the ages has many sources: envy, resentment, distrust, and suspicion. The differentiated ways of the observant Jews have bumped up against Gentile practices through the centuries, and Christianity's regular anti-Semitic opprobrium has been a disgrace. These spiritual forebears and continuing kin offer a legacy on which Christians depend, I would argue, now more than ever as the shared pursuit of religious liberty requires mutual respect. The continued conversation between these two expressions of faith enriches both.

Several years ago, I participated in the Christian Leadership Initiative, a program sponsored by the American Jewish Committee, which entailed a ten-day time of study at the Shalom Hartman Institute in Jerusalem, a leading center of research and scholarship. I recall one of the distinguished rabbis saying that God's relationship with Israel was an experiment by God, who decided to establish intimacy with a particular people to see if that might be a model for others. He concluded, sadly, that it had been a mixed effort as election proved a hard burden, intimacy even more so.

It is a significant step forward for New Testament scholars to scrutinize texts formerly read as supersessionist, now placing them in a particular sociocultural context of the separation of the gathered communities of synagogue and church, each an *ekklēsia* of God. It is also refreshing for Jewish scholars to pay attention to the Second Testament, for they interpret with bracing insight what non-Jews often miss.[5]

Paul's conviction that God intends to include Gentiles in the body of Christ, hence, God's election of all, places him at odds with his own Jewish kin, as we will witness in this correspondence as well as the larger arc of his ministry. Remarkably, he understood and preserved the historical privilege of his people, as Romans 7–9 argues, while determining that God always intended to include the whole of humanity.

The apostle wants the receivers of the letter to know that the gospel came in more than words, but "in power and in the Holy Spirit and with full conviction" (v. 5). Christian services of worship, entailing preaching, are so full of words that our eyes glaze over with the surfeit of language. More than mere words are in play as Paul reflects on how they first received the gospel; power and the Holy Spirit, with conviction, were the media of persuasion.

Evidently the proclamation was accompanied by miraculous signs as the word "power" indicates, which fueled the frenzy about the identity of the apostles. That they were sent away by night (Acts 17:10) suggests that their presence was considered dangerous as they proclaimed a different king.[6]

---

5. I find a good example of this fresh reading in Mark D. Nanos, *The Mystery of Romans: The Jewish Context of Paul's Letter* (Minneapolis: Fortress, 1996).

6. James R. Harrison, "Paul and Empire 2: Negotiating the Seduction of Imperial 'Peace and Security' in Galatians, Thessalonians, and Philippians," writes in Adam Winn, ed., *Introduction to Empire in the New Testament* (Atlanta: SBL Press, 2016), that Paul's apocalyptic gospel "competed with the Augustan conception of rule and its propagandist manipulation by his imperial successors. The Thessalonian politarchs accused Paul, Silas, and their converts of 'acting against the decrees of Caesar, saying there is another king, Jesus'. . ." (181).

We know when speech is authentic, even in the highly contrived news outlets, political addresses, TED talks, and, of course, sermons. Conviction about the message does come through, no matter the medium. In a world of slick rhetorical approaches, the apostles want the Thessalonians to know that their speech could be trusted because of the kind of persons they were. The empowering Spirit allowed their conviction to make a compelling argument for the message they embodied.

> From 1 Thessalonians . . . through Pliny's famous epistle (10.96) to the persecution under Decius and beyond, the clash of the gods ultimately determined the shape of the collision between (emerging) Christianity and paganism.
>
> C. Kavin Rowe, *World Upside Down: Reading Acts in the Graeco-Roman Age* (New York: Oxford, 2010), 17.

Paul recounts what kind of messengers they were among them—for their sake (v. 5b). We know that one's message can be compromised by one's character; Paul wants to assure them of proper motive and message. He even goes so far as to say that they were right to be imitators of the apostolic team, for it was actually imitating the Lord. This is a bold claim, and it is worthy of examination. Is this a bit of apostolic swagger, or is it an expression of humility, as the apostles know they can find such life only in the Lord?

We know that Paul understands his life in Christ as a total reorientation of all that went before; he has been called a Jewish Christ Mystic.[7] Although at times he pulls out his credentials (Gal. 1:13–17; Phil. 3:5-9) to give warrant to his message, the more regular tenor is that of humility, recognizing that the life he now lives he lives in the power of Christ who loved him and gave himself for him (Gal. 2:20).

When Paul says that the newly converted became "imitators" of them and of the Lord (v. 6), he is speaking primarily of the aggregation of suffering that all experience—the Lord Jesus Christ, the apostles, and the new believers. They received the word "in much affliction, with joy inspired by the Holy Spirit." Suffering plays a

---

7. This terminology comes from Marcus J. Borg and John Dominic Crossan, *The First Paul: Reclaiming the Radical Visionary behind the Church's Conservative Icon* (New York: HarperCollins, 2009), 19.

prominent role as the whole of the New Testament unfolds as paschal mystery. The stripping away of the old and putting on the new are always accompanied by a measure of suffering, and while not sent by God, it is the natural consequence of moving in a different direction than the prevailing culture, placing us in the company of Christ. It is also simply the reality of being a finite and frail child of dust. Even vivified by the Spirit, this mortal flesh is perishable and awaits imperishability in resurrection (1 Cor. 15:42–54).

How does one bear the reality of affliction in life, indeed in the life of faith? It is because the Spirit grants joy, a special expression of grace (v. 7). In August 2018, the Center for Faith and Culture at Yale sponsored a consultation on the Theology of Joy. I was struck by Willie James Jennings's description of joy as a work, not a sentiment. It was a work of resistance against fear and death, and his family "worked hard at joy." This required that one learn to make pain productive by rooting identity in the body of Jesus who endured because of "the joy set before him" (Heb. 12:2). The Thessalonians demonstrated joy in a hard circumstance, and Paul commends them for it.

Indeed, they became an example to all the believers in Macedonia and in Achaia. Paul wants them to know that their steadfast faith has "sounded forth," indeed has gone "everywhere." The reverberation of their conversion has made the air waves pulse with astonishing gratitude for authentic faith (*pistis*). All the newly formed congregations are naming the Thessalonian church as an example, and Paul is more than delighted. In the same way today, when congregations learn of the demonstration of Christian virtues by other congregations, it evokes encouragement to persevere in their own mission. My home church became engaged in Interfaith Hospitality Network, a project that welcomes homeless people to a week's stay in the church, after we learned of sister congregations who were participating. It was their demonstration of compassion that awakened us to participate. It has had a ripple effect in the congregation, as some came to assist with food provided by other members, some spent the night at the church for ready assistance, the youth opened their space, and some took home bedding to launder. We practiced the Benedictine virtue of "receiving all as Christ" and were thereby strengthened.

Paul says he does not need to describe the faithful witness of the Thessalonian Christians further, as it is clearly known throughout the region. Yet he does say more as he overflows with gratitude for their willingness to be transformative bearers of the gospel. It had become known that the Thessalonians had been willing to risk it all to be hospitable to the sojourning apostles (v. 9). They had turned to God, forsaking idols, "to serve a living and true God." They evinced "believing allegiance," a term used by N. T. Wright.[8]

Publicly visible acts were part of their transformed identity.[9] This prompts me to wonder what publicly visible acts Christians do today that distinguish them from the cultural mainstream? We advocate for racial justice—but many who do not believe do it more. We give to charity—but many religiously unaffiliated give more. We volunteer in our communities, working for food kitchens, tutoring, canvassing for political candidates—but so do those who do not name Christ as Lord. We gather for communion; others seek other forms for community, for they share the same hunger for belonging as Christians do. We listen to Scripture; others listen to many sources of wisdom that come from the rich intellectual heritage of philosophers, historians, spiritual writers of other ways of faith, and political analysts. Yet I contend that Christianity has a particular and enduring charism to offer. One of the tasks of this commentary is to clarify the distinctive identity of being Christian in our day and to challenge us to more demonstrable faith, without our claiming to be the only source of goodness in the world.

Throughout the ages, Christians have hoped toward a God-directed summing up of human history while others have scientific analysis or tout doomsday scenarios. It will be the contention of this commentary that good scientific data about the length of time our sun will last is not inimical to a theological vision of the consummation of the age. Important to remember is that history is in God, and God's eternality encompasses all that is finite.

The service Paul asks of the Thessalonians included that they wait for God's Son from heaven, whom God "raised from the dead,

---

8. N. T. Wright, *Justification: God's Plan and Paul's Vision* (Downers Grove, IL: InterVarsity Press, 2009), 181.
9. Gorman, *Becoming the Gospel*, 70.

Jesus who delivers us from the wrath to come" (v. 10). This verse is
packed with meaning and moves us into the heart of the theme of
this epistle. It assumes that the risen Christ dwells in the presence of
God yet will return to earth to collect those who name him as Lord.
The "wrath to come" is a startling prediction, and readers of this text
wonder how to think of divine wrath even as they sense the gravita-
tional movement of the New Testament toward great grace.

Michael Gorman offers perspective here: "The coming (and perhaps already-present) wrath of God (1:10; 2:16; 5:9) is real, but it
is not God's intention or preference for people. The reality of divine
wrath is, in fact, the 'flip side' of divine righteousness, in the sense of
God's saving, restorative activity."[10] Paul is not inserting a theory of
atonement here that requires divine appeasement by Christ; rather,
Christ is the agent of deliverance for God's own.

Divine wrath and the violence it conjures have long been a vex-
ing topic in biblical and theological discourse. Before Theopaschite
theology reoriented the landscape, it was normative to think of God
as one who cannot feel. While it is a good thing instead to think of
God as having emotion, how do we consider the violence that the
wrath of God suggests?

It is much too simplistic to play off a God of wrath in the Old
Testament against a God of mercy in the New Testament as did Mar-
cion; yet there is a movement across the scriptural landscape toward
the triumph of a nonviolent image of God. A contemporary theologian who has given sustained attention to this evolving rendering of
the character of God is J. Denny Weaver. When speaking of divine
violence, he calls it, "Bible versus Bible."[11] He works his way through
the various vignettes of the Old Testament and concludes that they
"picture a God who uses violence as punishment and judgment."[12]
Further, he observes how smoothly such claims of a God who uses

10. Gorman, *Becoming the Gospel*, 80.
11. J. Denny Weaver, *The Nonviolent God* (Grand Rapids, MI: Eerdmans Publishing, 2013),
    89–122. Another significant study comes from Jerome F. D. Creach, *Violence in Scripture*,
    Interpretation: Resources for the Use of Scripture in the Church (Louisville, KY:
    Westminster John Knox Press, 2013). He acknowledges that the "tension between the
    Testaments is real." Because Jesus place new demands on his followers, they must read
    Scripture with a keen eye for the "illusion of power through violence," rejecting it as not
    worthy of the reign Jesus proclaims. See 238–39.
12. Weaver, *The Nonviolent God*, 95.

war and natural disasters as punishment seem to transition from the Old Testament accounts through the parables of Jesus to United States history to the present, and to see how prevalent the idea of a God who exercises violence is in North American society.[13]

When Paul speaks of the coming wrath, he is drawing on a scriptural legacy that sees God actively engaged with those who oppose God's own elect as well as when they are a wayward people themselves forsaking covenantal obligation. Using opposing forces, natural disaster, or corrupt external or internal leaders, the various modes of experiencing God's wrath require sober assessment.

Andy Johnson offers a tempering characterization of the wrath of God: it is in the Bible "not an attribute of God but rather a response to human actions that harm oneself and others, destroying human relationships or God's good created order. It is a response of 'ferocious love' that seeks restorative justice."[14] Paul's encouragement to wait for deliverance utterly depends on God's gracious act of raising Jesus from the dead. Because of that radically transformative event, believers can be assured that the risen Christ is able to deliver them, ultimately securing their future. The resurrection of Jesus is the linchpin for Christian hope.

2:1–8

Paul's Reflection on Their Ministry in Thessalonica

The apostle begins this section with ringing confidence that his team's visit to Thessalonica had not been in vain. Obviously, he was worried about this, as the apostolic vanguard came there from their traumatic episode in Philippi. Probably still healing from the wounds of their arrest and imprisonment (they had been flogged), they came suffering yet persisted in declaring the gospel. He writes, "... we had courage in our God to declare to you the gospel of God in the face of great opposition" (v. 2). He is referring to the great uproar their presence summoned, the detail of which is found in Acts

---

13. Weaver, *The Nonviolent God*, 101.
14. Johnson, *1 and 2 Thessalonians*, 55.

17:1–9. Because the gospel received a favorable hearing, likened to "turning the world upside down" (Acts 17:6b), a crowd convulsed to run them out of town. Jason, a believer who was housing them, took the brunt of the attack. That he receives mention in Luke's narrative speaks of his notable sacrifice.

The apostolic witness persuaded many to believe, including "many of the devout Greeks and not a few of the leading women" (Acts 17:4). This is an interesting recounting from Luke. It appears that he is attempting to commend the worthiness of the gospel by calling attention to the significant ones it could attract. This appears to be a regular strategy throughout Acts,[15] raising questions about class and status in the body of Christ, something Jesus did not countenance, indeed explicitly forbade (Matt. 20:26; Mark 9:35).

Paul assures the Thessalonians that the appeal they offered "does not spring from error or uncleanness, nor it is made with guile." (v. 3). Pure motives drive their witness. Why else would they subject themselves to physical hardship, economic precariousness, itinerant fatigue, and regular suspicion? Paul was a learned scholar, a student of the renowned Gamaliel, who had set aside what could have been an illustrious rabbinical career to follow the call of Christ Jesus to be his emissary in the fledgling Christian movement. His willingness to "count it all loss" gives steely authenticity to his proclamation.

He reverts to his claim to authority by saying, "We have been approved by God to be entrusted with the gospel . . ." (v. 4). What is the basis of this bold assertion? In many respects, it is because of the Thessalonian response to the gospel that he can say this. The sounding forth of their faith is a demonstrable expression that faithful apostolic witness has been effective. This reciprocity is a mark of the interdependence between the congregation and apostolic team. This is a critical relationship through which gathered communities can flourish.

Recently I participated in a farewell Zoom chat for a departing pastor. He had served a congregation for nearly twenty-four years, first planning a new church and then incorporating another congregation into it that made for a thriving church. Person after person

---

15. See Willie James Jennings, *Acts*, Belief: A Theological Commentary on the Bible (Louisville, KY: Westminster John Knox Press, 2017), 172.

talked about what his ministry had meant to their own faith and hope as a Christian. Couples whom he had married told of his gracious pastoral care. Persons long skeptical of faith told how they had come to belief because of his remarkable ministry. They were testifying to the reality that this pastor was approved by God through the fruit of his labor. A gay pastor, he had created space for marginalized sexual minorities who were not too sure they were welcome at church. They had learned to belong because of genuine Christian hospitality, as led by this gifted minister. It was a reciprocal relationship, mutually interdependent to the conclusion of this epoch of ministry.

Paul's testimony is that their speech is not simply to please other humans; rather, their intent is to please God "who tests our hearts" (v. 4b). Above all else, the desire to please God is what pleases God. Paul's surpassing desire is to please God, so that with clear conscience he can say that the testing of his heart adjudicates that he is found faithful.

But I believe that the desire to please you does in fact please you. And I hope I have that desire in all that I am doing. I hope that I will never do anything apart from that desire. And I know that if I do this you will lead me by the right road, though I may know nothing about it . . . you will never leave me to face my perils alone.

Thomas Merton, *Thoughts in Solitude* (Gethsemani: Abbey of Our Lady of Gethsemani, 1956), 83.

The ethics of what the mission is is not clear: they are not flatterers; they do not seek to profit from the ministry; they were not desiring glory from those who received their proclamation (v. 5). They were not greedy, in it for themselves. Paul is explicitly contrasting their mode of speech and behavior to traveling charlatan orators "out for money and public honor and who abandon their pupils when the going gets tough."[16] Evidently there were many of this reputation passing through. Rather, Paul states the ethics of the

16. Johnson, *1 and 2 Thessalonians*, 58.

mission most clearly in the well-known "love chapter" of his letter to the Corinthians (1 Cor. 13).

Success in ministry often breeds self-interest as the inflated salaries of megachurch pastors, evangelists, and Bible teachers corroborate. Fancy homes and cars, private planes, and hefty entourages suggest that ministry can become "a cloak for greed," as the apostle puts it (v. 5).

It is not surprising that highly paid religious figures in our era such as Jim Bakker, Joyce Meyers, Benny Hinn, and Randy and Paula White have come under federal scrutiny for lavish lifestyles. That they profited greatly while maintaining a nonprofit tax status led Iowa Senator Charles Grassley to pursue an investigation of these and others.

Paul reminds the Thessalonians that they did not seek glory from those to whom they ministered by proclaiming the gospel, although they could have rightfully expected certain things "as apostles of Christ" (v. 6). They made no demands, however, and functioned in a humble manner like the one they followed and preached. They were "gentle" (other ancient authorities read *babes*) among them, "like a nurse taking care of her children" (v. 7). Even though this "like a nurse" is a simile, it is a startling way for an adult male to refer to himself.

These are striking metaphors that have drawn noteworthy interest from scholars.[17] Beverly Roberts Gaventa regards the maternal imagery in Paul's correspondence as an essential part of his theological vision.[18] Hardly a conventional description, this perception of apostolic work as dependent and nurturing deconstructs any imperious claim.

Whether to translate the description Paul offers of the apostles as "gentle" (*epioi*) or "infants" (*nēpioi*) has been debated. Early textual evidence leads to the conclusion that "infants" is probably correct, although it mixes the metaphor and is the more difficult rendering.[19] What could Paul possibly mean by referring to himself and his

---

17. See Jennifer Houston McNeel, *Paul as Infant and Nursing Mother: Metaphor, Rhetoric, and Identity in 1 Thessalonians 2:5–8* (Atlanta: SBL Press, 2014).

18. Beverly Roberts Gaventa, *Our Mother Saint Paul* (Louisville, KY: Westminster John Knox Press, 2007).

19. Gaventa, *Our Mother Saint Paul*, 20. See also Sandra Hack Polaski, *A Feminist Introduction to Paul* (St. Louis: Chalice, 2005), 24–25.

colleagues as "infants?" We tend always to think of babes as innocent, and the language that precedes this imagery declare Paul's innocence of improper motives or underhanded decorum in their execution of the mission. Linking infants and nurse displays a remarkably reciprocal relationship. Paul was not the sole source of Thessalonian perseverance in faith; indeed, his own apostolic calling relied on their responsiveness as a testament to his work.

I recall a story, perhaps apocryphal, of how the president of Hebrew Union College in Cincinnati always brought an ordination service to a close by asking: "Who will bless the people?" The congregation would respond: "The rabbi will." "And who will bless the rabbi?" he would ask, and they would respond, "The people will." This mutuality is the mark of fruitful relationship.

Such is the reciprocity of this section of 1 Thessalonians. Neither apostles nor people could grow in Christ apart from such interdependence. Whereas some have seen Paul as much more authoritarian in his approach to the new churches he helped found, some argue for a different power dynamic that was counter to prevailing structures. Surely his countercultural approach is on display in this letter. He does not pull rank; rather, he cedes authority to a larger wisdom embedded in community with deep familial ties.

> Paul's emphasis on mutuality, weakness and suffering, and his opposition to factionalism and boasting are indication of such an alternative power and leadership discourse in the context of a society which was dominated by competition for status, domination, and control.
>
> Kathy Ehrensperger, *Paul and the Dynamics of Power: Communication and Interaction in the Early Christ-Movement*, Library of New Testament Studies 325 (London: T & T Clark, 2007), 97.

The tender language continues as he describes their feelings toward their spiritual kin in Thessalonica: "Being affectionately desirous of you, we were ready to share with you not only the gospel of God but also our own selves, because you had become very dear to us" (v. 8). It was never just about information sharing; it was about forming a relationship that allowed seed sown in the fertile ground of friendship to take root and bear fruit. Giving the best they had to offer, which was the gospel of God through the graceful instruments of their very selves, was for the benefit of these who had become very dear to the apostles. Once again, this declaration underscores "the inseparability of speaking the good news and embodying it."[20] That these Gentiles had made a home in the Jewish hearts of the apostles speaks of the boundary transgressing that is inherent in the gospel of God. The ethnic diversity of this church sets a standard.

2:9–16

Paul Recounts the Strenuous Effort in Thessalonica

Labor and toil were necessary for the apostolic sojourn to be successful. Not only did they instruct about the gospel, but they also worked at their own craft to support themselves. They were not "preachers for hire"; rather, they lived circumspectly, "holy and righteous and blameless" (v. 10). Both God and the Thessalonians were witnesses of this behavior.

Now Paul shifts from being an infant or a nurse and compares himself to a father with his children, encouraging and guiding them toward leading "a life worthy of God" (v. 12). While we do not really sense a radical patriarchal shift toward authoritarianism, the balance it provides is constructive. It seems to be a continuation of the gentle tone of nurture. The author stresses that God is calling them into God's own "kingdom and glory." "Calling" (*kalountos*), translated "calls" in the RSV, is a present tense participle, which speaks of the durative invitation God is offering. It beckons an "ongoing covenantal response," and the recipients continuously participate in God's own glorious reign.[21]

This is cause for great thanksgiving on the part of the apostles. The Thessalonians heard their word as coming from God, a powerful active word that persuaded them to become believers (v. 13). This is not a fabricated human word meant to deceive; the word of God prompted them to endure the same sort of suffering as those churches in Judea. Paul says that they had become "imitators of the

20. Johnson, *1 and 2 Thessalonians*, 67.
21. Johnson, *1 and 2 Thessalonians*, 69.

churches of God in Christ Jesus" (v. 14) who suffered at the hands of their own people, just as the Thessalonians had done. It is only by the power of the Spirit that people can persist in faith when opposition grows.

The next few verses are dense with accusatory language as Paul excoriates fellow Jews for the many ways they have opposed God's overture of reconciliation in Jesus. Not only did they kill the Lord Jesus, he writes, but he reaches back into their ancestry and recounts the killing of the prophets. Then he notes that they "drove us out," most likely referring to being shunned, to put it delicately, by his own people for his allegiance to Christ as Lord. His own history of persecuting converts had become his own painful experience as he received the same treatment for his newly found faith.

We need to be clear that this is "an intra-Jewish polemic" and is specific in its target.[22] The reader should not surmise from this harsh language that Paul has forsaken his own religious heritage. He has been wounded by this opposition, and he retaliates with the strongest linguistic weapon he has by calling them anathema and maximally sinful. Has he withdrawn his Jewish identity? By no means.

Rhetorically he is building up to his passionate concern that Jews and Gentiles become one in Christ. His opposition is intent on "hindering us from speaking to the Gentiles that they may be saved" (v. 16). He avers that the attempts by Judean Jews to hinder his mission to the Gentiles eventuates in "heaping up their sins to the limit" (NIV). This kind of text has often been used for anti-Semitic purposes, and this is a trajectory we must not follow. This is an internal dispute that has no bearing on the ongoing legitimacy of Jewish faith. The separation of Christian and Jewish forms of *ekklēsia* is grievous to him, and he seeks ways to draw them together or at least to allow them a parallel movement into God's future.

My own belief is that Jesus started an internal reform within Judaism, rather than the forming of a new faith. The separation of synagogue and church remains a wound to these spiritual kin, and we are still finding our way to remembering the original covenant and the grace by which Gentiles participate. The continuing challenge

22. Johnson, *1 and 2 Thessalonians*, 80.

of finding common ground as we think about the messianic hopes of Israel persists. Christians remain responsible for finding ways to think about shared history with Jewish forebears that will not conclude that the Jewish faith is no longer viable. This invites significant interfaith work in our time, and we return to the original schism to understand better what is at stake.

Paul finishes this diatribe with these chilling words: "But God's wrath has come upon them at last" (v. 16). The wrath of God is manifested not simply at the eschatological sorting of good and bad but also when people reap the consequences of poor choices that betray the holiness God desires. The idea that God "gives them up" to the consequences of destructive actions (Rom. 1:18) is a form of justice that acknowledges human responsibility and divine displeasure at compromised behavior that betrays covenantal promise.

2:17–20

Paul's Anguish over Being Unable
to See the Thessalonians Face-to-Face

The letter arises out of deep affection for the Thessalonians and a sense of being bereft because he cannot see them. Malherbe suggests that verse 17 should read, "But we, brethren, having been orphaned by being separated from you for a short time, in person but not in heart, most earnestly endeavored to see you face to face with great longing."[23] Longing (*epithymia*) is an intense word that describes the anguish of absence. The metaphor shifts once again. Paul is no longer infant, nurse, or father; now he is orphan. This is most likely because he had to leave Thessalonica against his will, and he determines to see them again if at all possible. The orphan metaphor "resonates well with an audience who, in turning from the idols of their pagan past, may have experienced a similar separation from their households."[24] He believes that this separation is only for a season, and, clearly, he knows and states that his heart

23. Abraham J. Malherbe, *The Letters to the Thessalonians*, Anchor Bible, vol. 32B (New York: Doubleday, 2000), 182.
24. Johnson, *1 and 2 Thessalonians*, 83.

remains with them. This is an important statement. We understand that at times all we can do is send greetings, especially by way of a friend to a friend. Geographical space need not hinder deep connection, especially as we invest abiding care through prayer and faithful communication. When I hear from friends in Myanmar, I know that their greeting has a global resonance as they wish to be remembered, even as I do. When I visited with an elderly deacon in a historical Baptist church in Moulmein, Myanmar, he repeated the phrase: "Do not forget us." When I returned a couple of years later, I reminded him that I had not.

Paul wants to come to see the Thessalonians. On more than one occasion he made such plans, but he is forthright in saying that "Satan hindered us" (v.18b). Silas and Paul are explaining why they have been absent and why sending Timothy will have to suffice (3:1–2). They do not want their converts in Thessalonica to think they are deserted, orphaned; hence it is rather disingenuous that Paul names themselves as such. Yet his longing to be with them is palpable in this section of the epistle. We can sense his distress as he simply cannot keep from thinking about them and their own prospects for flourishing in a context adverse to their faith. His pastoral sensitivity is full of pathos and care.

Paul has an active sense of the powers and principalities, which likely include Satan or other evil figures in his theological worldview. He believes that since he has been commissioned by God to do a very hard thing in proclaiming the gospel to the Gentiles, there will be opposition, "many adversaries" as he puts it in 1 Corinthians 16:9. He has experienced this personally and wants the Thessalonians not to be naive about what they are facing.

Walter Wink has helped us today to think about the powers as we do not recognize the spirited nature of our universe: "Nothing commends Satan to the modern mind. It is bad enough that Satan is spirit, when our worldview has banned spirit from discourse and belief. But worse, he is evil, and our culture resolutely refuses to believe in the real existence of evil, preferring to regard it as a kind of systems breakdown that can be fixed with enough tinkering."[25]

25. Walter Wink, *Unmasking the Powers: The Invisible Forces That Determine Human Existence* (Philadelphia: Fortress, 1986), 9.

On this text, he writes, "Paul probably does not have in mind an actual confrontation with Satan as a figure blocking his path but means simply that circumstances were such as to frustrate his attempt to come."[26] He gives no indication of how he was hindered from returning to them, but he has moved beyond Jewish opposition to a supernatural level by suggesting that his ministry was oppressed by Satan. "Again and again" (*kai hapax kai dis*) he attempts to revisit them. Departing from Corinth to return to Thessalonica may have been impossible given the fractious realities he was confronting there, and clearly the apostle is torn over his absence from the Thessalonians.

> Paul holds the view that his own eschatological hope is bound up with his converts' spiritual condition as they jointly stand before the Lord.
>
> Malherbe, *The Letters to the Thessalonians*, 185.

Prizing this community greatly, the apostle describes them as his "hope," "joy," and "crown." His own authenticity as missionary is dependent on their faithful expression of following Christ, a concession that demonstrates a most significant humility. Remarkably, he is willing to put his own apostolic credentials in the service of the possibility of the vibrancy of the Thessalonian Christians.

When the Lord Jesus comes, the apostles want to present this congregation, presumably the first they successfully founded, as an expression of their own fidelity to their calling. Laden with theological meaning, these words sum up the goal of conversion. Hope establishes their perseverance; joy arises through the companioning of the Holy Spirit and fellow believers; and crown (*stephanos*)[27] allows the apostles to see the completion of their work, a cause for boasting at the Parousia of the Lord Jesus.

A crown held an auspicious meaning in the Greco-Roman world, especially as an award for victory in an athletic contest. The venerable

---

26. Walter Wink, *Naming the Powers: The Language of Power in the New Testament* (Minneapolis: Fortress, 1984), 138–39.

27. The apostle (and post-Pauline tradition) is fond of this language because it symbolizes the glory that Christians share by their participation in redemption. See these other texts: 1 Cor. 9:25; Phil. 4:1; 2 Tim. 4:8.

Olympics used the laurel wreath worn on the head as the sign of surpassing honor for the one who prevailed to win. Gail Ramshaw's perceptive thinking about "the myth of the crown" shows how patriarchy has often dictated the symbolism; however, there is a definite flattening of hierarchy as the Christian faith, "by honoring every individual before God, specifically leads away from pyramids."[28] Ramshaw's thesis is that a male deity is required to offer stability to society. The "son of this god" is granted power, the "crown," to keep a hierarchical kingdom in order. Whereas Jesus offered revolutionary witness against the status quo, his followers shaped his proclamation to uphold their desire for this version of God's reign. I agree that the communal focus of the Thessalonians and the radical reorientation the apostles present in their style of leadership allows "crown" to become corrected by the incarnation and their own embodiment of mercy.[29]

In verse 19 Paul is now introducing what will become a prominent theme of the letter, the coming of Christ. As the epistle unfolds, we will learn of the pastoral situation he is confronting. Parousia would be a common term in that sociocultural context. It simply means the visitation of high-ranking persons such as emperors, kings, provincial leaders, and, in this sense, the coming of deity. Paul appropriates this language to speak of the most significant coming of all.

The highest compliment he can pay the Thessalonians is his insistence that they themselves are his "glory and joy" (v. 20). It takes a secure leader to grant such approbation to others, and good leadership is always about empowering others to reach beyond what they thought possible. Good leadership is never solely about the interests of the leader. Paul knows that he will not stand before God as an isolated individual, but as one who has fostered the flourishing of others at great personal expense. His decentering of self on behalf of the Thessalonians grants him the privilege of oversight and counsel as the letter unspools further. The next chapter will recount both his anguish and exhilaration as he dispatches Timothy to strengthen their faith and as he receives a report of their fidelity.

28. Gail Ramshaw, *God beyond Gender: Feminist Christian God-Language* (Minneapolis: Fortress Press, 1995), 67.
29. Gail Ramshaw, *God beyond Gender.*

FURTHER REFLECTIONS

The Emerging Doctrine of the Trinity in the New Testament

The Trinity remains the central mystery of Christian faith, and it is not surprising that in the earliest literary deposit of the Christian movement we discern the influence of Trinitarian thinking on its formation. The christological emphasis of this epistle (and Second Thessalonians) requires theological imagination that moves toward a full-blown affirmation of God's own history with humanity as threefold in expression.

The first letter to the Thessalonian congregation highlights the "Father and the Lord Jesus Christ." It also mentions the Holy Spirit, but not necessarily in any triadic formula. There is a Trinitarian grammar at work, however, and it displays the emerging doctrine of the Trinity. Paul operates as if a Trinitarian consensus is already at work, and this belief shapes how he speaks of God. There are theological judgments operative in all of his writing, and his syntax about God is evidence of his developing view of God who reveals identity as Father, Son, and Holy Spirit.[30] That Paul will use "Lord" of each of the three underscores a sense that God can only be understood in light of the activity of these three expressions of divine life. In 1 Corinthians 12:4–6 Paul offers a succinct parallelism, a key theological vision, that describes a "relational determination of God's identity":

> There are varieties of gifts—but the same Spirit (*to auto pneuma*).
> There are varieties of service—but the same Lord *(ho autos kyrios)*.
> There are varieties of working—but the same God *(ho autos theos)*.[31]

This structure implies that there is no competition among these manifestations of the life of God, and that to speak of the Christian

---

30. See "Hebrews and the Pauline Letters," in *The Oxford Handbook of the Trinity*, ed. Gilles Emery, OP and Matthew Levering (Oxford: Oxford University Press, 2011), 49. See also Elaine M. Wainwright, "Like a Finger Pointing to the Moon: Exploring the Trinity in/and the New Testament," in *The Cambridge Companion to the Trinity*, ed. Peter C. Phan (New York: Cambridge University Press, 2011), 33–48.
31. Emery and Levering, *Oxford Handbook of the Trinity*, 50.

God requires we use this kind of language. As Rowe writes, "Trinitarian reasoning proves to be exegetically illuminating—indeed the requisite language by which to receive Scripture's grammatical moves."[32]

It is important to remember that the recognition of the canon is subsequent to the time when Trinitarian doctrine is coming to fruition. Yet there is a mutual shaping at work, and moving toward an acknowledgment of how God is identified as triune binds the testaments together and sets the trajectory of a unifying belief for Christian profession. The conversations that transpired in the fourth century as the first great ecumenical council, Nicaea, convened were primarily textual and exegetical. The recognition of the canon of the New Testament later in that century (367 CE)[33] is intertwined with the theological conclusions offered by two councils, the Nicene (325 CE) and the Constantinopolitan (381 CE) about the identity of Jesus Christ and the Spirit.

The development of the notion of "canonicity" helps solidify the perception that the God of the Old Testament is the same as the God of the New Testament. Scripture offered certain norms of identity, and the unified yet distinctive work of God as Creator, Christ, and Spirit press toward understanding God as Trinity. The experiences of witnessing the resurrected Christ and the outpoured Spirit at Pentecost led early believers to reflect on the differentiated ways they are encountering God.

One may wonder how the Old Testament helps fund this emerging belief as the declaration of monotheism is paramount. Christopher Seitz contends that we should not look for "threesomes hidden away inside the activity of God"[34] in the Old Testament, a particularly lexical approach. His larger project entails reading the Hebrew Bible in a way that points beyond itself as it summons language, for example, of the means by which God creates—by Word and Spirit

---

32. Rowe, *World Upside Down*, 53.
33. Athanasius, Bishop of Alexandria, issued an Easter letter in 367 that named the twenty-seven books of the New Testament. While there are later skirmishes over the rightful inclusion of Jude, James, and Revelation, his listing has predominated.
34. Christopher Seitz, "The Trinity in the Old Testament," in *The Oxford Handbook of the Trinity*, ed. Gilles Emery, OP, and Matthew Levering (Oxford: Oxford University Press, 2011), 30.

and Wisdom. These are not competing figures of deity; rather they serve to articulate the ways in which God operates:

> The terms the OT uses to express this Living character are manifold but not limitless. God creates through wisdom. God speaks through his word. God enlivens through the spirit. God is present in holiness and yet remains transcendent. God relates to an elect people and to creation as a whole, but also has a beloved son. . . ."[35]

God's character is dynamic and personal; thus, varied ways of speaking of God's action through diverse means are understandable. This adumbrates what will later be thought of as hypostases, the idea that there is a shared underlying reality of Christ with God or the Spirit with Christ as opposed to simply being attributes, that which lacks substance.

The kind of monotheism found in the Old Testament presages Trinitarian teaching, for God is never thought of as a static monad. Monotheism for the faith of Israel meant that they did not worship multiple gods; it did not mean that God cannot reveal the divine life in multiple forms of self-communication. The New Testament is primary witness to God's self-revelation in the Son through the Spirit. These two hands of God, as third century theologian Irenaeus famously described them, are the means of God's redemptive mission, and they continue to reach toward all the world.

Paul is very comfortable moving in the semantic landscape of Trinitarian thinking, a remarkable theological feat given his fierce monotheism. Yet he understands that thinking of how God discloses the divine self in the Son and the Spirit does not need to threaten the foundational confession that God is one. His understanding of resurrection, baptism, eucharist, spiritual gifts, the body of Christ, and eschatology is suffused with language of the unity of Father, Son, and Spirit, as well as their distinctive roles in creation, redemption, and consummation.

Theologians conclude that the economic (*oikonomia*) Trinity has epistemological priority over the ontological (*theologia*) Trinity. In other words, how one encounters God in the action of redemption

---

35. Seitz, *The Trinity*, 50.

as Spirit, Christ, and the Sending One leads one to reflect on the unity of the Trinity and, ultimately, who God is immanently, in God's own divine life. While this further reflection moves beyond the scope of the New Testament, the foundation for such theological construction is laid in the Pauline tradition, in addition to other New Testament texts.[36] We are in debt to Paul for this early thinking.

36. While the feminist critique of much of the doctrine of the Trinity in traditional theology is an important corrective, I will not pursue it here, rather confining this section to thinking about the emerging doctrine. It might be argued, however, that the patriarchal context for shaping both canon and creed leaves a lasting mark on the divine identity. See Patricia A. Fox's critique, "Feminist Theologies and the Trinity," in *The Cambridge Companion to the Trinity*, ed. Peter C. Phan (New York: Cambridge University Press, 2011), 274–90. Elizabeth A. Johnson offers the most sustained critique and constructive proposal about how to use emancipatory language to speak of God in *She Who Is: The Mystery of God in Feminist Theological Discourse* (New York: Crossroad, 1992).

1 Thessalonians 3:1–13

Strengthening Those Suffering for the Gospel

Paul wanted to be with his friends and fellow believers but could not, and he has grown apprehensive over how they are faring as they, too, suffer persecution for the name of Christ. Most likely an interval of several months has transpired since he last saw them, and difficult events have occurred in the community as members have died before the expected return of Christ. His premature departure meant that further teaching was needed to confirm the new believers in their faith, and he is eager to advance his catechetical work. He does the next best thing by sending his colleague Timothy to see how things are going in Thessalonica; the younger missionary would offer his own gifted ministry there and grow in his own pastoral work.

3:1

Paul's Sacrifice for the Sake of the Thessalonian Church

The apostolic team is willing to endure his absence, "be left behind at Athens alone" in the poignant words of 3:1. There are thick bonds between these early missionaries, and they lean on each other to maintain their common work. There is a sacrificial relinquishment on Paul's part that Andy Johnson calls "Paul's cruciform action."[1] Paul is willing to be bereft of his stalwart companion Timothy for the sake of the Thessalonians. We do not know if Silvanus

---

1. Andy Johnson, *1 and 2 Thessalonians,* The Two Horizons New Testament Commentary (Grand Rapids: Eerdmans, 2016), 87.

made the journey to Athens; we simply think that Paul dispatches Timothy for this visit, which expresses concern for their well-being, offers further instruction, and lays the groundwork for bringing cheering news to the anxious apostolic team. They knew they had left too soon, albeit under duress, and their care is demonstrated in this deliberate follow-up with those who may have felt abandoned.

This is a methodical approach to planting a church. Rather than simply tallying up numbers for apostolic boasting, there is genuine concern for this outpost of Christian belief. Paul well knows that mature faith takes time, and it is not easy to persevere when so many forces would seek to derail their journey of faith, love, and hope. One missional church scholar offers perspective on this reality: the "church faces a challenging polarity. On the one hand, it needs to live out its inherent translatability into every context, and on the other hand it must avoid the pitfall of becoming overly contextualized."[2] For the Thessalonians, this requires a profile that does not seek to overthrow existing structures of governance while, at the same time, making the break with idolatry so clear that the new community has a sense of boundary as to what is acceptable. In a society shaped by family relations, trade associations, clubs, and cultic assemblies, "social identity is secured by group adherence, and status is maintained in a vertical pattern of social alliances and public loyalties."[3] Disentangling themselves from this web of connections mandates great intentionality and nuance. Fatum offers further insight: "In such a society it is a comprehensive and risky project, indeed, to change one's faith and way of life; in a very literal sense it means a radical change of social identity in order to adjust to a new pattern of adherence and independence."[4] Her acute perception prompts awareness of the extremity of social/familial cost, potential alienation, and actual political threat in exchange for this new religious conviction.

The apostolic team is intensely aware of what the Thessalonians are facing; they have had their own taste of how disruptive their

2. Craig Van Gelder, *The Ministry of the Missional Church: A Community Led by the Spirit* (Grand Rapids: Baker Books, 2007), 124.

3. Lone Fatum, *First Thessalonians, Searching the Scriptures: A Feminist Commentary*, ed. Elisabeth Schüssler Fiorenza (New York: Crossroad, 1994), 254.

4. Fatum, *First Thessalonians*, 254.

proclamation was during their sojourn there. To challenge idolatry in whatever form threatens the status quo, usually giving rise to significant opposition. We can think of brave persons who have challenged regnant expressions of idolatry: Dietrich Bonhoeffer's resistance to Hitler's Aryan propaganda; Dorothy Day's critique of materialism that ignored the poor; Martin Luther King Jr.'s prophetic denouncement of racism; Elizabeth Johnson's discernment of the ravages of sexism in biblical studies and theological construction in her own church; and Harvey Milk's protest against the treatment of LGBTQ persons. Each suffered in unique ways, some even giving their lives at the hands of malignant forces who wanted their idols to go unchallenged. This kind of leadership entails great personal cost, and many shrink back from the precipice of risk. I will point to some contemporaries who have found the cost of discipleship dear in a further reflection.

Who offered leadership to this Thessalonian community as it continued its pilgrimage in faith? While Jason is not mentioned within the epistle, we know from the account in Acts that he was an influential leader. Presumably he was a new believer also, still growing in his understanding of how the resurrection of Jesus has transformed his horizon of hope. Paul does not want a vacuum of leadership, particularly his own absence, to thwart the witness of the community. He knows that stable and mature leadership is what can sustain a community under threat.

We wonder what kind of structure developed in the interval between Paul's departure and Timothy's visit. Did they have deacons who served the congregation along the order we see in Acts? Most likely not, as that was a later development. Who led in baptism and Eucharist, the initiating and sustaining sacraments for a Christian *ekklēsia*? We cannot be sure. Was there regular proclamation and confession that Christ has risen, the very foundation of their faith? This would be critical to their continuation. The reader is left to ponder what indeed, other than the Spirit of God, assisted the church to persevere. The Spirit always gifts the body of Christ to do the work to which it is called. We can presume such occurred in Thessalonica, and there are hints of an emerging structure in 5:12–13 as Paul speaks of "those who labor among you and are over you in the Lord . . ."

When I was a pastor of a very small church in rural Kentucky as I was completing doctoral studies, I marveled at the aggregation of spiritual gifts that spurred good ministry in the community. Tutoring children who were behind in their studies, visiting the sick, feeding visitors to their church, helping other farmers bring in the crops, this faithful community offered its many gifts in service to neighbors. Because I was only there two times a week, Sunday and Thursday, the seasoned lay leadership—who were accustomed to helping train newly minted pastors—carried the load of ministry. They were acquainted with the supply of the Spirit and offered their spiritual resources to those in need, and somehow, with grace, they continued to make an impact.

While Paul well may have appointed leaders prior to departing, it is more likely that they emerged in his absence (5:12–13). Those who were the first converts (*aparche*), literally the first fruits, of Thessalonica may have led the congregation. Hans Conzelmann makes this argument in his treatment of 1 Corinthians. Those "first baptized enjoy special esteem."[5] At this point there is no formal order of deacons, only functions or services that arise from gifts (*charismata*).

We sense an improvisatory approach going on as this reciprocal relationship between apostles and community reveals great interdependence. Their continuing relationship serves all concerned. Clearly, there is not a fixed doctrinal deposit that gives clear parameters for belief, and the ethical understanding of Christian living is still taking form, especially for those of pagan background. The Jewish converts would have guidance from Torah; yet living in the diaspora made their enactment of distinctive practices more exigent, and they would have had to adapt. This kind of improvisation, under the guidance of the Spirit, occurs in every epoch, with God entrusting frail humans to carry the gospel in earthen vessels (2 Cor. 4:7) for their historical horizon. While the guardrails of tradition and creedal deposits offer a centering understanding, believers have to face new issues in their day and find a way to confess their faith contextually. If Phyllis Tickle, an insightful contemporary interpreter, is correct, that is the urgent task of our day: "Every time the incrustations of

---

5. Hans Conzelmann, *1 Corinthians*, Hermeneia—A Critical and Historical Commentary on the Bible, trans. James W. Leitch (Philadelphia: Fortress, 1975), 298.

an overly established Christianity have been broken open, the faith has spread—and been spread—dramatically into new geographic and demographic areas, thereby increasing exponentially the range and depth of Christian's reach as a result of its time of unease and distress."[6]

I believe Phyllis Tickle has been prescient in her analysis, and heeding her wisdom can benefit ecclesial identity in our time. Essential change is never easy, and the conserving impetus too often endemic in churches quenches the Spirit's holy nudge toward the future. Every congregation faces the "temptation of playing it safe," in the words of Gil Rendle.[7] Too many compromises of the gospel and too many lost opportunities to express God's loving forgiveness to estranged ones result from this. Many younger adults have lost patience with this self-protective modus operandi and are departing the church in droves. Only initiatives for social justice have any hope of turning this around, and there are many options other than churches to accomplish this work. Working to become more relevant on the social landscape is a critical task.

3:2–5

Sending Timothy for Encouragement to Beleaguered Thessalonians

Timothy, "our brother and God's servant in the gospel of Christ," travels to Thessalonica for exhortation and "to establish" in faith those whose conversion now puts them in direct conflict with their former ways. Paul commends Timothy as *synergon tou theou*, which is nothing less than coworker with God. The apostle believes that a visit from Timothy would be of great assistance and does not lack confidence in his gifts or suitability for the task. Since he had not been a part of the initial visitation of the apostles, Paul wants to make sure that the time Timothy spends among the Thessalonians is of maximum benefit. Deeply rooted in faith from his family and

6. Phyllis Tickle, *The Great Emergence: How Christianity Is Changing and Why* (Grand Rapids: Baker Books, 2008), 17. See also her *Emergence Christianity: What It Is, Where It Is Going, and Why It Matters* (Grand Rapids: Baker Books, 2012).

7. Gil Rendle, *Quietly Courageous: Leading the Church in a Changing World* (Lanham, MD: Rowman & Littlefield, 2019), 155.

significant association with Paul, Timothy could bring fresh perspective and perhaps be a less intimidating presence than his men-
tor. The lengths to which Paul goes to describe himself in maternal
imagery, in addition to weak and dependent as infant and orphan,
may be intended to offset suspicion that he had been overbearing in
his approach. Perhaps his great anxiety over their well-being in his
absence arises from some guilt on how he behaved, what accelerant
to persecution he helped fuel, and presumption that more of their
flourishing was up to him rather than the Spirit. (This may sound
like my own hermeneutics of suspicion at work, and I could be
accused of layering contemporary psychological assessment on to a
very different culture.)

There is no such thing as a minister without flaws. Pride or insecurity may stalk the pastor, with faithful leaders doing what they can
to repair damage done by intemperate speech or self-preoccupation.
Even though the Spirit strives to help pastors and people bear the
strains of their differences, uneasy relationships are not uncommon.
Part of this arises from the many expectations congregants place
on their ministers; they want perfection in performing the myriad
tasks: proclamation, administration, evangelization, community
leadership, education, pastoral care and visitation, to mention only
a few.

His own travail and imperfection notwithstanding, Paul does not
want the church to be dissuaded by the afflictions that accompany
faithfulness. Not only did the apostles expect to be persecuted, but
they also warned these converts that their pathway would include
similar suffering (vv. 3–4). Suffering for the name of Christ is a
prominent theme in Pauline correspondence.[8] We are astonished at
his own capacity to perdure when adversaries are regularly at hand.
Indeed, it appears that when adversaries challenge his ministry, he
believes that he is following the will of God (1 Cor. 16:9). Without
suffering, he would not be conformed to the image of God's Son, in
his judgment. That he bears this as a signet of his calling stamps his
calling as authentic.

---

8. E.g., Rom. 5:3; 2 Cor. 12:10; Eph. 3:1–6; Phil. 1:29; and Col. 1:11. He believes suffering
   conforms one to the image of Christ.

Avoiding suffering seems to be endemic in our time. Any small hardship such as power going out, delay in home services, some pain accompanying recovery after surgery, less than a stellar performance review, is often seen as unnecessary and burdensome. The affluent are especially susceptible to the notion that they should be exempt from the common fate of humankind, where suffering has the possibility of being braided with life-giving energy. Without trying to glorify suffering, it is a regular theme in the Pauline literature that one takes one's share in suffering. The mythology that modern medicine has mastered palliative care so that no pain is borne remains popular, particularly if you can afford the best medical care. The recent pandemic has laid bare the disparities people of color endure when seeking care. Compounding factors such as systemic health problems arising from food deserts, neglect of prophylactic measures, and a medical community that caters to white persons all contribute to unnecessary suffering that could be avoided. We cannot avoid addressing these issues if we would be just.

The extent to which some parents will go to make sure little negative comes into the lives of their children does not prepare them well for the reality of human exigencies that comes with finitude. Cosseting children and preventing them from experiencing the consequences of poor choices undermine the development of virtue.[9] Suffering is a part of being human, and, as we learn to receive it, we become part of the paschal mystery of dying and rising, putting off the old and finding newness of life beyond suffering.

I am not suggesting that we should labor under a martyr complex about suffering like poor old Polycarp of Smyrna who, some suggest, actively sought to be a spiritual paragon by the manner of his death.[10] Prior to the Constantinian Edict of Milan in 313 that permitted Christianity to be tolerated as a legitimate religion of the empire, it was much more dangerous to confess the Lordship of Christ. The idea of being a martyr, a burning witness, encouraged the faithful to stand fast. Early Christians said it should not be

9. See the important working of Alasdair MacIntyre, *After Virtue* (Notre Dame, IN: University of Notre Dame Press, 1981).
10. Polycarp, disciple of John and Bishop of Smyrna, at age eighty-six was burned at the stake and then speared to finish him off in 155 CE. See *The Martyrdom of Polycarp* for a presumably eye-witness account.

sought, but neither should it be avoided.[11] The first martyr, Stephen, remained the exemplary model for how to forgive even as one was dying for faithful following; Christian martyrs were to die as had their Savior, bearing the suffering and forgiving their enemies. They were to exemplify God's own welcome even of persecutors who opposed the way of Christ.

While more progressive Christians may not entirely trust contemporary blaring claims about the persecution of Christians around the globe, often because of missionaries' refusal to live within governmental guidelines about proselytizing, there clearly are instances where Christians are targeted as a vulnerable minority. I see this most clearly from the protracted time I have spent in Myanmar, where active measures are taken against ethnic groups that are largely Christian, in particular the Karen people.

Years of displacement into refugee camps along the Thai-Burma border have blunted the hopes of generations of Karen, and this forcible removal from their property continues unabated. Without papers and little hope for return to their property, the Karen remain a people without rights to their homeland and slim hopes for immigration. In a December 2018 opinion piece in the *Wall Street Journal*, Hollie McKay quotes Ephraim Mattos, East Asia operations manager at the Nazarene Fund, who said, "The Burma Army has already moved in hundreds of troops, dozens of heavy weapon systems and multiple mechanized vehicles in what appears to be in preparation for an imminent onslaught against the Karen people."[12] The persecution is ongoing.

Systematically, the military destroys churches, looting offerings, violently raping women in the sanctuaries, thus desecrating both, and prohibiting worship at home. They want to exploit the public vulnerability of a gathered community, which they relentlessly attack. Because of the years of obscurity for the nation after the

---

11. Well-known is Tertullian's statement, "the blood of the martyrs is the seed of the Church." In *To the Martyrs* he writes that some Christians "eagerly desired it" (*et ultro appetita*)—martyrdom.

12. The Karen are not the only targeted group; the brutality against the Kachin people has been especially gruesome. Hollie McKay, "Myanmar Persecutes Christians, Too," *Wall Street Journal*, December 6, 2018, https://www.wsj.com/articles/myanmar-persecutes-christians-too-1544138518.

British departed, ethnic groups in Burma (Myanmar) have had little recourse. Genocide is occurring, and the world seems to care too little. Regrettably, it is often when people of color are being killed that the global community turns a blind eye.[13] Persecution both challenges and refines faith.

Paul's concern that the labor of the apostles might have been in vain is understandable, and he is eager to learn of the state of the nascent church. He writes passionately about their spiritual well-being: "when I could bear it no longer, I sent that I might know your faith." (v. 5). Truly his heart remains with them, and he desires that the Thessalonians endure in their calling. He believes that his own reputation is on the line, apparently, and he yearns for their spiritual health.

I have a pastor friend who writes his congregation every week. He calls them "beloved," and he offers words of blessing and encouragement. He is not afraid to tell them that he loves them, misses them, and carries them in his heart all the while. Especially as churches are not able to easily gather in person during the COVID-19 pandemic, his messages are treasures to the congregants—particularly those who are vulnerable to the virus and even more cut off from their community of faith. As I have spoken with members of this congregation, I have learned of the significance of this straightforward pastoral care. His accompanying presence—primarily through social media—is sustaining the congregation's sense of corporate identity as well as the valuing of individuals. I imagine that this form of pastoral care will continue long after fears of contagion have ebbed, because it allows the minister to provide care for more persons.

The apostle names his fear of what might have befallen the Thessalonians: "that somehow the tempter had tempted you . . ." (v. 5). Once again, we read Paul's acknowledgment that malign spiritual power is working against God's purposes. He does not use the language of "Satan" here as in chapter 2; rather, he uses "tempter" (*ho peirazōn*), which connotes the same force of testing the faithful. Indeed, this places the Thessalonians in the same company as Jesus, who did not escape having his faith tested by the adversary (cf. Matt.

13. Hollie McKay, https://www.wsj.com/articles/myanmar-persecutes-christians-too-1544138518.

4:5; Mark 1:13; Luke 4:2). It appears that, like their Lord, these new believers also remained faithful in the face of such temptation.

Paul concludes this pericope with his concern about whether the apostolic labor has been in vain. He has worked with a sense of urgency, and his desire to form faithful communities has driven him onward. In this instance, however, his anxiety is nearly crushing as he yearns over the Thessalonians, feeling helpless to accompany them further.

We are anxious only about those things we cherish, and clearly Paul cherishes this community in which he labored for their conversion. It could be that some of his anxiety arises from the tenor of his proclamation there. It would appear that his preaching "had contained fairly explicit reference to the return of Jesus."[14] This was causing great consternation in the congregation, and he must rethink his eschatological approach. He will take up this topic in chapter 4 of this first epistle, seeking to allay their fears.

I wonder if he thought of this early part of his ministry when later he penned 1 Corinthians 15:58, "Therefore, my dear brothers and sisters, stand firm. Let nothing move you. Always give yourselves fully to the work of the Lord, because you know that your labor in the Lord is not in vain"(NIV). He has moved from the anxiety over his work in Thessalonica to resounding confidence that God establishes human labor, and God is always working for good with those who love God, called by God's own purposes (Rom. 8:28).

3:6–10

Receiving a Good Report of Faith and Love

Timothy returns with good news of their faith and love. He brings a report that a fairly well-established mission is going forward and, important for the agenda of the rest of the epistle, he brings requests for further teaching. That they remembered the apostolic team kindly is deeply reassuring (v. 6) even though the community suffered for extending welcome to them. The Thessalonians are as eager to see

14. Michael Walsh, *The Triumph of the Meek: Why Early Christianity Succeeded* (San Francisco: Harper & Row, 1986), 112.

Paul as he is to see them. The congregation's faithfulness comforts the apostolic team even as they continue to bear affliction and distress.

Verse 8 is a stark declaration: "For now we live, if you stand fast in the Lord." Paul and his companions can also remain faithful as they witness their spiritual progeny pressing forward in their righteous pursuit. It is a "mutual mediation of grace."[15] This is a very rending statement from Paul; it suggests that his team gravely needs encouragement at this juncture of their ministry. Having departed Athens and arrived in Corinth, the apostles face great obstacles once again. Knowing that others are standing firm inspires them to press on. Without a sense that others can persevere, it is not likely that the apostolic mission can withstand the onslaughts from varied sectors.

I remember as a second-year seminary student serving as a Baptist summer missionary in Israel, attempting campus ministry at the Scopus campus of the Hebrew University. At that time in my theological formation, I believed that Jews needed to be converted, and I was zealous in my efforts for that to occur.[16] More seasoned leaders talked about simply learning to live peacefully with both Jews and Muslims, striving for the common good, indeed, the peace of Jerusalem. I remember how thickly connected the Christian community was there. Denominational lines were permeable, with Protestants, Catholics, and Orthodox believers finding common cause in seeking to preserve early Christian origins and the places they called holy while remembering that an even more ancient people had significant claim to the land. These rock-ribbed Baptists relished any news of other Christians flourishing, and they sought ways of collaborating even when fractious divides threatened. They put a higher priority on a humble witness that genuinely cared about the complex religious setting that all faced rather than a triumphal need to be ultimately the only righteous before God. I sense a similar humility in Paul's response to Timothy's report.

Paul tries to summon language of gratitude sufficient to describe his joy at the report. He thanks God for the faithfulness of the

---

15. Johnson, *1 and 2 Thessalonians*, 90.
16. Today, I simply believe that Jews are following a different pathway to salvation. The relationship between Christians and Jews is most constructive when there is both mutual respect and a measure of "holy envy," as Krister Stendahl famously put it.

Thessalonians (vv. 9–10). I. Howard Marshall translates Paul's exuberance in this way: "Paul means 'I am tremendously grateful to God—and yet I realize that I am incapable of giving him the gratitude which he deserves.'"[17] Ben Witherington likens Paul's statement to Psalm 116:12, "What shall I render to the LORD for all his bounty to me? (RSV)"[18] The joy that Paul and his companions feel for the sake of the Thessalonians before God is intense, and the intercession that they offer is unflagging, night and day (v. 10).

The prayer of the apostles is that they might see their beloved friends face to face and "supply what is lacking in [their] faith," (3:10), which is a hint that some of Timothy's report is not quite as glowing. Evidently, he learned of theological concerns in the community, and he will defer to Paul to add further teaching. The overall rhetorical strategy has been to praise the Thessalonians copiously, but now a shift in tone prepares for an instructional section beginning with chapter 4.

Correcting others is subsequent to correcting one's own perspective. I cannot help but speculate that Paul may have needed to reconsider how he spoke to the Thessalonians about his vision of the summing up of the age. Apocalyptic language, which he surely used, has the effect of kindling enthusiasm for a literal enactment of the prediction and may contribute to lax behavior or escapist fantasies. Even as the writings of Tim LaHaye have perpetrated alarmist perspectives on the way history will conclude, the apostle's earlier teaching may have stoked similar alarm.[19]

Persons are eager to have a roadmap for the future. They want to "crack the code" of the image-laden and metaphorical writings of Scripture.[20] Popular writers have become rich off of the gullibility of those

---

17. I. Howard Marshall, *1 and 2 Thessalonians*, New Century Bible Commentary (Grand Rapids: Eerdmans, 1983), 97.

18. Ben Witherington III, *1 and 2 Thessalonians: A Socio-Rhetorical Commentary* (Grand Rapids: Eerdmans, 2006), 96.

19. LaHaye is the author of sixteen novels of apocalyptic fiction, the Left Behind series, which has sold millions of copies. Written between 1995 and 2007, these books have captured significant attention because of the angst many feel about the condition of the world. They represent a dispensationalist view of biblical prophecy, focusing on literalistic interpretations of Revelation, Daniel, Isaiah, and Ezekiel. The theological system he purports and has popularized subordinates a more careful reading of Scripture. Scholars of Protestant, Catholic, and Orthodox traditions have widely panned his construction.

20. Coming out of a very conservative background myself, I have been helped greatly by

who believe something is true just because it is in a book! Especially in an accelerated time of global pandemic, which includes the SARS (of which COVID-19 is a variation) and Ebola epidemics, readers want some assurance of what the future holds. It is a temptation to use the present challenge as a lens from which we read a larger swathe of human history, forgetting that recurring calamities bedevil every epoch.

Albert Camus wrote *The Plague* in Oran, a French Algerian city, during World War II. Illness and the virus of war were for him "the plague," as he writes the story of the city's experience of the cholera epidemic in the mid-nineteenth century in the context of his own reflection on the French resistance to the Nazis. His novel is most interested in how persons can cultivate compassion rather than practice disregard for the suffering in such a cataclysmic time. The characters in the book fail both at being of concrete assistance as well as in finding ways to alleviate the anguish of their neighbors. The narrator, the supposed objective observer of these dynamics, concludes with an acute observation: "There are more things to admire in men than to despise."[21]

Camus's well-known quotation is regularly summoned in this season. This is the call of the present moment in our context, also, as we seek to strengthen our common life. Whether we see this time as that of God's judgment on a wicked world or merely the result of humans living in close proximity to one another and other infecting agents, we have lessons to learn. Paul offers guidance about how to live with "end of the world" frenzy, which is still relevant.

3:11–13
Offering Apostolic Blessing of Affection

Paul concludes this section with rich words of blessing, asking God and the Lord Jesus to "direct our way to you . . ." continuing the theme of their longing to be present once again with the Thessalonians. He

---

Northrop Frye's *The Great Code: The Bible and Literature* (San Diego: Harcourt Brace, 1982), as he delineates the words, types, myths, metaphors, and language of the Bible. His literary critical approach to scriptural texts he highly esteems for their continuing cultural importance orients the reader beyond dogmatic and literal interpretations.

21. Albert Camus, *The Plague* (New York: First Vintage International Edition, 1991), Kindle Edition, Location 4076 of 4174.

exhorts them to allow the Lord to make them "increase and abound in love to one another and to all," and he reminds them that this is the pattern the apostles have exhibited toward them. Such love is not generated simply by good-hearted humans. It is the power of the Holy God who desires Christians to become unblamable in their own expression of holiness before God (v. 13). Here we hear the echo of participation in God's own holiness, which is an invitation to become the gospel to others.[22]

Of this idea, Lone Fatum cites Halvor Moxnes: "The extensive purpose of Paul's communication is to guide his new converts through a steady progress of moral improvement onward to that state of pure holiness"[23] so as to be prepared for the coming of Christ. An ingredient to this improvement is tangibility of their love toward one another and to all, as the apostles hold forth such love for them (v. 12). There is nothing as winsome as a hospitable congregation, and people who feel truly welcomed experience something like a resurrection.

"Holiness" may sound like an old term that is more connected with certain ecclesial tribes that go back to the eighteenth century. We recall that Charles and John Wesley founded a "Holy Club" (so called in mockery by fellow students) while enrolled at Christ Church, Oxford, in 1729. Strict discipline, accountability, and vigorous study and service all contributed to the formation of young men who would prove themselves prodigious advocates for their faith (e.g., George Whitefield). Their methodical approach to discipleship led to the founding of Methodism, which remains a global expression of Christianity. Nazarenes and other traditions carry this legacy forward.

Holiness has to do with sharing life with God; it is not an expression of being better than others or condemning of all that is "this worldly." It is the pursuit of living in accordance with God's intent for human flourishing. It relates to an increase in love toward others and faithful action in the midst of their tribulation.[24] Paul knows that this is not possible without God's own action in Christ to empower persons to become embodied holiness (*hagiōsynē*). God will "establish

---

22. See Michael J. Gorman, *Becoming the Gospel: Paul, Participation, and Mission* (Grand Rapids: Eerdmans, 2015).

23. Halvor Moxnes, ed., *Constructing Early Christian Families: Family as Social Reality and Metaphor* (New York: Routledge, 1997), 185, quoted in Fatum, *First Thessalonians*, 254.

24. Johnson, *1 and 2 Thessalonians*, 97.

their hearts" so that they will be presentable before God at the "coming of the Lord Jesus with all his saints" (v. 13). In other words, they will be conformed to those who accompany their savior, the saints.

Like "holiness," the word "saint" suggests one not fully rooted in the common demand of living life in a human body. While we may love Frederick Buechner's lyrical image of God's "holy flirtation with the world" as God drops handkerchiefs—the saints—such a description makes it appear that these persons are not grounded in the same reality as the rest of us. Paul's vision of those persons (saints) who accompany Jesus in his coming is not clear, and he simply writes "with all his saints" (v. 13).[25] Some debate whether these are angels or Christians who have already died;[26] and likely Paul depends on Zechariah 14:5 that prophesies, "the LORD your God will come, and all the holy ones with him." More likely, it is an image that ties the two testaments together; God is redeeming God's own in God's eternal redemptive project. That saints accompany the Parousia offers assurance that God is gathering faithful people to share life in God's presence.

Paul echoes an apocalyptic tradition, "which connects the holy ones with the end,"[27] as in Daniel 7. The holiness of the Thessalonians has an eschatological orientation: it will only come to completion at the coming of the Lord Jesus Christ (5:23). The work of sanctification has been ongoing in their lives yet awaits its full revealing.

FURTHER REFLECTIONS
Costly Discipleship in Our Time

The long shadow of Dietrich Bonhoeffer falls across any discussion of discipleship. Capturing the imagination of generations through his writing and his martyrdom, he was unflinching in thinking about

---

25. Frederick Buechner, *Wishful Thinking: A Theological ABC* (New York: Harper & Row, 1973), 83.
26. Abraham J. Malherbe, *The Letters to the Thessalonians*, Anchor Bible, vol. 32B (New York: Doubleday, 2000), 211–14, contends that the "holy ones" are most likely Christians, but he does not see this as an example of some hidden rapture. Paul may have written it this way to assure the Thessalonians that their loved ones who have already died are in the safekeeping of their Lord.
27. Malherbe, *The Letters to the Thessalonians*, 215.

the cost of following Jesus. Wedded in his life were contemplation and action. He was not content to theorize about discipleship, nor could he avoid the demands of his conscience when confronted with the horrific savagery of Adolf Hitler. We remember him with gratitude, knowing that it would have been very easy for him to fall in line with many other German Christians in supporting the Third Reich. In retrospect, we revere him more as we learn more of his immense sacrifice.

It is always risky to call attention to the life of a disciple prior to its conclusion, for even the best sometimes betray their confession of Christ through behaviors unworthy of their Lord. And while there are other key prophetic figures in our time, I will draw attention to only one: John Lewis, of blessed memory. His discipleship was life-threatening and long-standing, an expression of his commitment to faith in Jesus Christ.[28]

John Robert Lewis (1940–2020) was a civil rights leader and American statesperson, serving as a member of the U.S. House of Representatives from Georgia's 5th district from January 1987 until July 2020. Prior to serving in the House, his primary work was as a leader of the Student Nonviolent Coordinating Committee, a Freedom Rider, and an organizer of the 1963 March on Washington. Most notable was his leadership of three Selma-to-Montgomery marches across the Edmund Pettus Bridge. This action to end legalized segregation nearly cost him his life on "Bloody Sunday," when he was beaten brutally, fracturing his skull. And it was not the only time he endured violence, arrest, and imprisonment for his advocacy for the dignity and civil rights of minority citizens.

Even in this he found hope. Reflecting on this march he observed how difficult it was to bring about change quickly: "Selma is a place where we injected something very meaningful into our democracy. We opened up the political process and made it possible for hundreds and thousands and millions of people to come in and be

---

28. Many of the details of the life of John Lewis come from his book *Walking with the Wind: A Memoir of the Movement,* written with Michael D'Orso (San Diego: Harvest Books, 1999). Most of what it cited in this section of further reflection is simply public record.

participants."[29] John Lewis found hope in every movement toward crossing bridges of promise toward racial reconciliation.

The work of civil rights was a key expression of his faith, and he pursued it with candor and nonviolent passion. As a child, he aspired to be a preacher, his first congregation consisting of chickens, as he liked to recount. He preached his whole life long through his work for justice for Black Americans and getting into "good trouble" was costly but necessary. Lewis said that "the civil rights movement was based on faith. Many of us who were participants in the movement saw our involvement as an extension of our faith. We saw ourselves doing the work of the Almighty. Segregation and racial discrimination were not in keeping with our faith, so we had to do something."

Lewis first heard Martin Luther King Jr. on the radio as a fifteen-year-old boy and was deeply moved by his courage and principled approach to civil rights. Later, meeting Rosa Parks and ultimately King helped spur his own involvement in the movement, following their example of nonviolence.

For seventeen terms Lewis served his district, which was primarily Atlanta. Called the "conscience of Congress," this distinguished representative had encompassing concerns that included national health insurance and the rights of LGBTQ+ individuals. His commitment to nonviolence led him to oppose the 1991 Gulf War, attempts at limiting welfare, and other dehumanizing policy moves. "Where is the sense of decency?" was his frequent retort to such political gambits. He knew who would benefit and who would suffer, and his commitment to justice frequently put him at odds even with members of his own Democratic party.

He lived to see the first Black American become president in 2008 and offered this perspective: "If you ask me whether the election . . . is the fulfillment of Dr. King's dream, I say, 'No, it's just a down payment.' There are still too many people fifty years later, there's still too many people that are being left out and left behind."

John Lewis departed to be with God the summer of 2020 after a few months battling pancreatic cancer. Duly honored in the Capitol, in his district, and at the bridge he crossed, this indefatigable

---

29. John Lewis, oral history interview conducted by the House historian, Dec. 11, 2014.

warrior has an enduring legacy. Faith and hope sustained his long obedience, and we can give thanks for this witness to graceful forgiveness, a true mark of discipleship. It was this strength of character that so inspired.

I met Congressman Lewis at an American Baptist meeting in the summer of 2005 just outside the convention center after he had addressed the gathering. He walked alone down the street as if a person of much less notoriety. I asked if I might shake his hand as I was so honored to meet him. His usual humble response was, "I am grateful to meet you too."

1 Thessalonians 4:1–18

Exhorting toward Maturity in Christian Living

We move beyond thanksgiving into the heart of the epistle as Paul begins his instruction on how the Thessalonians ought to live in their uncertain time, how they ought to walk. He reminds them of instructions already given and, evidently, he has become aware through Timothy that the Thessalonians are having a hard time fulfilling the expectation of participating in their own sanctification (vv. 1–2). Thus, he will be very specific in his exhortation. We may be reminded how concretely ethical exhortation can be expressed and whom it benefits.

4:1–2

Apostolic Exhortation for How to Live in a Liminal Time

The apostle reminds them that they have learned how to live from the presence and instruction of the apostolic team when they were with them. They had set an example worthy of emulation. The apostolic concern is not simply about correcting behavior for a legalistic purpose; indeed, the goal of transformed living is to please God. Paul notes that the medium of their instruction is "through the Lord Jesus." Higher authority than apostolicity is in play, and no claim to independent teaching could suffice. The apostles see themselves as the authorized conduit for the gospel of Jesus.

A Christian leader must be very careful in making such a claim. Of course, a wise spiritual guide relies on the Holy Spirit and the example of Jesus to offer instruction; however, one must be vigilant in discerning whether one really has "a word from the Lord" about matters of substance. Paul will make such a disclaimer in 1 Corinthians 7:25 and then proceed to offer his "opinion as one who by the Lord's mercy is trustworthy." The real danger comes when one cannot distinguish personal opinion from the grounded teaching that flows from God.

Claiming spiritual authority can be a treacherous enterprise, and there is a seductive element to the power that accrues to positions of leadership. Talking more and listening less are the twin qualities that can shipwreck one's vocation, the Scylla and Charybdis of ministry. Being less watchful about character also threatens credibility, and we all must grow in vigilance as we guard our hearts.

Paul will use this injunction again later in chapter 4 as he emphasizes that he is declaring to them "by the word of the Lord" (v. 15). He knows that any teaching he offers must have the sanction of being in line with the earliest Christian traditions. How he has access to these is a further question, yet we know that his interaction with the "pillar apostles" in Jerusalem, as well as other witnesses such as Priscilla and Aquila, were significant for him.

Paul had met the risen Christ on the way to Damascus. Klaus Haacker notes that this encounter does not lead to divine judgment, as the tradition of prophetic language would suggest an indictment. Instead, "Paul is called to serve the one whose memory he had tried to erase."[1] His experience of grace in this encounter shapes all of his thinking. For this "untimely born" apostle (1 Cor. 15:8), the death and resurrection of Jesus provided the foundational certainty. His resurrection was the "great eschatological event" that propelled

> What was the role of Paul in the foundation of Christianity? Was Paul the true interpreter of Jesus? Or was he a maverick innovator who invented a new religion, nothing to do with what Jesus had intended, in which the figure of "Jesus" happened to play a central role?
>
> N. T. Wright, *What Saint Paul Really Said: Was Paul of Tarsus the Real Founder of Christianity?* (Grand Rapids: Eerdmans, 1997), 22.

---

1. Klaus Haacker, "Paul's Life," in *The Cambridge Companion to St. Paul,* ed. James D. G. Dunn (Cambridge: Cambridge University Press, 2003), 24.

Paul to rethink his interpretation of the Hebrew Scriptures.[2] Seeking to understand a crucified messiah within the context of Judaism was his hermeneutical challenge, yet he passionately concluded that Jesus is the Jewish Messiah, "the one in whose life, death, and resurrection Israel's destiny was summed up and brought to fulfillment."[3]

Paul's experience of the risen Christ "brought with it the recognition that his people's messianic hope was fulfilled, that the new age of the kingdom of God and the resurrection had begun, and that the time of God's blessing through Abraham to all nations . . . had come."[4] Preaching Christ to the Gentiles flowed from this conviction and this endeavor became his all-consuming concern.

The continuity between the teaching of Jesus and the theological construction of Paul is clear, in my judgment. I turn to N. T. Wright's perceptive analysis:

> Jesus believed it was his vocation to bring Israel's history to its climax. Paul believed that Jesus had succeeded in that aim. Paul believed, in consequence of that belief and as part of his own special vocation, that he was himself now called to announce to the whole world that Israel's history had been brought to its climax in that way. When Paul announced "the gospel" to the Gentile world, there, he was deliberately and consciously implementing the achievement of Jesus.[5]

C. H. Dodd argues that Paul received the fundamentals of the gospel at a date that "cannot be well later than some seven years after the death of Jesus Christ."[6] This claim contends for great continuity with the earliest traditions while leaving room for Paul's own genius in structuring his proclamation and writing, as well as significant improvisation in intertextual reading.

2. Wright, *What Saint Paul Really Said*, 22.
3. Wright, *What Saint Paul Really Said*, 174.
4. Stephen C. Barton, "Paul as Missionary and Pastor," in *The Cambridge Companion to St. Paul*, ed. James D. G. Dunn (Cambridge: Cambridge University Press, 2003), 35.
5. Wright, *What Saint Paul Really Said*, 181.
6. C. H. Dodd, *The Apostolic Preaching and Its Developments* (London: Harper & Brothers, 1936), 16.

4:3–8

Living in the Bounds of Sexual Purity

Paul gets right to the point about what sanctification (*hagiasmos*) needs to look like in the Thessalonian community: "that you abstain from unchastity" (v. 3). That this is the first thing Paul addresses suggests that some blatant behavior was transpiring, manifestly known in the community for it to be included in Timothy's report. While some may have attempted to keep secret their expressions of unchastity—a word that means sexual immorality (*porneia*)—there may also have been a lack of distress among these new believers about this aspect of their lives, and they were openly flaunting their promiscuity. Those of Jewish background would be more attuned to thinking of Torah teaching about avoiding sexual relations outside of marriage, but the Gentiles who were now "turning to God" required further instruction.

We recall that the first criteria for including the Gentiles in the one people of God were that they abstain from things related to idols and from sexual immorality (Acts 15:19–20). This apostolic decree provided foundational guidance for those who came out of the imperial cult or other mystery religions. The stipulations were both minimal requirement—no circumcision—and food prohibition, to lessen offense to their Jewish forebears in faith by not eating things polluted by being sacrificed to idols. The decision of the Jerusalem Council also called the Gentiles to new standards of sexual behavior.

> Amid its historical suspicion of sex, the church has sometimes behaved as if sex were the *most* important dimension of Christian life."
>
> David H. Jensen, *God, Desire, and A Theology of Human Sexuality* (Louisville, KY: Westminster John Knox Press, 2013), ix.

Christians have regularly elevated "sexual sin" to the highest level of moral concern. A certain nervousness about human bodies has shaped much of Christian thinking,[7] and the notion that

---

7. Early church fathers such as Basil of Ancyra and Gregory of Nyssa wrote of sexual activity as granted "to humans by a merciful God in light of the loss of original blessing." In other words, it is only because of sin that marriage and its concomitant sexual expressions came into being. They prized asceticism and monastic pursuits, which advocated for celibacy and

celibacy is a higher form of spirituality has endured in some traditions. Rather than seeing human sexuality as a joyful gift to be offered
in covenantal relationship, a restrictive attitude has prevailed, rel-
egating sexual intercourse to the sole purpose of procreation while
denying its unitive and celebrative functions. As Sarah Coakley
perceives, "Institutional Christianity is in crisis about 'sexuality.'"[8]
The inability to articulate a theology of desire that is deeply rooted
in God's own Trinitarian relations severs sexuality and spirituality,
she argues. When a thick relationship between the two no longer
obtains, immorality ensues. Granting desire a privileged status,
Coakley believes the longing for God and longing for intimacy with
another are of one piece.

Once known for their restrictive instruction on matters of sexuality, churches have of late been more shaped by culture than ever
before. Christian ethicist David P. Gushee critiques the sexual-
ethical perfectionism of previous times, believing that for today an
ethic of covenantal realism both resists libertinism and promotes
the wisdom of Scripture, history, and tradition without the negative
condemnations of earlier times.[9]

Paul is quite forthright in his instruction to the "brothers," who
evidently were the offenders. Debate over the meaning of "possess his vessel [*skeuos*]" (KJV) in verse 4 is nearly as old as the letter itself.[10] While some translate the word "vessel" as referring to a
wife, which Linda McKinnish Bridges says hearkens from rabbinical Judaism,[11] most scholars today will say that the word refers not
to living with a wife in honor, but simply to gaining control over
one's sexual urges so that boundaries in the community could
thrive. It is important not to skew this interpretation by forcing

---

other practices. See Teresa M. Shaw, *The Burden of the Flesh: Fasting and Sexuality in Early
Christianity* (Minneapolis: Fortress, 1998), 198.

8. Sarah Coakley, *God, Sexuality, and the Self: An Essay 'On the Trinity'* (Cambridge: Cambridge
University Press, 2013), 1. Also see her edited volume, *Faith, Rationality, and the Passions*
(Oxford: Blackwell Publishing, 2012), which focuses on how Christian practice takes
seriously the interface between reason and passion, a wholistic approach to humanity.

9. See his recent work, *After Evangelicalism: The Path to a New Christianity* (Louisville, KY:
Westminster John Knox Press, 2020), 119.

10. Augustine, with his penchant for suspicion about all things sexual, argues for "wife" rather
than the male organ, which had given him so much anguish.

11. Linda McKinnish Bridges, *1 & 2 Thessalonians*, Smyth & Helwys Bible Commentary
(Macon, GA: Smyth & Helwys, 2008), 98.

Paul's admonition to align with the text of 1 Peter 3:7, "Likewise you husbands, live considerately with your wives ["vessels" in other translations], bestowing honor on the woman as the weaker sex." Besides, to render "vessel" as "wife" takes a very low view of a woman's significance as if "her *raison d'être* was solely to provide a means by which her husband might satisfy his sexual appetite without infringing the divine law."[12] The brothers need to gain discipline over their passions, indeed learn to control their bodies, chiefly their sexual organ.

Reading this text today with egalitarian lenses moves us beyond thinking of men as controlling women's sexuality. Thus, the language of "possessing," as some interpreters contend, belongs to a patriarchal system that commodifies women, and readers today can summon this text to reject that hierarchical structure. Women are not responsible for men who are unable to control their sexual urges, although women are often blamed in rape cases for what they were wearing or for acting provocatively, as judged by men.[13] It is a remarkable repudiation of patriarchy for Paul to place responsibility for constructive sexual activity squarely on the shoulders of the men.

A new congregation was sure to be of interest to surrounding neighbors, and if its profligacy in sexual practices were known, the claims to following a better pathway would be nullified. If those within the community were taking advantage of each other, as Paul alludes in verse 6, it would become common knowledge, as this kind of scandalous word tends to travel the community grapevine. Paul wants

> It is, then, a matter to be learnt, and that diligently, not to be wanton. But we possess our vessel, when it is pure; when it is impure, sin possesses it. And reasonably. For it does not do the things which we wish, but which sin commands.
>
> John Chrysostom, *Homilies on Galatians, Ephesians, Philippians, Colossians, Thessalonians, Timothy, Titus, and Philemon*, in Nicene and Post-Nicene Fathers, ed. Philip Schaff (Edinburgh: T & T Clark, 1994), 344.

---

12. F. F. Bruce, *1 & 2 Thessalonians*, Word Biblical Commentary (Waco, TX: Word Books, 1982), 83.

13. Many would argue that rape has little to do with satisfying sexual desire and altogether to do with degrading power that men exercise over women.

nothing to sabotage the good reputation circulating about the faithfulness of the Thessalonian Christians.

In recent years as information about sexual practices in cults has
come to light, such as in the communities around David Koresh or
Jim Jones or Warren Jeffs, we see that an abusive pattern persists.
Underage girls are often the target of these so-called religious leaders, and these girls as well as young women are vulnerable to their
sexual proclivities. Already suspect, these exploitative actions tar-
nish further any shred of credibility in public opinion about these
communities. That predatory behavior shatters the lives of female
victims is often overlooked.

Living within the bounds of sexual purity grants a distinctive
identity and differentiates them from their culture. Paul is not advo-
cating celibacy or denying the reality of the importance of human
sexuality. He is setting boundaries that will allow human flourishing. If a man in the community is soliciting or demanding sexual
favors from the wife of a brother in Christ, he is transgressing marital
vows and sinning against another member of the body of Christ. As
McKinnish Bridges writes, "The first boundary is that sex is to be
placed in the context of holiness and honor."[14] Concerned about both
individual and communal practice, the apostle knows that without a
disciplined approach, neither will be commendable in their culture.
Clearly Paul wants them to be identified as holy, not heathen. Holiness is his goal so that when the Lord comes, the believers will bring
honor to God by their circumspect living.

The apostle offers a stark warning that the Lord "is an avenger in
all these things" (v. 6). He reminds them of his previous forewarn-
ing about how God holds persons accountable in this aspect of their
lives. God's calling is to holiness, which requires forsaking uncleanness. If one refuses to adjust behavior toward holiness, it is an affront
to God, an act that "disregards" God because the Holy Spirit has
been given to them (v. 8).

Paul believes that the Christian must be careful about what they
may do that compromises the Spirit. After a long section on immorality in 1 Corinthians 6:12–18, Paul concluded, "Do you not know

14. McKinnish Bridges, *1 & 2 Thessalonians*, 102.

that your body is a temple of the Holy Spirit within you, which you have from God? You are not your own; you were bought with a price. So glorify God in your body" (vv. 19–20). This is a more refined way of seeing how the Spirit of God interacts in our bodily lives. The emerging pneumatology, doctrine of the Spirit in the First Testament, did not allege that Holy Spirit was sullied by sinful human spirit.[15] God could indwell a Samson or a Saul and remain holy; such is the humility of God. Nevertheless, Paul regards the Spirit as God's chief good gift to humanity, whom we should welcome by offering the wholeness of self as an instrument of grace. We can see that the apostle is moving toward a wholistic theological anthropology. It is not possible to separate embodied actions from a person's identity, from who one most truly is.

4:9–12

Living in Love and Industry

Loving one's spiritual kin in Christ is at the heart of transformed living. Paul is assured that God has continued to instruct the Thessalonians with this essential teaching.

The whole of the arc of redemption is about God's unwavering love for creatures, and that nothing can separate humans from that love (Rom. 8:38).

Being loved changes persons. Paul knows that because God's love has been poured out on this community, they have become more loving. It is the sine qua non of following Jesus, and it is to be extravagant in circumference, reaching throughout Macedonia (v. 10).

There are yet supplementary acts that demonstrate this Christian life, Paul avers, by exhorting them to do "more and more." Presumably, he means for them to grow in their concern for others. One way the members of the community can do this is by working with their own hands so as not to be reliant on the charity of others. He knows that this approach grants dignity to the worker and relieves others of needing to provide patronage. This has been his pattern, and he

---

15. See my *Joining the Dance: A Theology of the Spirit* (Valley Forge, PA: Judson, 2003), 39–40.

knows what freedom and commendation it evokes; he can proclaim freely, and others can see his own industry. His reticence to receive support from others has set a model, and he dignifies work as an essential part of Christian vocation.

A remarkable example of this principle has occurred in Chiang Mai, Thailand, where tribal women from villages have set up micro-businesses by reviving crafts of weaving and sewing, as well as investing in agricultural development. Because village life is so peril-ous for women and girls—with much sexual abuse and little control over their destinies—these initiatives prevent them from being traf-ficked as sex slaves, as if that could be their only source of income, their lives reduced to commodity. Their desire for a self-determining future in a horribly abusive culture is transforming their own sense of agency and reliance on God's synergistic partnership in the gos-pel. Educating these women and girls is making a profound differ-ence in their future prospects, and they have found ways to support themselves through the dignity of their work. Some of the girls have been able to pursue further education, often returning to continue the transformative work of developing these enterprises.

Lacking citizenship papers as they have been displaced from Myanmar or Laos, their refugee status has not prevented them from courageous acts of charting a new course. They are living the truth of what Paul encourages: "to aspire to live quietly, to mind your own affairs, and to work with your hands, as we charged you; so that you may command the respect of outsiders, and be dependent on nobody" (vv. 11–12). Collaborating with NGOs and each other, these women are creating an economy that lifts their families out of poverty and prostitution. They are powerless no longer as they envi-sion a different future story.[16]

The apostle wants the Thessalonian community to be respected by outsiders. As they live chastely, diligently, and equitably, they will most likely attract new believers who admire their way of life. These are sustaining practices, and Paul is eager for them to grow the com-munity's capacity to care for their own and others by prudent living.

16. Andrew D. Lester, *Hope in Pastoral Care and Counseling* (Louisville, KY: Westminster John Knox Press, 1995), offers a sustained reflection on the power of constructing a hopeful future story, a new narrative that can actually reshape one's life.

They will honor Christ as they live into the resurrection life that is promised by their baptism.

4:13–18

Living in Hope for the Coming of the Lord

This is a difficult text to comprehend fully as we only hear one side of the conversation; apparently some members of the community have died and there is considerable grief in the Thessalonian church, even a sense of hopelessness. What is the fate of those who have died prior to the return of Christ? Are they consigned to Sheol, a place of less-than-full life inhabited by shadowy remnants of earthly life?[17] Are living members of the community cut eternally off from these loved ones? Will they be together at the Parousia, or will those still alive have advantage? Paul needs not only to clarify earlier teaching and offer further instruction but also needs to provide pastoral care for a troubled congregation. In this section the theme of hope surges to the forefront.

The destiny of departed ones, "those who are asleep" (v. 13), is unconditionally related to the confession that "Jesus died and rose again" (v. 14). Any hope for resurrection of believers is bound to his overcoming of death. His resurrection is the premise of his lordship, the focal dimension of apostolic proclamation. Because Paul has met the risen Christ on the way to Damascus, he can write with assurance because of his call and commission to apostleship.[18] Where did he get his conviction that Christ would return?

According to C. H. Dodd, Paul worked within the Jewish doctrine of the two ages, "This Age," and "the Age to Come." By "virtue of the death (and resurrection) of Christ the boundary between the two ages is crossed, and those who believe belong no more to the present evil age, but to the glorious Age to Come."[19] The coming of Israel's Messiah, Jesus, shifts the language from the "Day of YHWH"

---

17. Most descriptive are the following texts: Job 10:18–22, Ps. 88:2–10, and Ps. 94:17.
18. See J. Christiann Beker, *Paul the Apostle: The Triumph of God in Life and Thought* (Philadelphia: Fortress, 1980), 5.
19. Dodd, *The Apostolic Preaching and Its Developments*, 11.

(OT) to the "Day of the Lord" (NT), according to N. T. Wright, yet it remains the ancient Jewish hope.[20] Paul's great challenge is that few Jews believed that their Messiah had come, thus Paul must create eschatological architecture that includes a crucified Messiah and the welcome of Gentiles.

Paul's rhetoric "clearly assumes his audience's belief in the Lord's royal coming."[21] Most likely they are making the shift to thinking about the Day of the Lord as the demonstration of Jesus as Messiah. Paul would not have taught them about the resurrection of Jesus without referring to their own hope of also being raised. As a Jew steeped in the Hebrew Scriptures, he would know the language of the coming one, such as found in Daniel 7:13.[22] Because he is persuaded that Israel's hope is fulfilled in Jesus, he can easily apply this expectation to the Parousia of the risen Christ.

We know that Paul spent time in the company of foundational witnesses in Jerusalem who would have claimed to be eyewitnesses of resurrection appearances and ascension. He makes a similar claim about having seen the risen Lord. They would have shared these remarkable and mysterious events with him prior to any account in the four Gospels. Perhaps the apocalyptic language of Matthew 24 and Mark 13 had been a part of what he learned from them, although we have no means of verification. In 1 Corinthians 15:11 he declares a summary of the gospel, which he has received. While we cannot precisely retrieve the oral tradition, we know that there was a significant body of testimony circulating that Paul would have inherited as a convert to the Way. He truly believes that his kerygma is in line with the primitive testimony, and in Galatians 1:11–18 he says his gospel did not come from a human source, and in the next chapter he recounts that he submitted "the Gospel which I preach" to Peter, James, and John at Jerusalem (Gal. 2:2), evidently receiving their approval. It is probable that both the inspiration of the Holy Spirit and the teaching of these earlier apostles shape his theological

20. N. T. Wright, *Paul and the Faithfulness of God*, parts 3 and 4 (Minneapolis: Fortress, 2013), 1094.

21. Andy Johnson, *1 and 2 Thessalonians*, The Two Horizons New Testament Commentary (Grand Rapids: Eerdmans, 2016), 122.

22. For further explication of the significance of this text see Adela Yarbro Collins, *Cosmology and Eschatology in Jewish and Christian Apocalypticism* (Leiden: Brill, 2000), 171.

perspective, in addition to his own unique training and experience as a diaspora Jew.

Without the letters to the Thessalonians, we would have little teaching on the coming of the Lord. Paul mentions it six times in 1 and 2 Thessalonians and only one other time specifically (1 Cor. 15:23), although there are allusions in the other epistles. Parousia was not a foreign thought to the Thessalonians, as it carried the cultural connotation of a royal parade as an important person came to the city.[23] It meant a public disclosure of honor and power, and Paul surely had that in mind as he wrote about the return of the reigning Christ. He does not want his friends to be uninformed, so he delineates what he can imagine will occur as the appearing sums up the present age. Both his contemporary culture and his deep knowledge of the Old Testament texts shape these spare predictions.

In the time the apostolic team spent with the Thessalonians they spoke urgently about eschatological things to the extent that, evidently, they believed the Christ would return before any of the community died. That was not the case, however, and the apostle wants them to lean into hope even as they grieve. Once again, according to Beverly Roberts Gaventa, Paul wants this congregation to be distinguished from those around them,[24] "so that you may not grieve as others do who have no hope" (v. 13). How Christians handle death is a telling sign of faith in God's faithfulness. Hope will differentiate the Thessalonian community, just as abounding love and sexual propriety will. Hope is the telos that draws Christians forward in times of unknowing.

It is the most radical act of trust to accompany a loved one to the point of death and then entrust that one to the care of God. I experienced this profoundly when my husband died over a decade ago. Everything we believe about hope, resurrection, and God's future intersects in the movement through death to life.

Faith deepens as Christians trust God's own capacity to overcome all that would threaten to overcome us, especially that last enemy, death. That boundary between life as we know it and the life to come

23. Johnson, *1 and 2 Thessalonians*, 123.
24. Beverly Roberts Gaventa, *First and Second Thessalonians*, Interpretation: A Bible Commentary for Teaching and Preaching (Louisville, KY: John Knox Press, 1998), 63.

has been traversed by Jesus, who as pioneer points the way through the treachery of death to life everlasting.

In straightforward language Paul contends that because of the resurrection of Jesus, God "will bring with him those who have fallen asleep" (v. 14). This answers their question about the fate of the deceased, whether they were in the safekeeping of their Lord and whether they would participate along with the living in this summative event. He uses his earlier warrant "by the word of the Lord" to assure them that those who remained alive "shall not precede those who have fallen asleep" (v. 15). It is not clear why this matters theologically except perhaps it invites humility for the Thessalonians to think that those who have been in Christ's presence longer (in whatever form) have been given priority of status. While no intermediate state is spelled out in this brief epistle, it is in keeping with the rest of Paul's writing to think of those asleep in Christ as already held in his body even while awaiting final consummation. So deep is Paul's belief that resurrection is not a solitary event, past tense and involving only Jesus, he cannot imagine Christ's triumphant return not including those who have entrusted themselves to his Lordship and its new realm.[25] The raising of Jesus precedes these others, but it is his intent to envision a great corporate harvest.

Then the startling description of Paul's vision of the Parousia unfolds:

> For the Lord himself will descend from heaven with a cry of command, with the archangel's call, and with the sound of the trumpet of God. And the dead in Christ will rise first; then we who are alive, who are left, shall be caught up together with them in the clouds to meet the Lord in the air; and so we shall always be with the Lord (vv. 16–17).

We cannot lose sight of the sheer grandeur of his apocalyptic language and the danger of concretizing a literal interpretation, which has too often been the case as authors sensationalize this imagery.

---

25. See Nancey Murphy, "The Resurrection Body and Personal Identity: Possibilities and Limits of Eschatological Knowledge," in *Resurrection: Theological and Scientific Assessment*, ed. Ted Peters, Robert John Russell, and Michael Welker (Grand Rapids: Eerdmans, 2002), 202–18, to think about continuity in embodied life through death to resurrection.

"The seriousness of apocalyptic language lies less in the details than in the dazzlement of the vision as a whole."[26]

Conventional apocalyptic descriptions included a loud shout, a mighty trumpet, or other cataclysmic sounds from heaven.[27] This scene would remind Jewish readers of Scripture of Daniel 7, as mentioned above. Gentile readers would be struck by the images of power. The trumpet signals arrival of a royal figure; it may also be a summons to a final battle. That the descending one would bridge both heaven and earth in this powerful display indicates that Christ is bound by neither and triumphs over all, unlike the Roman emperor who has limited territories over which he can preside.

The imagery is difficult to parse. Literal interpretations in popular fundamentalism suggest that "Paul envisaged Christians flying around in midair on clouds,"[28] a fantastical scene. The departed seem to come with the Lord, yet those "dead in Christ" rise first. Paul does not spell out if this is a joining of earthly bodies "sown in dishonor" (1 Cor. 15:43), with the eternal spirits of those in Christ's company. Most likely he is not suggesting that those who have previously died are enjoying the fullness of resurrection life in heaven. He simply says that the dead will rise first and those alive will be "caught up" or "snatched." The dramatic language suggests how great an enemy death is, with snatching from the jaws of death requiring great power.

The idea of "rapture" has long dominated this passage, deriving from *rapio*, the Latin translation of *harpazō*, the word that means to snatch or carry away. There is no hint of a "secret rapture" here as popularized by premillennial dispensationalists. This nineteenth century theological aberration has the purchase of conspiracy, selectivity, and secrecy, thereby tantalizing the imaginations of folk seeking to make sense of their cultural space, often on the margin. I will write more about this in the further reflection on "Eschatological Hope in Our Time."

---

26. Beverly Roberts Gaventa, *Our Mother Saint Paul* (Louisville, KY: Westminster John Knox Press, 2007), 182.
27. Cf. 2 Esd. 6:23; Dan. 10:6; 1 En. 14:8; and Rev. 1:10.
28. N. T. Wright, *The Resurrection of the Son of God* (Minneapolis: Fortress, 2003), 215.

Christ's appearing (as Parousia can also be rendered) has appropriate fanfare: the archangel's call and the trumpet of God. This serves to alert the faithful that the long-awaited day has arrived. There are several ways of thinking about this text. First, it is the consummation of the age; the present age is winding down, and the Lord returns to earth to gather up the faithful, leaving the others to fend for themselves in a wicked and destructive world. On the surface this text does not suggest that Christ lingers long; the goal, it appears, is to gather up the faithful and depart, closing the present age. A second option is to not see this as a literal physical return, but rather to think of one's going through death to life and encountering the glory of Christ at the end of the journey. The appearing is the result of one coming to the Lord in the life beyond. This is a rather solitary reading and probably holds less promise even if it subdues the literalism of the physical return.

Andy Johnson considers a third way of reading this. Rather than seeing this as taking all the saints out of the world or the voyage of the individual through death to the presence of Christ, Johnson affirms "that this community who goes to honor the Lord by meeting him in the air shares that honor as they escort him back to earth, where he publicly consummates his reign as Lord of the cosmos."[29] Rather than this being some sort of interim millennial rule, it is about the ultimate redemption of all that God created. God, through Christ, is bringing about the desired end for the world God so loves.

The imagery of meeting in the air and being surrounded by clouds offers a mysterious theophanic (God-disclosing) vision. Clouds often shroud mysterious presence in Scripture, whether the leading of the Israelites to the land of promise, the cloud over the tent of meeting, the holy presence on the Mount of Transfiguration, or the ascension. One who was taken up in a cloud now returns with the same portent. It is no less mysterious here as Paul realizes that to speak of this kind of eschatological scenario requires ancient tropes and futuristic hopes. Its mystery cannot be fully articulated.

The ending of this pericope is the most profound: "and so we shall always be with the Lord" (v. 17). This is the great hope of redeemed

29. Johnson, *1 and 2 Thessalonians*, 133.

life, to live in God's presence in an unhindered way, confident of welcome and the sheer ecstasy of becoming what God has purposed for individuals and community, gathered into the one body of Christ. We cannot fathom eternity, so the language of "always" transcends our temporal frame. Yet the idea of always being with the Lord has the reassuring tone of Isaac Watts's beloved hymn "My Shepherd Will Supply My Need": "Here I would find a settled rest . . . no more a stranger, nor a guest, but like a child at home."[30] God's eternal welcome lifts us beyond the exigencies of suffering and death and gives a lasting home.

The chapter ends with these words of reassurance, "Therefore comfort one another with these words" (v. 18). The apostle wants them to ruminate on his teaching and remind other members of the community that they are not forsaken, and that God is accomplishing the divine intent. He also wants them to know that they have the power to tend one another in grace and hope. Comfort is contagious, and they can extend it to others grieving in their midst. God does not leave them comfortless, and the presence of other community members is a sign of God's own care. As Theresa of Ávila reportedly said, "Christ has no body but yours. No hands, no feet on earth but yours. Yours are the eyes through which he looks compassion on this world." As instruments of grace, Christians offer Christ's own comfort to their neighbors.

FURTHER REFLECTIONS
Sanctification as the Goal of the Christian Life

Much of this epistle is about growing toward holiness, or the process of becoming sanctified, becoming a saint. This cannot happen in isolation, for it is within a community that the disciplines of compassion, self-control, and forbearance are exercised. How can we ask God for patience and overlook those who come our way that require it? Holiness is not about withdrawal from the community but a deeper immersion into it.

---

30. Text: Psalm 23, paraphrased by Isaac Watts (1674–1748).

Those early *ammas* and *abbas* who departed the cities for the desert in the fourth to sixth centuries thought that if they could escape the baleful influence of contemporaries, they could in isolation pursue holiness in an unhindered way. Yet, as St. Anthony said, it was not so much the battle of the eye or the ear, external battles, but the battle of the heart, the interior challenge that shaped their spiritual destinies. On whom would they lean their whole being? Along the way they learned that isolation ultimately was not the best way to become holy. Their neighbors were the means of Christian formation rather than a hindrance to it. As Dorotheos of Gaza illustrated with his wheel in the sand, where the center represents God and the spokes represent human beings, the closer one gets to God the closer one gets to one's neighbor. And the closer one gets to one's neighbor, the closer one gets to God.[31] Inseparable movements draw us with neighbor to God.

Sanctification is a lifelong process that requires the interface of divine and human agency. The Protestant Reformation's insistence on *faith alone* has unfortunately fostered a deep suspicion about the efficacy of any human effort in matters of salvation. "Only believe" became the watchword of those shaped by a tradition that accented the justifying action of God to the neglect of "growing in grace," the transforming movement of sanctification. In addition, the Reformed tradition has treated the biblical idea of perseverance as a logical corollary of God's unilateral election; there, "working out one's salvation with fear and trembling" (Phil. 2:12) has not always been viewed as the essential expression of personal redemption.

Alongside this theological legacy is our acquisitive culture's preoccupation with achievement, programmed outcomes, and easily won certitude. Give us the formula, the opinion of the expert, or the right software, and we are certain we can solve any presenting challenge. Thus, the acute spiritual longing of contemporary persons is vulnerable to purveyors of spiritual methods that promise quick solutions to the unfathomable emptiness that characterizes the spiritual lives of many, even among those who claim Christian identity. The idea of a patient, receptive, collaborative process in which one's true spiritual

31. *Dorotheos of Gaza: Discourses and Sayings,* translation and introduction by Eric P. Wheeler (Kalamazoo, MI: Cistercian Publications, 1977).

identity is forged over time seems strangely out of sync with today's instant communication, instant credit, and instant gratification.

A monk friend of mine, now in his nineties, speaks of the process of sanctification as sitting by the same monk in the choir for over fifty years (who has bad breath and is tone-deaf) and finding ways to love him. This mundane activity is just the sort of thing God uses to call us to maturity in Christ. Our lives remain "unfinished symphonies," in the words of Ronald Rolheiser.[32]

Put briefly, the theology of sanctification with which I work includes these four affirmations: (1) sanctification is God's work and ours; (2) sanctification is a lifelong process; (3) sanctification actualizes our calling as truly the image of God and truly ourselves; and (4) sanctification occurs best in community.[33] This cannot be a purely linear process, yet these aspects of becoming holy are essential.

We are called to be saints, and, according to John Wesley, it will not come to pass unless we *intend* to become saints.[34] As Thérèse of Lisieux exhorts, "Begin now . . . believe me, don't wait until tomorrow to begin becoming a saint." The community of faith is the context where our lives are bound together by the Spirit of God, who uses every aspect of our common life as a means to sanctification. This Paul knows well and urges participation in a community that leads to holiness.

FURTHER REFLECTIONS
Eschatological Development in Paul

A perennial question in Pauline studies is the degree to which his eschatology develops. Is the Thessalonian correspondence an outlier—alarmist and apocalyptic—or is it the foundation for his further thinking about the return of Christ and the summing up of the age? That he explicitly mentions Christ's return only in one

---

32. Ronald Rolheiser, *The Holy Longing: The Search for a Christian Spirituality* (New York: Doubleday, 1999), 156.

33. For a lengthier treatment of this outline, see my chapter "Spiritual Formation: The Journey toward Wholeness," in *Central Thoughts on the Church in the 21st Century*, ed. Thomas E. Clifton (Macon, GA: Smyth & Helwys, 1998), 121–33.

34. See his generative work, *A Plain Account of Christian Perfection* (London: Epworth Press, 1955).

other text outside 1 and 2 Thessalonians provokes curiosity about his extended proclamation. While we may assume that the entire authentic Pauline corpus (seven letters) is written within a fairly short time frame, most likely CE 49–57, nonetheless the delay of the Parousia becomes an interpretive challenge for the Thessalonian epistles, if not a primary concern for subsequent letters.

N. T. Wright argues that Paul's thinking in the Thessalonian correspondence does not really differ from his later writings. "Jesus' resurrection; his present location in heaven; his future return, and his deliverance of his people from wrath: these are commonplace in Paul's developed thinking . . . and were central from very early on in his writing . . ."[35] The whole of the Pauline corpus takes its bearings from the resurrection of Jesus.

Again, Wright states his view:

> to suggest a straightforward "development" of his eschatology is in fact a further oversimplification which acknowledges neither the subtle complexity of all his thought nor the situational dynamics which called forth (for instance) a good deal of eschatological teaching in 1 Thessalonians and hardly any in Galatians. The rich, dense coherence which we have seen in his vision of monotheism and election is once again on view as we contemplate his eschatology.[36]

The development of Paul's eschatology has, apparently, been more in the minds of his interpreters. Misunderstanding about Parousia that details "the Lord descending, believers going up on the clouds, and meeting the lord 'in the air'" has, according to Wright, been "drawn, not from the Bible at all, but from the world of pagan usage, where it was almost a technical term for this kind of imperial visitation."[37] Schemes that conflate Revelation with these early Pauline writings only serve to confuse.

What is most important in Paul's thinking is that he models the hope of resurrection for Christians on the resurrection of Jesus. There is continuity with the imagery of "waking and sleeping" found in Daniel 12:2 and Paul's inaugurated eschatology. What Israel

35. Wright, *The Resurrection of the Son of God*, 214.
36. Wright, *Paul and the Faithfulness of God*, 1047.
37. Wright, *The Resurrection of the Son of God*, 217.

longed for came to pass in the resurrection of Jesus; this will also come true in the lives of Christians. Paul has modified Jewish eschatological beliefs by naming Jesus as the crucified and risen Messiah and pointing to the gift of the Spirit as the demonstration of the inauguration of the last day, the day of the Lord Jesus.[38]

Wright poses the interesting idea that there was an interval between Jesus' death and resurrection.[39]

> As far as Paul was concerned, resurrection, for Jesus as for Christians, was a new life *after* a period of "life after death," not a new state into which he had slipped at bodily death, leaving his body to be buried as irrelevant. He does not say that Jesus had been "asleep" between his death and resurrection, but he implies that there must have been a period between the two events . . . [and] that for Paul, the resurrection of Jesus was the sharp, shocking fulfillment of the hope of Israel.[40]

We usually think of Jesus passing through death to life in an instantaneous process, even though there is the Petrine witness of him "descending into hell" (1 Pet. 3:19, 4:6) to preach to captives there. Once an important part of the Apostles' Creed (inserted in the fourth century), it has come to occupy a more dubious status since the Reformation.

Wolfhart Pannenberg believes that neglecting this article of faith constricts a vision of how expansive the lordship of Christ really is, as well as God's intention to save all. "Salvation from future judgment is still made available in the realm of the dead to those who during their lifetime encountered neither Jesus nor the Christian

---

I believe in God, the Father Almighty, Creator of Heaven and earth; and in Jesus Christ, His only Son Our Lord, . . . He ascended into Heaven, and sitteth at the right hand of God, the Father almighty; from thence He shall come to judge the living and the dead.

Apostles' Creed

---

38. Wright, *Paul and the Faithfulness of God*, 1046.
39. Wright, *The Resurrection of the Son of God*, 218.
40. Wright, *The Resurrection of the Son of God*, 218–19.

message."[41] God's revelation in Jesus is not confined to a first-century audience but spans all of time, according to the descent narratives. Accenting his proclamation to the multitude who came before him sharpens the idea of faith coming by hearing (*fides ex auditu*), as well as the universal scope of salvation. While Paul does not address the topic of the descent, there is a similar sense that the cosmic lordship of Christ will be manifest to all (Phil. 2:10–11).

That the expected "end" had broken into history required that Paul rework his eschatological vision. Although the end was inaugurated with the resurrection of Jesus, he is clear that there is a further consummation to occur. There are hopes carried by Israel that do not seem realized in the coming and resurrection of Jesus—justice had not yet fully arrived, people still sin, the Messiah is not what they expected—and the future of the ancient people of God is at question. The fact that most of Israel rejected Jesus as the promised Messiah challenges Paul to creative theological construction.[42]

He works with the dualism of the present age and the age to come, a popular notion with the rabbis of his epoch and Second Temple Judaism. His belief in resurrection derives from Daniel, 2 Maccabees, and perhaps the Wisdom of Solomon, and his own encounter with the risen Christ; then he has the profound responsibility of proclaiming that Israel's hope had been realized in the resurrection of Jesus.[43] Already ruling, a significant affront to Caesar's empire, Jesus will make this rule known throughout the realm through his own appearing. The age to come is already breaking into the present, and Paul's writing reflects this affirmation.

FURTHER REFLECTIONS
Eschatological Hope in Our Time

The orthodox statement about the coming of Christ is stated in the Councils of Nicaea, Constantinople, and Chalcedon: "he shall come

---

41. Wolfhart Pannenberg, *The Apostles' Creed in the Light of Today's Questions* (London: SCM Press, 1972), 93.
42. Wright, *Paul and the Faithfulness of God*, 1048.
43. Wright, *Paul and the Faithfulness of God*, 1062.

again, with glory, to judge the quick and the dead; whose kingdom shall have no end," according to the Nicene Creed. These venerable words cannot be said to convey a sense of urgency in our time as the centuries have unspooled since they were codified. Only the more fringe groups in recent centuries—Plymouth Brethren, Millerites, dispensationalists, fundamentalist contemporary Zionist Christians—seem to find this confession compelling or give it much notice. Yet we must not dismiss this confession out of hand, for it speaks about human hope, God's providence, and the Lordship of Jesus Christ.

Each of the affirmations in the conciliar formulations carries considerable freight. What does it mean to "come with glory?" What does judgment before God's emissary, Jesus the Christ, look like, especially for those who have already died? Do we know of any kingdom that does not end? These are but a few of the questions that arise as we think not only about our own destiny beyond death, but that of the cosmos and humanity as a whole.

Most needed of recovery in our time is a sense of accountability before God. The scenarios surrounding the summing up of humanity's history epoch remind us that there is a transcendent intention at work. The Triune God has been moving creation toward its desired end since its beginning. At times humanity has been a true partner in this endeavor, but more often humans resist God's movement toward justice and mercy. We do not balance the needs of the community with our own individual desires, which usually proves disastrous.

It was not until about 200 BCE that personal eschatology came to the fore, with the book of Daniel shaping the trajectory. Prior to that, it was primarily the nation that was focal. The martyrdom of the Maccabees sharpened the question about the fate of the righteous, moving beyond the primitive notions of Sheol toward strong belief in resurrection. Their deaths in the service of the people of God, warring against the desecration of the temple by Antiochus Epiphanes (c. 180–161 BCE), led to this affirmation from the mother of the seven martyred sons: "Therefore the Creator of the world, who shaped the beginning of man and devised the origin of all things, will in his mercy give life and breath back to you again, since you now forget yourselves for the sake of his laws" (2 Macc. 7:23). It was a thoroughly Jewish understanding of resurrection, with the New Testament being dependent on this construction.

Eschatological thinking has always been context specific. When apocalyptic texts emerged, for example, the book of Revelation, a great persecution of Christians was transpiring under the reign of the Roman emperor Domitian from 81 to 96 CE. Scholars now debate about whether the Revelation version of apocalypse was only concerned about its timeframe or whether it had a futurist connotation; this remains a perennial concern as interpreters deal with the nature of apocalyptic writing. It may be that all apocalyptic writing finds a way to blend this-worldly prophetic eschatology with an other-worldly, more transcendent vision for the completion of creation and redemption.

Laura Turner has asked the question, "Why are so many Christians obsessed with predicting the rapture?" Simply because it is in the Bible, she believes. Citing the "Rapture Index," which has a scoreboard of factors that point to the nearness of this cosmic event, it measures how many think the time is at hand. She contends that the early church "believed that Jesus would return very soon, even during their lifetimes, and Christians have been revising that prediction ever since."[44] This publication also confronts its fears about the apocalypse by celebrating Armageddon Awareness Day in conjunction with Earth Day, a curious juxtaposition.

The challenge with most visions of the end is the abandonment of this world for the sake of heading heavenward, wherever that is. Such a view imagines that God is elsewhere and that this good earth is not worth preserving. It also suggests that our true home is not here but in a transcendent realm. A critical theological idea is that the earth is in God, even as God suffuses our globe with presence.[45] God is at home with us even as God is not confined to creation as we know it, the essential meaning of panentheism.

Over the last forty years, leading theologians have been attentive

---

44. Laura Turner, "Why Are So Many Christians Obsessed with Predicting the Rapture?," *Pacific Standard*, April 19, 2019, https://psmag.com/news/why-are-so-many-christians-obsessed -with-predicting-the-rapture.

45. See the fine analysis of Sallie McFague, *A New Climate for Theology: God, the World, and Global Warming* (Minneapolis: Fortress, 2008), 80.

to the reality that the whole of theological thinking is eschatological. At the forefront of this movement has been Jürgen Moltmann,
who began his *Theology of Hope* with these words: "From first to last,
and not merely in the epilogue, Christianity is eschatology, is hope,
forward looking and forward moving, and therefore also revolu-
tionizing and transforming the present."[46] His understanding is that
eschatology is not about predicting the future but is the mainspring
of all human history. It is the realization that God is always ahead of
us, drawing us toward ultimate meaning out of participating in the
Trinitarian history. God invites humans to share in the divine life on
the historical plain; indeed, our participation becomes part of God's
own story of reclaiming those God loves.

At the very least, eschatological thinking taps into the unre-
quited longings humans have for justice, for the world to be put
to rights, as N. T. Wright likes to put it.[47] In every epoch, each Christian generation has pondered if it were living in the "last days" as it
surveyed the cataclysms of its time. Somehow, we think our epoch
carries a larger burden than ever before, displaying our ignorance of
history and the degree to which we are curved in on ourselves. The
delay of the Parousia challenges confidence about divine action in
bringing creation to its true purpose through the return of the Son.

How may we find a balance between obsessive preoccupation with figuratively checking the skies for imminent return and
utter neglect of doctrinal understanding of how God might bring
our world to its true destiny? In my judgment, linking our scientific
understanding of our globe with thoughtful theological understanding is a fruitful pathway.[48] We know that our home, the planet
Earth, is finite and that its future as we know it is dependent on how

46. Jürgen Moltmann, *Theology of Hope* (New York: Harper and Row, 1967), 16.
47. See his *Simply Christian: Why Christianity Makes Sense* (San Francisco: HarperCollins,
2006), especially chapter 1.
48. I have been helped greatly by A. R. Peacocke in his 1978 Bampton Lectures, *Creation and
the World of Science* (Oxford: Clarendon Press, 1979). As both scientist and theologian, he
concludes: "The wisdom of the Bible in setting its 'salvation history' within a trans-temporal
framework is thus made manifest to our scientific perspective in a way impossible to many
of our immediate forebears who conceived of infinite space enduring for an infinite time as a
kind of unlimited stage for the dance of matter, energy, and life. . . . Hence the wisdom of the
biblical setting of the Beginning and End as a trans-temporal framework for salvation history,
yet included in God's work, for it is essential to God being God that he is the first and last
(the Alpha and Omega), that his activity includes everything" (347).

long our sun will last. We know that climate change is a major factor shaping the future of our habitation, which makes "humanizing the eschaton" a possibility, at least in its most basic material sense. Our destructive ways shorten the time span of our planet.

Sallie McFague calls us to become partners with God "in maintaining the health of creation."[49] Rejecting an agential model of God (as if God were the only actor) that places all responsibility for the future of the earth on the deity, she believes that global climate change requires a new sense of the interdependence of all things and that we take our proper place in tending this world. That was the original human assignment, and our refusal to think beyond individual concerns has plunged our planet toward a deathly crisis. Because God has invited humans to be God's own representatives in the world, this is our work to do. Empowered by the Spirit, following the model of Jesus, we strive toward life overcoming death.[50]

49. McFague, A New Climate for Theology, 75.
50. McFague, A New Climate for Theology, 80.

1 Thessalonians 5:1–28
Maintaining Eschatological Vigilance

After his message of comfort to grieving community members, the apostle writes more about how they are to prepare for the ultimate disclosure of the day of the Lord.[1] He does not want them to be deluded by false claims. While he says they have no need of having anything written to them "as to the times and the seasons," he proceeds to do exactly that. Of course, it draws the desired attention with that disclaimer.

This final chapter of 1 Thessalonians is not only for its first-century recipients; it also calls the current reader to discernment about what is actually transpiring in our day. Falsehoods about the current pandemic, politics in the election season, climate catastrophes, immigration policies, and racial injustice require sober assessment.

This first-century letter offers insight about how to live a vigilant life in the bonds of community, and we know that community is hard to sustain. Yet it is only in the bonds of community that Christians can stay on course as ethical beings who live in expectant hope of Christ's coming.

5:1–11
Living in the Light, Awake and Prepared

Paul reminds them of what they already know, that the day of the Lord will be unexpected, "like a thief in the night." Andy Johnson

---

1. The "day of the Lord" is a familiar term to this congregation, and it is a christological revision of monotheism.

says that this metaphor, which we find twice in the Synoptics, "suggests to many that Paul is here drawing on the Jesus tradition."[2] Stealthy, dangerous, invasive, and a menace to the household, a thief poses a great threat. If persons are lulled into a false sense that peace and security reign, a state presumably assured by the Roman Empire, they will be in danger of not recognizing the true season at hand. Like a pregnant woman at full term, there is no escaping the imminent travail. Labor will come, and hopefully a healthy baby as a result. Yet Paul refuses to speculate about the timing, as he knows that this is beyond human calculation, entrusting it to God.[3] Most important in this hortatory writing is his caution that these new converts not presume it has already occurred. He knows the disconsolation that would accompany a false belief.

Beverly Roberts Gaventa says that the shift from 4:13–18 to 5:1–11 is jarring; however, the two passages belong together, the first passage saying that the Parousia can be trusted and the second saying it cannot be predicted. The believers should not find this threatening, as it remains in God's hands rather than theirs.[4]

Paul contrasts light and darkness repeatedly in this section; those that live in the light will not be surprised when that day arrives. Because they have been living wakeful and sober lives, the sleep of darkness does not occlude their recognition of redemption. Affirming the community as beloved children of the light who "belong to the day" (vv. 5, 8), Paul calls them to persevere in vigilant living. He assures them that although it may be sudden, they will not be caught by surprise when the day of the Lord arrives, for they have been living with unquestionable preparedness. The significance of the ethical exhortations comes into view as he surveys the quality of their communal responsibilities.

Those that are "of the night," preferring darkness for their drunken pursuits, are living careless lives and will be judged accordingly.

---

2. Andy Johnson, *1 and 2 Thessalonians*, The Two Horizons New Testament Commentary (Grand Rapids: Eerdmans, 2016), 136.

3. Abraham J. Malherbe, *The Letters to the Thessalonians*, The Anchor Bible, vol. 32B (New York: Doubleday, 2000), 291, stresses the continuity between the testaments in Paul's writing: "What is said of the Day of Yahweh in the OT is said of the Day of the Lord Jesus by Paul."

4. Beverly Roberts Gaventa, *First and Second Thessalonians*, Interpretation: A Bible Commentary for Teaching and Preaching (Louisville, KY: John Knox Press, 1998), 69.

Sleepwalking through life, indulging their baser appetites, they are blithely unaware of their accountability before God. Our lives are always before God (*coram Deo*), as Luther liked to say. While it appears that the wicked prosper, this text warns persons that there are surprising outcomes to living dissolute lives. Perduring in this form of living destines them for wrath (v. 9). Although Paul does not spell out the grim implications, he warns the readers to stay vigilant, alert to their real circumstances.

This contrast between light and dark is a frequent theme in biblical parlance. The idea that "the darkness is passing away and the true light is already shining" (1 John 2:8) was part of the New Testament vocabulary in speaking of the coming of Jesus. Paul's own conversion as recounted in Acts 26 was a turning from darkness to light, which would be a significant aspect of his message to the Gentiles (v. 18). In Ephesians 5:8 he exhorts: "walk as children of light." This was to be a defining hallmark of followers of Jesus. As children in my Baptist tradition we sang, "The Light of the World Is Jesus," giving voice to the conviction that he illumines the shadowy places that need illuminating by the brilliance of God's own glory. The shining of God through Jesus casts light in even the darkest places.

"Sleep" carries several connotations, also. "Those who have fallen asleep" (4:15) simply means those who have died. In chapter 5, "sleep" carries a more ominous meaning as Paul warns them not to sleep "as others do" (v. 6). He wants them to exhibit the kind of self-control worthy of the habitation of the Spirit. They are not to resemble the debauchery of their pagan neighbors. Ordering one's desires "is a Spirit-given ability for those who belong to Christ to crucify the inappropriate passions and the excessive and destructive desires of the flesh."[5] Paul does not say that human desire is a negative human quality; rather, he speaks against excessive and destructive desires. Desire for intimacy with another is not dissimilar to the longing that we have for God. Sarah Coakley, as noted earlier, points to the "messy entanglement" of sexual desire and desire for God but argues that they are inseparable.[6] Clarifying the relationship

---

5. Johnson, *1 and 2 Thessalonians*, 141.
6. Sarah Coakley, *God, Sexuality, and the Self: An Essay 'On the Trinity'* (Cambridge: Cambridge University Press, 2013), 155.

between these is paramount, especially as we desire to grow both ethically and spiritually.

How will the Thessalonica congregation be able to stay on this sanctifying journey? Paul suggests that they "put on the breastplate of faith and love, and for a helmet the hope of salvation" (v. 8). Once again, the trilogy of faith, love, and hope appear, and he instructs how to gird for the ensuing challenges. These are the same "weapons of light" that Paul describes in Romans 3:12. God is a divine warrior (Isa. 59:17) and comes not only to do battle for God's own but also equips those who will join in the defeat of evil. The coming wrath is not for them, Paul assures; rather their hope is to obtain salvation through the Lord Jesus Christ (v. 9). God will protect them even as they join in the battle for the righteous cause of the Divine. Their present lives and future hopes are in God's hands, yet they must do their part.[7]

The brief statement about Christ's mission, the One "who died for us" (v. 10), is the early credo that gives confidence.[8] This was an integral part of the tradition that Paul had received (1 Cor. 15:3) and, in shorthand here, he stresses that any escape from the impending wrath of God is dependent on this act of self-giving by Jesus. While there is no extended reflection on the meaning of Christ's death here, Paul assumes that they have a sense of its significance. We will explore this idea in the further reflections section below.

He wants them to know that their confession of the Lordship of Jesus Christ obtains salvation (v. 9). Christ's work, not theirs, becomes their protection so that whether they "wake or sleep," they "might live with him" (v. 10). If they remain alive or if they die in faith, they have the same assurance that they are in the safekeeping of their Lord. Paul wants them to consider that there is a sense in which they cooperate with this grace. Yes, he has died for their sins, but they are not to be passive in their appropriation of this reality. Far too many Christians ignore the participatory reality of atonement.[9]

7. Cf. Eph. 6:10–20.
8. For an extended analysis of this formula, see Arland J. Hultgren, *Christ and His Benefits: Christology and Redemption in the New Testament* (Philadelphia: Fortress, 1987), 104, 114.
9. Molly T. Marshall, "On a Hill Too Far Away?: Reclaiming the Cross as the Critical Interpretive Principle of the Christian Life," *Review and Expositor* 91 (1994): 247–59.

Christ's action invites response, and his faithfulness becomes the human conduit so that they might grow in faithfulness themselves. Incarnation, the word ever becoming flesh, models how one joins God's redemptive work. As we observed earlier, sanctification includes both grace and effort. Paul has reminded them of who they are and calls them to persevere.

Michael J. Gorman calls Christians to this kind of participation: "*theosis*—Spirit-enabled transformative participation in the life and character of God revealed in the crucified and resurrected Messiah Jesus—is the starting point of mission and is, in fact, its proper theological framework."[10] It is a remarkable thing that God invites our participation—another way to translate *koinonia*—for it grants our lives their ultimate dignity to share with God this redemptive mission to restore humanity and the earth.

5:12–22

Final Exhortations and Greetings

Paul beseeches them to respect those who labor among them, presumably those who have pastoral responsibility for the congregation. It is fitting that they "esteem them very highly in love because of their work" (v. 13). Since Paul is no longer in the community, this can hardly be an appeal for himself. He knows the strains of leadership and how easy it is to scapegoat those called to this task when the community wavers or is under threat. Loving a leader does not compel blind obedience; however, faithful love and prayerful intercession does offer the encouragement needed to continue the strenuous task of being a wise spiritual guide to a community. The work of leaders is of inestimable value as they point the way toward committed living amid a challenging ethos that would discourage public Christian affiliation and practice. Pastors form congregations, and their presence carries impact for generations. It is amazing what congregants remember from those who labor among them, key

---

10. Michael J. Gorman, *Becoming the Gospel: Paul, Participation, and Mission* (Grand Rapids: Eerdmans, 2015), 4.

phrases, special visits, tender listening, and their gentle role in those life events of birth, baptism, marriage, spiritual crises, and death.

The apostle further exhorts them to "be at peace among your-selves" (v. 13). Nothing erodes a healthy community like rancor does. In my experience, churches are often the most gossip-filled of human institutions. Under the pretext of "speaking the truth in love," gossip can be like a wildfire in a congregation. I recall the damage of rumormongering in a congregation where I served as interim pastor. There was a prominent, long-married couple who after many years of struggling to hold the marriage together sought a divorce. The congregation took sides, and the tales continued to mount as to who was really at fault. Even though the members of the church were actually bowed down with grief over the suf-fering of their friends, their propensity to pounce on any whiff of scandal exacerbated the wounds to the body of Christ. If there is sexual misconduct suspected, it fans the flames of the anxieties of those who sit in judgment, even as they deny their own frailty. It requires maturity and humility to be at peace with those with whom we share our lives in faith. Especially in a community that faced oppression from the outside, living in harmony for the Thes-salonians became a sustaining buffer against outside forces. It also bore good witness to what the Spirit can bring about, a peaceful coexistence.

That Paul feels compelled to instruct them about admonish-ing "the idlers" suggests that Timothy has reported that some who expected the imminent return of Christ had become slack in their own work habits. They probably reasoned, "What does it matter if we forsake industry if the day of the Lord is to come any day? Why put in the daily grind if it all will end quickly?" This is the great problem of presuming to know when the end will come, which Paul sought to discourage. Rather, he wanted them to build each other up, and thus he set forth a straightforward pathway for them to fol-low by focusing on their responsibility to the community.

After this directive about the importance of being faithful in their work, he offers a litany of clear guidance about how their conduct can reflect their conversion. In verses 14–22, he states that these practices will be lifegiving in building a community that is worthy of the name of Christ. In short declarative sentences, he offers his apostolic counsel.

This is as practical a catechesis as we can find in Scripture. In the Greek text, the listing in verses 16–22 are set apart to highlight the stress on concrete instruction. They are terse parenetic words of ethical instruction that require some explication given the context of the writing.

Because of the specificity and significance of these exhortations, I will treat them in turn. After his call to respect those who are "over them" in the Lord, to live in peace, and to sustain healthy work habits, he then offers almost cryptic words of direction for living in the liminal meantime before the coming of the Lord. As Malherbe writes, "Paul heaps up terms from the lexicon of exhortation that he uses pastorally."[11]

1. Encourage the fainthearted. Paul believes that a mutual ministry within the congregation is possible and necessary. He knows what powerful effect comes when encouragement flows from one member of the community to another. It is a contagious blessing, and lives are strengthened. There are always the fainthearted among us as persons have different life experiences that threaten their well-being. Rather than shunning them as a drain on the community, believers should come to their assistance. Part of the reason why Paul will develop his body of Christ imagery is that he wants the interdependence of stronger and weaker members of the body to support each other. Reciprocity is a key marker of Christian identity.

---

1. Encourage the fainthearted.
2. Help the weak.
3. Be patient with them all.
4. Do not repay evil for evil.
5. Always seek to do good.
6. Rejoice always.
7. Pray constantly.
8. Give thanks in all circumstances.
9. Do not quench the Spirit.
10. Do not despise prophesying.
11. Test everything.
12. Hold fast to what is good.
13. Abstain from every form of evil.

Paraphrase of 1 Thess. 5:14–22

---

11. Malherbe, *The Letters to the Thessalonians*, 301.

2. Help the weak. This exhortation naturally flows from the prior one. Those with resources are to put them at the disposal of those who need them: namely, the weak. Luke Timothy Johnson has argued that it is the need of the weak that determines what we give rather than our desire to give a certain amount.[12] The Bible always draws attention to the weak: widows, orphans, poor, and ill. These seem to be the relentless object of God's concern, and those who love God must also love these. It is not only with financial resources that we are to help the weak, yet that remains a tangible demonstration of where our hearts reside. The weak may be the ill among us, the vulnerable child at school, the harried parent, or the immigrant. Stephanie Paulsell reminds us that all bodies matter to God. "Convictions about creation, incarnation, and resurrection hold the body at the center of Christian life."[13] Whatever embodied form the weak take, they remain of concern to God and, consequently, to those who follow the Incarnate One. Important to remember is that we are also the weak, if not now, inevitably.

3. Be patient with them all. I saw a cartoon recently of Dennis the Menace and Mr. Wilson. It shows the elderly neighbor shaking a fist as Dennis scurries home, asking why Mr. Wilson claims to have lost his patience when he never uses any of it. Patience is not easy for many of us, yet it is a central virtue of following Jesus. It is not clear what the referent for "them all" is here. Perhaps Paul is referring to the fainthearted and the weak; or it may be a more general appeal to engage both community members and external neighbors with this kind of forbearance. We know that it is characteristic of God to be patient with wayward humanity, the Bible being replete with stories of God's forbearance. God's own are called to imitate the divine patience. In the *Life and Miracles of St. Benedict,* Pope Gregory the Great reflects on how patience is expressed by a religious superior. That one "ought to bear patiently with a community of evil men as long as it has some devout members who can benefit from his presence. When none of the members are devout enough to give

---

12. See his "The Life of Faith and the Faithful Use of Possessions," Lake Lectures, The Center for Philanthropy, Indiana University, 2006, 10–11.
13. Stephanie Paulsell, *Honoring the Body: Meditations on a Christian Practice,* The Practice of Faith Series (San Francisco: Jossey-Bass, 2002), 8.

any promise of good results, his efforts to help such a community will prove to be a serious mistake."[14] Paul offers no such limits to patience. It is an ongoing fruit of the Spirit (Gal. 5:22).

4. Do not repay evil for evil. One of the most enduring traits of sinful humanity is to "get even" when feeling wronged.[15] An eye for an eye, the *lex talionis*, resides deep in us, and retaliation is a temptation for us all. Marjorie Suchocki calls this "the fall to violence," which she believes is the original sin of humanity.[16] When threatened by the actions of another, we seek to secure our own lives by aggressive defense that mirrors what was done to us. Indeed, one becomes like the one who did evil in the first place by returning it in kind. We know that violence incites further violence. The rampant violence against Black persons when accosted by police is often met with protest that sparks additional violence, and situations spiral out of control. The question of reparations arises, as it should, since racial discrimination continues educationally and economically. Nonviolent resistance, as practiced by Gandhi and Martin Luther King Jr., is difficult to sustain, yet if we practice an eye for an eye and a tooth for a tooth, we will be a "blind and toothless nation," observed King.

5. Always seek to do good. This is the rejoinder to the prior exhortation. Rather than repaying evil for evil, one should strive always to do good. Discerning what that good is remains challenging, given human finitude, exhaustible resources, and great need. The refrain from Acts 10:38, "he went about doing good," is both the summary of Jesus' ministry and the model for us to follow. A seminary professor of mine suggested that usually people can carry only one justice cause effectively. By narrowing focus to one area, greater energy can be devoted, and one can accomplish transformational good. Sometimes doing good is simply refraining from judging another. One of the desert fathers, Abba Poemen, was asked, "If I see my brother

---

14. *Life and Miracles of St. Benedict* (Collegeville: Liturgical Press, 1949), 14.
15. Miroslav Volf writes at length about the biblical mandate to "love one's enemy" in his important work *The End of Memory: Remembering Rightly in a Violent World* (Grand Rapids: Eerdmans, 2006).
16. Marjorie Hewitt Suchocki, *The Fall to Violence: Original Sin in Relational Theology* (New York: Continuum, 1994), 162, writes, "Violence is the defiance of mutual-well-being, and is a consequence of the competitive nature of existence in a world where 'life is robbery.' The bent toward aggression that is exercised through violence is an essential aspect of the structure of sin."

committing a sin, is it right to conceal it?" Poemen answered, "At the very moment when we hide our brother's fault, God hides our own, and at the moment when we reveal our brother's fault, God reveals ours, too."[17] This kind of mercy is at the heart of doing good.

The focus of the exhortations shifts at this midpoint. The apostle moves from appealing to community members to live in unselfish ways toward one another to how one should seek to relate to God. These instructions guide one toward spiritual health in faithful pursuit of holiness.

6. *Rejoice always.* This is a favorite theme of the apostle, and we hear the echoes especially in Philippians 4:4. Paul knows that joy and grace are closely related, and his exhortation to rejoice accents the lavishness of God's grace to which Christians respond by rejoicing, indeed, in all circumstances. To rejoice is to preserve perspective even amid persecution. One can "count it all joy" because of the knowledge that Christ has overcome all that would threaten. Joy joins patience as a fruit of the Holy Spirit, and it is also a choice.

I remember a story from Kathleen Norris's *The Cloister Walk* about the delight an old infirm monk had on the occasion of a simple visit after taking a bad fall. As Norris and a younger monk stuck their heads in his room, he weakly welcomed them with, "Ah, . . . It's a sweet life." And he said it again. Norris reflected on the significance of his response. A lifetime of monastic practice had formed him to find joy in every situation, and his rejoicing led to theirs.

7. *Pray constantly.* Once again, Paul summons the community to constant communication with God. Prayer is about shared life

---

His welcome refreshed me and made me see something that's easy to lose sight of in our infernally busy lives. That we exist for each other, and when we are at low ebb, sometimes just to see the goodness radiating from another can be all we need in order to rediscover it in ourselves.

Kathleen Norris, *The Cloister Walk* (New York: Riverhead Books, 1996), 366–67.

---

17. Cited in Roberta C. Bondi's *To Love as God Loves: Conversations with the Early Church* (Philadelphia: Fortress, 1987), 54.

with God, as Roberta Bondi puts it.[18] The sense that all of life can be an intentional conversation in the presence and power of the Triune God calls one to a new level of existence. Closer than our very breath is God; closer than we are to ourselves is the Holy One (*interior intimo meo*), in the words of Augustine.[19] Even our breathing can become a synchronicity with the Spirit, the Holy Breath of God, who vivifies our lives. John Wesley calls prayer "the breath of our spiritual life."[20] I will explore this exhortation in further reflections below.

8. *Give thanks in all circumstances.* This is an exceedingly hard exhortation to practice, as complaining can arise very easily when the way is hard. Especially in these days of pandemic when families cannot celebrate birthdays, holidays, or even the homegoing of beloved family members together, it is hard to remember to give thanks. And there are other circumstance that beset us. How can one give thanks when a longtime friend forsakes the relationship? How can one summon gratitude when an unexpected and overwhelming diagnosis comes? How can one thank God in the midst of grave concern over a beloved son's mental health issues? It is important to note that Paul advocated for thanksgiving in the midst of every situation—*not* to give thanks *for* every situation. Paul knows from his own experience that gratitude is a transformative practice. When he later writes in 2 Corinthians 9:6–15 about giving, his ultimate argument for their stewardship is gratitude, as generosity produces a great thanksgiving to God (v. 11). While we may think our good fortune comes through our industry and exceptional character, this can be only partially true. When suffering comes, it cannot be solely because of sloth or bad character, either. Bad things happen to good people and good things happen to bad people. Learning to be present to what our discrete circumstances are and seeking, with God's help, to be grateful in them all helps us relax our grip and acknowledge that we do not determine utterly the outcomes of our lives.

18. Roberta C. Bondi, *To Pray and to Love: Conversations on Prayer with the Early Church* (Minneapolis: Fortress, 1991), 27.

19. Augustine, *Confessions* 3.6.11, *Nicene and Post-Nicene Fathers of the Christian Church*, vol. 1, ed. Philip Schaff (Edinburgh: T & T Clark, 1994), 63.

20. John Wesley, *Explanatory Notes upon the New Testament* (Kansas City: Beacon Hill, 1981), 155.

Grace upon grace has come upon us. Giving thanks reveals more of this divine munificence, this lavish generosity.

9. *Do not quench the Spirit.* The Apostle Paul has a robust theology of the Spirit. It is a key part of his theological perspective, and he is the first New Testament writer to give the divine name "the Lord" to the Spirit (2 Cor. 3:17). That the Spirit shares the fully personal and fully divine character of Christ moves theological construction toward Trinitarian confession. Paul cannot think of the body of Christ without the breath of God, the Spirit. He cannot think of gifts of grace apart from the chief charism, which is the Spirit. He knows that he cannot do his apostolic mission in his own power; he remains reliant on the supply of the Spirit (Phil. 1:19), which he clearly states. Quenching the Spirit is the quickest way to stifle ministry and faithful living. Martin Luther, who drank deeply at the Apostle's well, wrote these insightful words in *A Mighty Fortress Is Our God:* "Did we in our own strength confide, / Our striving would be losing." Luther, like the one from whom he had learned so much, understood that power from beyond himself sustained his reforming work. Quenching the Spirit can take many configurations: ignoring a minority voice in a church business session, suspecting the sincerity of a fellow Christian, neglecting one's own spiritual gifts, or refusing to take the needed time to discern what really is of the Spirit.[21] The Holy Spirit and the human spirit are so closely related that divine presence never overwhelms human decision, yet our decisions can serve to stifle what the Spirit is seeking to accomplish.

10. *Do not despise prophesying.* Some scholars speculate that after the departure of the apostolic team of Paul, Silvanus, and later Timothy, other "prophets" visited the community and gave their own version of the apocalyptic future. While it would be very tempting for Paul to say that the community should not listen to anyone but him as their founding leader, he trusts that God continues to speak. We know that there is a larger tradition at work than what we find in the undisputed letters of Paul, and he is aware that he is the beneficiary of other prophetic teachers who have preceded him. This is also a

---

21. See my chapter "Breathing, Bearing, Beseeching, and Building: Reading Scripture with the Spirit," *The Lord and Giver of Life: Perspectives on Constructive Pneumatology,* ed. David H. Jensen (Louisville, KY: Westminster John Knox Press, 2008), 51–53.

strong recognition that there will be members of the community who have this spiritual gift of prophecy. It is not about their capacity for foretelling the future as much as it is about affirming those who will offer sensitive reflection on how God is moving in the community toward the vision of faith, love, and hope. Paul is clear in this writing that he "assumes, along with other New Testament witnesses (e.g., Acts 2:16–18), that there will be the giving and receiving of Spirit-inspired prophetic messages within the community."[22] God has more to say to a community than any one person can convey, and trusting that God will continue to offer guidance through faithful guides puts them in a "posture of receptivity," in the words of Richard Foster.

11. Test everything (dokimazete). This is an important corollary to the preceding exhortation. The members of the community must hear the prophetic word and then discern if it is of the Spirit. While this kind of examination lacks the precision that we would desire, as human emotion is an inevitable and not always helpful ingredient, with practice, attention to the ongoing guidance that the Spirit offers in the community can preserve the centrality of faithfulness (*pistis*). Luke Timothy Johnson believes that "Paul regards this capacity of judging, testing, or discerning to be a gift of the Holy Spirit that works in and through human intelligence."[23] It is more than secret knowledge revealed to a select few, but a matter that the community can sift with sound judgment. The charismatic nature of the community does not mean that careful thinking has been abandoned; rather, the Spirit heightens the capacity to think wisely together as the members of the community weigh issues that will advance their sanctification in the Lord.

12. Hold fast to what is good. How easy it is to lose sight of what is truly good amid competing invitations for our attention. Not too long ago, Madison Avenue sought to place before Americans a vision of what is good in terms of fashion, technology, culinary arts, housing, automobiles, travel—even commodifying the trappings of the spiritual life. Although its ad agencies no longer drive

---

22. Johnson, *1 and 2 Thessalonians*, 154.
23. Luke Timothy Johnson, *Scripture and Discernment: Decision Making in the Church* (Nashville: Abingdon, 1996), 109.

the consumer appetites as in earlier "Mad Men" days, it set a precedent in creating a sense of need for goods that only satisfied the egos of those who could purchase them rather than any essential requirement for thriving. The constant ads popping up on social media incite the same rapacious intent today. This exhortation suggests that one adopt a clear-eyed approach to what we, as followers of Christ, can actually name good. In these days of quarantining because of the COVID-19 virus, many have renewed their commitments to their families as being of inestimable value. Many have become more generous with their neighbors as the employment crisis has not treated all with even hand. Many have found that strengthening bonds with old friends through calls or emails (even letters!) has sustained them when many of the social conventions that we daily observe are not really possible. The situation of widespread illness has called for compassion, generosity, and fervent prayer. These are worth holding fast, for they are good. When we move out of this season of pandemic, we trust that good lessons learned will continue.

13. *Abstain from every form of evil.* This final exhortation echoes earlier prohibitions in the community as it seeks to differentiate the Thessalonian congregation from its oppressive culture. Although a believing community can never be extricated from its surrounding environs, it can begin to live into a vision that is distinct, a manifestation of God's reign rather than that of Caesar. Abstaining from evil in Thessalonica demonstrates confession of the Lordship of Christ, and thus habits of virtue form the community. Sexual promiscuity, indolent workers, conspiracy theories about Parousia, slandering another believer, and neglecting to attend to the Holy Spirit are examples of evil, according to Paul. The gospel is only believable if it can be demonstrated through transformed living. That Christ has been raised is the presupposition for newness of life for the baptized. Learning to abstain from evil is a lifelong project yet is the concrete realization of performing lives of resurrection in the already, as well as the not yet.

These crisp exhortations, similar to what we find in Romans 12:9–21, offer a pathway for living in community with other Christians. They are as valuable today as in the first century.

5:23–28

Closing Words of Blessing and Encouragement

This first epistle draws to a close with great assurance that God will continue to be at work in their midst. Paul offers a petitionary prayer through which he reminds that it is God who will "sanctify you wholly." While there are many things converts can do to strengthen their Christian discipline, there is also the sense of God's continuous activity that invites human participation. These believers remain unfinished, needing ongoing sanctifying attention. "May your spirit and soul and body be kept sound and blameless at the coming of our Lord Jesus Christ" (v. 23b). The language "be kept" points beyond the activities of these members of Christ. The one who called them is faithful and will do the keeping (v. 24). This is an ancient idea in the Hebrew Bible as God is the "keeper" of Israel, the *shamar* that neither slumbers nor sleeps in faithful watching (Ps. 121:4).

Just as God called the community into being, now divine action will preserve it for its desired end. As Andy Johnson observes, "it is *not the practices themselves* that sanctify, but the God who both enables them and is active in transformative ways in the midst of them."[24] Rightly, he is reminding that while constructive spiritual practices are formative, ultimately it is God who brings about transformation.

There is an interesting juxtaposition between personal and communal life in these verses. When speaking of "spirit and soul and body," the apostle seems to be constructing a theological anthropology of the individual, yet everything that has gone before in this chapter is about living wisely in Christian community. They are inseparable, of course. Thus, his first petition is that the whole community (*hymas*), "you all," as southerners of my family used to say, be sanctified. Paul knows that formation happens in community while individual responsibility remains. Even those who live in monastic communities have times of isolated presence before God, especially in private *lectio divina*, in addition to the regular communal prayer, meals, and fellowship.

In one of the few delineations of the human as "spirit and soul and body," Paul wants to think holistically. God wants to make the whole of

---

24. Johnson, *1 and 2 Thessalonians*, 156.

a person holy. These are inseparable aspects of being a human being and while this description seems to make them distinct from one another, they are aspects of the whole embodied reality of what it means to be human. This tripartite rendering has led to unwarranted theological speculation about what is of higher value—spirit or soul—often leading to a devaluation of the body that is the instrument of human presence in the world, which the incarnation of Jesus should dispel, as the word became flesh and continues to do so in his followers.

Paul reminds them that the One who calls is faithful. The wording does not place the call of God in the past tense, as if the final summons had been offered.[25] God continues to call so that persons may draw nearer to the Holy One that they might reflect more clearly God's own holy character. The Lord Jesus Christ is coming, and these early Christians want to share in the Parousia as sanctified handiwork of God's artistry.

Concluding words request prayer from the community. This is a humble petition, which reveals the degree of interdependence between the apostolic team and this community that they so love. Paul also instructs that they all greet one another with a holy kiss. This may be a rejoinder to that possibility that unholy kisses had been taking place; this exhortation furthers his aim of a chaste community. While this practice has varied cultural appropriation, it remains a sign of peace and affection for those with whom we share the bonds of love in Christ. I must admit, I do not mind being kissed by beloved sisters and brothers in Christ!

The current social distancing that preoccupies our every waking hour makes it much harder to offer the greetings of peace, the hugs of welcome, and the shared eucharistic meal. It is understandable that we have had to move most of our social interactions to screens, yet we viscerally remember the embodied expressions of care and unity. It is a part of being human to desire affectionate expressions of care as incarnations of God's own presence. As we return to a more normal form of being present to one another, we treasure anew what we once took for granted.

---

25. *Kalōn* is in the present tense, which implies God's own continuous action calling for faithfulness.

Paul then adjures the congregation to read this letter.[26] The whole congregation deserves to hear this communication, and it is a transparent overture in asking that all be apprised. It is also an egalitarian move to benefit those who may not have the skill to read it for themselves. To read it publicly ensures that all have equal access to this apostolic instruction. In a time when educational disparities are on display as financial futures are so uneven, with our contemporary "digital divide" that means some students do not have equal access to virtual learning, we can appreciate his concern that all receive his message.

One cannot help but wonder how far Paul's letters actually circulated. Can he assume that what he says to the Thessalonians will ever be available to the Galatians? Do the readers in Corinth know what he narrated to the beloved congregation of Philippi? These intriguing questions remain a source of interest and inquiry. Scholars argue that even as early as the mid-to-late first century there was a clear interchange between Christian communities, and the epistles would have been key artifacts in this (Col. 4:7–16).[27] I can imagine an emissary traveling to another Christian community with a treasured epistle and then learning of what that community might have received from apostolic witness. We know that the New Testament was built through this circulation of correspondence, and the literary deposit the Church curated is impressive, as even scholars of the classics will admit.

The letter ends with a benediction of grace "The grace of our Lord Jesus Christ be with you" (v. 28). This forms an *inclusio*, a parallel structure to the opening greeting of grace. What could be a more fitting summary of the whole letter than to think about how the grace of the Lord Jesus Christ has come to their city and formed a new community of faith, love, and hope? They respond to this benediction through faithful attention to all that this letter instructs, and they seek to be emissaries of their faith in their larger community. They can do this because of the inpouring of the grace of the Lord Jesus Christ. It is an inexhaustible flow of power and transformation for them and for all the world.

---

26. This is Gaventa's accent on Paul's instruction; see *First and Second Thessalonians*, 87.
27. For example, see the work of Larry Hurtado, *The Earliest Christian Artifacts: Manuscripts and Christian Origins* (Grand Rapids: Eerdmans, 2006).

FURTHER REFLECTIONS
Christ Who Died for Us

According to Andy Johnson, this is the first time such language "Christ who died for us" was used in New Testament documents.[28] Whether this is an early formula on the significance of Christ's death and whether it might be referring to a vicarious atonement is of interest in a theological analysis of this epistle. There is not a developed theological understanding of sacrificial offering at this point, but as Malherbe suggests, the clause "who died for us" (*tou apothanontos peri hymon*) "appears in the earliest strata of Christian tradition."[29] N. T. Wright says this verse is basically shorthand for longer expositions (Rom. 14:8; 2 Cor. 5:11–6:2; Gal. 2:13–15; Col. 2:14–15) of Jesus as the Messiah through whom God has reconciled the world. Building on Isaiah's prophecy, especially chapter 49, Wright contends that Paul makes this statement the center of his theology. This is a tradition received by Paul (1 Cor. 15:3), which is perhaps why he does not feel the need for a lengthy development of the confession here. Clearly, as Arland Hultgren assumes, "Its frequency in Paul's letters indicates that the formula became a part of the apostle's own proclamation."[30]

We should not press the spare language to say what it does not say. There is no suggestion that Christ is trying to placate God, rather he is offering himself for us because of our own need to be redeemed from our sins. Later atonement theories, such as that of Anselm that are predicated on the expiation of God's wrath so that God might be able to forgive, have no grounding here. It is human sin that pushes Jesus out of the world and onto the cross (a creative interpretation of original sin); human sin is taken up into the divine life as a means whereby God overcomes evil as well as God taking responsibility for creating a world in which such is even possible.

Theologians ponder the kind of death Jesus died. Was it truly god-forsaken, an abandoned death, as Moltmann contends?[31]

28. Johnson, *1 and 2 Thessalonians*, 144.
29. Malherbe, *The Letters to the Thessalonians*, 299.
30. Hultgren, *Christ and His Benefits*, 49.
31. Jürgen Moltmann, *The Crucified God* (New York: Harper & Row, 1974), 242.

Was the horrific reality of his death so exhaustive that no one else need die such a death since he was our substitute, as evangelical New Testament scholar Leon Morris argued?[32] What sign of God's presence with Jesus remained—only the faithful women, perhaps? The claim of forsakenness is hard to sustain if God's accompanying presence is embodied through those who followed to the end. The mystery of the inter-Trinitarian event is inscrutable, yet we consider the Abba's anguish, the Son's excruciating agony, and the Spirit's exigent desire to hold their communion intact. Truly, the cross is an inter-Trinitarian event.

The language that Jesus died "on behalf of us" suggests the focus of the redemptive work of the cross. That Paul does not elaborate here suggests that he had already erected the stanchions for this understanding when with them. Apparently, a sense of interchange is operative, as M. D. Hooker has suggested.[33] Christ stands in for us, even as we learn to stand in for him as body of Christ.

> **Christ became what we are so that we might become what he is.**
>
> Athanasius, *Contra Arianos*, iii, cited in *The Early Christian Fathers*, ed. and trans. Henbry Bettenson (London: Oxford University Press, 1956), 404.

Biblical interpreters and theologians have characterized the death of Christ in many ways. Naming him as substitute, propitiation, representative, sacrificial lamb, and one who died a death that we might not have to die—estranged and with ignominy—gathers up the transcendent grandeur of his self-giving.

Ben Witherington observes that Paul "already had an understanding of the salvific nature and importance of Jesus' death and of how it was the key to believers being joined together and with Christ at the eschaton."[34] It is his conclusion that Christ's death is vicarious, and that most likely Paul offers this understanding to the Thessalonians. That he places it in the context of the eschaton demonstrates how the death and resurrection of Christ is the key to their future.

---

32. See his comprehensive work *The Cross in the New Testament* (Grand Rapids: Eerdmans, 1965), 43, which offers a sustained argument for viewing Christ as our substitute in the atonement.
33. See M. D. Hooker, "Interchange in Christ," *Journal of Theological Studies*, n.s., 22 (1971): 349–61.
34. Ben Witherington III, *1 and 2 Thessalonians: A Socio-Rhetorical Commentary* (Grand Rapids: Eerdmans, 2006), 152.

FURTHER REFLECTIONS
Respecting Those Who Labor among You

Religious leaders are not immune from criticism; indeed, some of the harshest critique issues from those in their care. Projecting their own hopes or expectations on their pastors or other congregational leaders leaves many disappointed. Interrogating whether these projections are legitimate is often neglected. Remembering the humanity of our leaders is paramount, which we prefer to forget. Although they do represent the Divine for us in their priestly and prophetic roles, they are frail creatures of dust, as are the members of their flock.

Christian vocation is not simply about the ordained minister. All persons on the journey of faith can claim that their vocation is Christian if it contributes to the common good and reflects their giftedness. It is too limited in scope to think spiritual gifts are only exercised in the context of the congregation. Jürgen Moltmann is helpful in widening this aperture. He contends that any human endowment put to use for the well-being of others can be considered a spiritual gift.[35]

Christian vocation is a journey toward authentic living, and it is an ongoing concern of Paul. In a later writing, he exhorts "I . . . beg you to lead a life worthy of the calling to which you have been called" (Eph. 4:1).[36] Vocation begins with listening for a voice, indeed the voice of God that comes to us through Scripture, through proclamation, and through perceptive friends. Vocation is about a relationship with God and others, therefore deeply personal but not private.

Here is a summary of a theology of Christian vocation:

---

35. Jürgen Moltmann, *The Spirit of Life: A Universal Affirmation,* trans. Margaret Kohl (Minneapolis: Fortress, 1992), 180.
36. While most scholars consider Ephesians to be post-Pauline, nevertheless his concern for attention to calling is sustained.

1. God has called each of us—into life, into faith, and into purposeful living. This means that our lives have meaning beyond self-interest. Indeed, if we are curved in on ourselves (*incurvatus in se*), we are not able to find the larger mission that is uniquely ours. When we are self-preoccupied, the soul shrivels, for we are meant to be for others.

2. God can speak to us through the world's groaning need. Vocation often arises out of our concern about a deep need in the world. For me it was a clear sense that God wants the church to accept its daughters as well as its sons in ministry, that call to me being to assist theological education in teaching and embodying this new reality.

3. God has more to say to us than we can hear by ourselves. We must listen to the questions people ask us, for often there is imaginative insight to consider. As people receive and affirm our gifts, we also gain perspective about possibility for our lives.

4. Vocation allows us to be most fully ourselves—and most fully God's. It is constructive to ask, What makes our hearts rise up? Where do we feel most at home? Christian vocation welcomes the yoke of Christ (Matt. 11:29), which fits easily and is shared by him, the true yokefellow.

5. Christian vocation is that which keeps "making more out of us."[*] Our callings are not static, and there will be continuing opportunities to grow and learn. Our vocation is a key part of the sanctification process, especially if we seek to "find God in all things," as the Ignatian examen instructs. Our vocation is not simply for those we serve but is a means through which we experience God's love.

6. Christian vocation always requires the assistance of the Holy Spirit. If we think we can accomplish the Lord's calling in our own strength, we have not realized that godly work requires godly power. Throughout this first epistle to the Thessalonians, Paul links the presence of the Holy Spirit in the community and individual members with the capacity to persevere in their faith. The Holy Spirit continues the divine transformative work so that the Thessalonians become holy in their relationships and actions.

7. Vocation is for the body of Christ—and for the world; it is offered in community. We learn the significance of our vocation only as it is offered, received by others, and produces good fruit. Our gifts belong to everyone, and we must devote them to the upbuilding of God's people. Spiritual gifts that equip for our callings are not possessions; they are expressions of grace to assist the common good—both within and beyond the congregation.

[*]Gail Godwin, *Evensong* (New York: Ballentine Books, 2000), 12.

FURTHER REFLECTIONS
Pray Constantly

First Thessalonians 5:17 has prompted many to consider the question of how to fulfill the exhortation to "pray constantly." We know that *The Way of a Pilgrim* attempted through the Jesus Prayer to let the prayer descend from the lips into the heart so that it was as regular as breathing.

The pilgrim tells of his quest: "On the twenty-fourth Sunday after Pentecost, I went to church to pray at the Liturgy. During the reading of the Epistle of St. Paul to the Thessalonians, I heard the following words: 'Pray without ceasing.' The words made an indelible impression on me, and I began to wonder how it was possible to pray unceasingly since everyone must occupy themselves with other matters as well, in order to make a living . . . I thought about this for quite a while but was unable to understand it."[37]

> **Lord Jesus Christ, have mercy on me.**
>
> Jesus Prayer, in *Way of a Pilgrim*, 15.

While sermons reiterated this command, there was no instruction on how to do it. He sought spiritual guidance to learn unceasing interior prayer and finally some monks pointed him to the *Philokalia*,[38] which teaches the Jesus prayer. He became a faithful practitioner, submitting to their instruction so that he could, with God's help, fulfill this command. His whole life becomes prayer, and as a wandering pilgrim, he is able to share his discovery with all whom he encounters.

Religious orders, such as the Benedictines, seek to order their hours of prayer so that they might approach this lofty goal. The fact that Benedictine communities all around the globe are praying the

37. *The Way of a Pilgrim*, trans. and annotation by Gleb Pokrovsky (Woodstock: Skylight Paths, 2001), 3. This classic of Russian spirituality has, since the mid-nineteenth century, been a useful guide to notice and collaborate with the constant striving of the spirit toward God.
38. This great classic of Orthodox teaching on prayer is a collection of writings that span the fourth to the fifteenth century. A focal selection from the *Philokalia* that centers on teachings of the Jesus prayer is *Writings from the Philokalia on the Prayer of the Heart*, trans. E. Kadloubovsky and G. E. H. Palmer (London: Faber & Faber, 1992).

divine office gives a sense of the fulfillment of this apostolic appeal. Calling this the *Opus Dei*, the work of God, to which nothing else is to be preferred, communal and individual prayer shapes each day. As the Rule of St. Benedict instructs: "Let nothing, therefore, be put before the Work of God."[39]

Those of us who are neither wandering pilgrims nor living a cloistered life can also find ways to grow in this joyful discipline. Creating a structure for regular prayer is essential if we would allow the Spirit within us to draw us closer to God. Phyllis Tickle, of blessed memory, believed that there was no substitute for keeping the divine hours. Not a monastic herself, she nevertheless organized her manual for prayer around morning, noon, and evening practice. A contemporary reworking of Benedictine fixed-hour prayer, her manuals draw from Scripture, early Christian writings, hymnody, and *The Book of Common Prayer*.[40]

There are other approaches, to be sure. My own discipline over the years is to keep a yearly prayer journal through which I practice praying the Scriptures (*lectio divina*) as I work my way through the weekly lectionary readings. Writing my prayer helps sustain focus as well as keep faith with those for whom I said I would pray. These prayer journals also allow me to review points of struggle, new experiences of grace, and the ones God has called me to care for through prayer.

Praying without ceasing becomes the very pulse of Christian discipleship. As we open our hearts to the presence of God and the beckoning to care for others, we are fashioned ever more into the likeness of the one who prays for us unceasingly. It is the faith of Christ that gives us enduring life and hope to be gathered with all the faithful.

---

39. *The Rule of Saint Benedict*, trans. Leonard Doyle (Collegeville: The Liturgical Press, 2001), ch. 43, 101.

40. See, for example, Phyllis Tickle, *The Divine Hours: Prayers for Summertime* (New York: Doubleday, 2000).

2 THESSALONIANS

Introduction

When we move into the second epistle, we experience both continuity with the message of 1 Thessalonians as well as disjunction. It is important for contemporary readers to see the distinctions as they speak to different stages in faith and a dynamic first-century context. The mystery of the Parousia deepens, and the author wants to prepare the community for harder things. First Thessalonians accents its eschatological teaching primarily on a personal level, according to F. F. Bruce, focusing on the state of believers who have died prior to the Parousia.[1] Paul refers to the day of the Lord as it will impact persons in general: the ungodly will be surprised while the followers of Christ, who are children of the light, will be awake and prepared for it. The expanse of concern in the first epistle is more about piety and hope and does not encompass a cosmic perspective.[2] According to Abraham Smith, "Appreciating the signs of God's power already evident in the community lies at the heart of 1 Thessalonians."[3] It seeks to reinforce in this Jewish and Gentile community the teaching of the apostles about how to live when their whole orientation to life has been overturned by the message of the resurrection of Jesus. Eschatological credibility cannot be separated from belief in the resurrection.[4]

1. F. F. Bruce, *1 & 2 Thessalonians*, Word Biblical Commentary, 45 (Waco, TX: Word, 1982), xliii.
2. Bruce, *1 & 2 Thessalonians*, xliii.
3. Abraham Smith, "The First Letter to the Thessalonians," *The New Interpreter's Bible*, vol. 11 (Nashville: Abingdon, 2000), 685.
4. Michael Welker, "Theological Realism and Eschatological Symbol Systems," *Resurrection: Theological and Scientific Assessments*, ed. Ted Peters, Robert John Russell, Michael Welker (Grand Rapids: Eerdmans, 2002), 38, offers a compelling analysis of the New Testament witness that affirms "the objectivity of the transfigured body."

The Thessalonian congregation now stands out in their community as persons who no longer trust the keeping of Torah for their salvation (Jewish believers) or who have abandoned the pagan cult of Caesar (Gentile believers) for the living way of Jesus, who is truly *Kyrios* (Lord). They have the challenge of defining the boundaries of their community amid hostile environs, and we can only imagine the economic, cultural, and societal impact of their faithfulness to the overwhelmingly good news (*euangelion*) of Jesus. Their reputation is a key witness to the strength of the gospel and the power of believing in the Lordship of Christ, who is made present through the Spirit. Remembering the transformative power of the gospel remains essential.

In 2 Thessalonians, the writer offers further instruction about how to be prepared for the great day, the expected return of Christ. Apostolic teaching suggests how the church will be able to recognize the events that herald its approach, and the writer unspools critical incidents that they might anticipate. Inspired by the Spirit and a critical reading of the historical context, this additional epistle generates a supplemental call to vigilance. New characters enter the plot as description of the end times unfolds. The author moves into the historical realm when writing about the threatening scenario that will sum up the chronology of their time, and the first-century context comes more clearly into view as the influence of the Roman Empire is waning. Margaret Mitchell notes that the emphasis now is not on the assurance of salvation for the believers dead and living, as in the first epistle, but on "God's retributive justice against the enemies of the church at the eschaton (1:5–12; 2:10–12)."[5] As Smith affirms, "Remaining firm in one's convictions without being beguiled by enticing words or false hopes is paramount for 2 Thessalonians."[6]

Apparently false hopes have taken hold in the community, prompting unchristian behavior, and this is the reason for a further letter. N. T. Wright uses traditional language when he reminds us of the difference between inaugurated eschatology and the future

5. See the argument of Margaret M. Mitchell, "1 and 2 Thessalonians," *The Cambridge Companion to St. Paul*, ed. James D. G. Dunn (Cambridge: Cambridge University Press, 2003), 58.
6. Smith, "The First Letter to the Thessalonians," 685.

consummation of it.[7] Clearly they are living in between these events. Wild speculation about a realized form of eschatology, however, has destabilized the congregation. Believing that the day of the Lord has already occurred has led some to profligate practices that undermine the solidarity and witness of the community. This phenomenon has repeated itself throughout Christian history, as we will explore later in this chapter.

The matter of authorship of the second epistle is contested.[8] Some scholars believe that the similarity of word usage and a sustained theme argue for Pauline authorship, while others maintain that the author of 2 Thessalonians simply mimicked the first letter to give credibility to the second. Contending that a pseudonymous writer produced it, these scholars point to the lack of creativity that would align with other Pauline offerings. Bonnie Thurston perceptively states her lament: "The question this evidence [of literary similarity] raises is why Paul would so slavishly follow his own precedent. Why would Paul use his own work so unimaginatively?"[9] Evidence against Pauline authorship is significant on literary, historical, and theological grounds.[10]

Yet 2 Thessalonians has early attestation, according to Leon Morris, as Polycarp, Ignatius, and Justin "all seem to have known it, possibly also the writer of the *Didache*."[11] The statement in 3:17 claiming to be Paul's own signature, "I, Paul, write this greeting with my own hand. This is the mark in every letter of mine; it is the way I write" seems to be an attempt to underscore its provenance. It leaves questions, moreover, as it seems forced. It "doth seem to protest too

---

7. N. T. Wright, *Paul and the Faithfulness of God,* parts 3 and 4 (Minneapolis: Fortress, 2013), 1047.

8. Andy Johnson argues for the authenticity of Pauline authorship and suggests that the epistle was written a few months after Paul left Thessalonica and was engaged in mission in Corinth. Johnson believes that the pseudonymous theories "raise more questions than they answer." See his *1 and 2 Thessalonians,* The Two Horizons New Testament Commentary (Grand Rapids: Eerdmans, 2016), 7. See also the argument of Mitchell, "1 and 2 Thessalonians," 58.

9. Bonnie Thurston, *Reading Colossians, Ephesians, and 2 Thessalonians: A Literary and Theological Commentary* (New York: Crossroad, 1995), 160.

10. Mitchell, "1 and 2 Thessalonians," 58.

11. Leon Morris, *The First and Second Epistles to the Thessalonians,* The New International Commentary on the New Testament (Grand Rapids: Eerdmans, 1959), 29.

much!" Writing in the name of another in the first century did not receive the censure that contemporary plagiarism does.[12]

Educational practices about citation differ culturally. In my experience teaching in Myanmar, it is common for one to cite the words of a teacher verbatim. It is seen as a high honor for a revered scholar rather than intellectual dishonesty. It is more an expression of humility rather than theft. North American conventions about documentation do not prevail, and it appears that in first-century Thessalonica, writing in the name of another and using much material from the first epistle was not seen as a prevarication.

Linda McKinnish Bridges argues for a different writer for the second epistle but observes that placing the name of the leader of the apostolic team on the letter "assured the letter's delivery and acceptance by an anxious congregation. To place Paul's name on the document not only honored the apostle but also ensured the longevity of the tradition."[13] There were unscrupulous pseudonymous writers who did commit intellectual fraud for profit, but according to Beverly Roberts Gaventa, "such a motive is scarcely imaginable for the writing of 2 Thessalonians, since its sales expectations would be nonexistent."[14]

Those who hold to Pauline authorship for 2 Thessalonians suggest that he is correcting his own earlier writing, seeking to tamp down eschatological frenzy that the first epistle occasioned. Earl Richard suggests a different occasion and purpose for 2 Thessalonians. He believes that the letter was composed "to discredit the claims, made in Paul's name, of apocalyptic preachers which were causing alarm within the community (2:2) and social unrest within its ranks (3:6–12)."[15] It was not uncommon in the first century for a writer to use the name of a more famous author to ensure a reading, and the inclusion within the New Testament canon ensures its ongoing role in apostolic teaching. We know that the Pauline tradition is much larger than the seven undisputed letters, and there are varied ways

12. Bart Ehrman, *The New Testament: A Historical Introduction to the Early Christian Writings* (New York: Oxford University Press, 2000), 342, is helpful on the issue of pseudepigraphic writings.

13. Linda McKinnish Bridges, *1 & 2 Thessalonians,* Smyth & Helwys Bible Commentary (Macon, GA: Smyth & Helwys, 2008), 199.

14. Beverly Gaventa, *First and Second Thessalonians,* Interpretation: A Bible Commentary for Teaching and Preaching (Louisville, KY: John Knox Press, 1998), 95.

15. Earl J. Richard, *First and Second Thessalonians* (Collegeville: Liturgical Press, 1995), 299.

in "which Paul's authority was exercised in his absence."[16] Even after his death, the Pauline teaching continues, as his influence in the first-century Mediterranean world cannot be gainsaid.

While there are centers of gravity within the Scriptures,[17] the canon gives structure to our understanding of Christian origins in the Second Testament imbedded with the necessary and ongoing tradition within the Hebrew Bible. Indeed, as a Christian I cannot read the apostolic teaching and gospel narration without attentiveness to God's ongoing story with Israel. The one triune God is the same subject of both Elder and New Testaments, in the opinion of Christopher R. Seitz,[18] and we profitably read them together as Christians who are grateful to be included in God's family tree, grafted into it by grace. Seitz sounds a great deal like Luther's venerable Trinitarian hermeneutic when Seitz reads Scripture in canonical context.[19] He believes that the whole of the Bible points to the triune nature of God.[20] I agree and do not suggest that God's covenant with Israel is abrogated.

As Seitz writes, "The fact that the same word 'Lord' is used consistently and without predication for Lord, Lord Jesus, the Lord of the Spirit is not a matter to be sorted out but a cause for praise as such."[21] While I do not find "Lord of the Spirit" a constructive rendering of the Pauline language,[22] I affirm Seitz's Trinitarian hermeneutic and the way that he sees the relationship of the testaments as interdependent for this reading.

Similar to 1 Thessalonians, the second epistle construes an exordium, which is the opening of an argument, a proof section that is the central argument, and the peroration, the closing of the argument. The audience that received the letters may or may not be the

---

16. Margaret Y. MacDonald, *The Pauline Churches: A Socio-historical Study of Institutionalization in the Pauline and Deutero-Pauline Writings*, Society for New Testament Studies Monograph Series 60 (Cambridge: Cambridge University Press, 1988), 123.

17. For example, I would place 2 Corinthians 5:17 about God reconciling the world a bit ahead of "use a little wine for the sake of your stomach" (1 Tim. 5:23) in terms of salvific importance.

18. See his *The Elder Testament: Canon, Theology, Trinity* (Waco, TX: Baylor University Press, 2018), especially 183.

19. Christine Helmer, "Luther's Trinitarian Hermeneutic and the Old Testament," *Modern Theology* 18 (2002): 49–70.

20. See also the position of Walter Brueggemann in *Theology of the Old Testament: Testimony, Dispute, Advocacy* (Minneapolis: Augsburg Fortress, 1997), 731–32.

21. Seitz, *The Elder Testament*, 190.

22. Paul is much more likely to use descriptors like "Holy Spirit" or simply "Spirit."

same. The time lapse between the two letters may indicate another generation of readers.[23] Most striking, according to Gaventa, is the lack of language of deep affection that flows through the first epistle. The thick bond of familial language is not present.[24] This subsequent writer is more taciturn and less effusive in praise of the Thessalonians.

In my treatment of this second epistle, I will presume that an unknown author wrote in Paul's name. In my judgment, it does not detract from scriptural authority; indeed, it reinforces the significant weight given to Christianity's first theologian, the apostle Paul. His shaping of early Christianity is without demurrer, and how one assesses the "three Pauls"—the radical Paul, the conservative Paul, the anti-Paul—in the nomenclature of Borg and Crossan, only adds to the layers of interpretation and understanding.[25] That we can see development in the Pauline tradition as well as recontextualization of his thought prompts more careful analysis of the particular theological vision and application.

Elisabeth Schüssler Fiorenza offered the groundbreaking insight that rather than seeing positive development in Paul, we see in the later writings attributed to him that retrenchment is going on: "The praxis of coequal discipleship between slaves and masters, women and men, Jews and Greeks, Romans and barbarians, rich and poor, young and old brought the Christian community in tension with its social-political environment."[26]

This moves in the direction of a Faustian bargain as the post-Pauline tradition utilizes the Greco-Roman patriarchal order to structure the house churches as well as the Christian household.[27] Guess who gets sacrificed in order to keep the possibility of persecution from Rome at bay? Subjugating women and slaves became the norm and, as history attests, these texts have been the preferred source for those who find patriarchy God's enduring order.

---

23. Abraham Smith, "The First Letter to the Thessalonians," 681, contends that there is "no way of determining whether the same community actually received both letters."

24. Gaventa, *First and Second Thessalonians*, 91.

25. See Marcus J. Borg and John Dominic Crossan, *The First Paul: Reclaiming the Radical Visionary behind the Church's Conservative Icon* (New York: HarperCollins, 2009).

26. Elisabeth Schüssler Fiorenza, *In Memory of Her: A Feminist Theological Reconstruction of Christian Origins* (New York: Crossroad, 1983), 279.

27. Schüssler Fiorenza, *In Memory of Her*, 279.

The second epistle must wrestle with an enthusiastic brand of eschatological frenzy, an apocalyptic fervor that seeks to "compensate for the letter recipients' loss of power."[28] Even though the congregation perseveres amidst its many detractors, it appears that its claims about the day of the Lord and the subsequent lack of its realization has weakened its stature among those all too ready to criticize the fledgling movement. Part of the suffering of the community comes from this disjunction between expectation and fulfillment, and the consequent behavior this "delay" prompts.

Christian history is replete with sectarian groups setting the date for the imminent return of Jesus Christ. A kind of esoteric Gnosticism ensues, as only those with the secret knowledge within the group can hope to transcend the worldly clutches of outsiders who are oblivious to the real signs of the times, according to the conspiring group of true believers. When each group has folded up its ascension robes with grave disappointment after standing on a hillside awaiting the Parousia, its critics have been quick to condemn the group's certitude or gullibility as a revered leader has set the timetable for the ending of human history. (What is left to do but have a "white sale" of their prepared garments to salve their disenchantment?)

Doomsday theorists have operated since apocalyptic entered the biblical lexicon—and beyond—as astrologers and other religions, such as the Mayan tradition, have their own vision of the winding up of the present age. For thousands of years, people have been certain that they know when the end will come and have prepared accordingly. This presumption flies in the face of the caution of Jesus about trying to pin down the date of culminating events.

It seemed only logical that 1000 CE, the end of the first Christian millennium, would welcome the second coming of Jesus.[29] Primarily a grassroots movement, true believers sold their goods, abandoned their homes and livelihood, and waited. Disappointed, they recalculated the return to be 1033, yet no appearing. We hear no more of this loosely organized adventist group. Usually when a prediction

---

28. Smith, "The First Letter to the Thessalonians," 683.
29. While it is a disputed idea, evidence for apocalyptic expectations at the turn of the first millennium is in ascendence. See Richard Landes, "The Fear of an Apocalyptic Year 1000: Augustinian Historiography, Medieval and Modern," http://www.jstor.org/stable/2887426.

fails, the group disperses or forms another sectarian expression of apocalyptic hope.

Writing shortly after 1000 CE, Wulfstan II, Archbishop of York, saw the regular attacks by Vikings as a sign that the world might soon end. He offers a sermon to the English people, *Lupi Sermo ad Anglos*, which is the Latin translation of the first line, "the sermon of the Wolf to the English, when the Danes were greatly persecuting them, which was in the year 1014 after the Incarnation of the Lord Jesus." Alister McGrath notes that his words "evoke the possibility of the end of the world being near, reflecting the millenarianism which appears in a number of words written around this time. Since a thousand years had passed since the coming of Christ, the expectation of an imminent 'doomsday' was widespread, based on a literal reading of Revelation 20:2, 5."[30] We see that he read the trauma of his epoch as portending the end, a hermeneutic that will be repeated.

Other dates have been set, such as February 1, 1524, when London astrologers believed that the alignment of the stars as a great fish (Pisces) meant an imminent flood. People moved to higher ground, built arks, and waited on dry ground for what was a false prediction. The date was reset to 1624 without avail. The Shakers thought 1780 would usher in the Day of Judgment, but they were also deluded. They were able to adapt their prophecy and continued as a millenarian communal movement.[31]

Most notable in more modern time is the great ruse of William Miller, a self-educated Baptist farmer-preacher from Low Hampton, New York, who declared that the world would end between March 21, 1843, and March 21, 1844.[32] His calculations were based on his exegesis, a "detailed attention to the minutest parts of the Bible, including its numbers, and so well fit into the American enthusiasm for scientific endeavor that loomed large before the Civil War."[33] Chagrined at the failed outcome, the Millerites moved the date

---

30. See *Christian Literature: An Anthology*, ed. Alister E. McGrath (Oxford: Blackwell, 2001), 168.
31. Timothy Miller, *When Prophets Die: The Postcharismatic Fate of New Religious Movements* (Albany, NY: SUNY, 1991).
32. E. Brooks Holifield, *Theology in America: Christian Thought from the Age of the Puritans to the Civil War* (New Haven, CT: Yale University Press, 2003), 301.
33. Mark A. Noll, *A History of Christianity in the United States and Canada* (Grand Rapids: Eerdmans, 1992), 193.

to October 22, 1844. Jesus did not arrive, a nonevent, which was called the "Great Disappointment," with some of the flock departing to form another sectarian group. Christopher Hitchens acerbically calls this the "closing up of religion." Further, he notes "The once-apocalyptic 'Millerites', for example, survive only in the reduced form of the 'Seventh Day Adventists.'"[34] We remember Miller because of the widespread interest his prediction generated, and he stands as a cautionary note against seeking to know what is known only to God.

Others have set ensuing dates: Charles Taze Russell, the founder of the Jehovah's Witnesses, in 1914; Herbert W. Armstrong, the founder of the Worldwide Church of God, in 1936; Hal Lindsey, the author of *The Late Great Planet Earth*, vaguely in the 1980s; and many more. Of recent interest was the fear of Y2K, January 1, 2000. Anxious that computers would not calibrate the "00" ending, many expected that the technological web might shred. Obviously, it did not occur, as we continue to use the same tools prior to the turn of the millennium, with a few upgrades, of course. The world has not ended, although in the current pandemic, some fear that an ultimate reckoning is at hand. The kind of stockpiling of goods for homes that we have witnessed in 2020 suggests that many view history as it has been known as being over.

In a recent article in *The Atlantic*, Olga Khazan suggested that the real sickness in our time is a lack of empathy. The precipitous death spiral of Americans—not to mention the global impact—suggests that the demise of the elderly is seen as expendable. She cites Lori Peek, a sociologist at the University of Colorado Boulder, who queries: "Is our national empathy—our care and love and concern for one another—at such a low level that we are not truly feeling, in our bones, in our hearts, and in our souls, the magnitude of the loss?"[35] The fact that it is mostly the elderly and persons of color who are dying results in "compassion fade," in her words. Not surprising, they are less likely to receive prioritization for treatment as their resources to pay medical bills are diminished.

---

34. Christopher Hitchens, *God Is Not Great: How Religion Poisons Everything* (New York: Twelve, 2007), 169.
35. Olga Khazan, "A Failure of Empathy Led to 200,000 Deaths. It Has Deep Roots," *The Atlantic*, September 22, 2020, 2.

This lack of empathy has been demonstrated from the highest levels of the current presidential administration. Even as the virus surges through school districts, college campuses, meat packing plants, and retirement centers, the political powers of our nation have downplayed the severity of the crisis and given more attention to personal political ambitions than the common good. It appears that something vital—a sense of the common good—is ending and, while it may not be the end of the world, a significant measure of care for the well-being of neighbors is fracturing.

As of February 2022, the pandemic is far from over, and we cannot predict the lingering impact of these *anni horribiles*. Urgent efforts resulted in the rapid development and delivery of effective vaccines in the United States. However, many did not live to receive this therapy, as their health was already compromised by the economic disparities of being poor or a person of color. As of early 2022, more than nine hundred thousand people in the United States have died of COVID-19. This current situation will pass, we believe; hopefully the lessons we learned will not. While I trust careful scientific endeavors, the politicization and profit motive of the pharmaceutical industry leaves one skeptical about fair medical treatment. As Anthea Butler writes, "In debilitating congruence, 1 in every 1,000 Black people in American has died from COVID-19 since this coronavirus began to spread here. The dual pandemics of racism and the virus have been devastating for African Americans."[36] It is not surprising that their experience of this time has apocalyptic overtones. The significance of these epistles is that they speak to different epochs when apocalyptic thinking is rampant.

Retaining a sense of watchfulness about the Parousia is challenging given the many years of expectation and the long lapse from the New Testament writings until now. As we have seen, different epochs have handled the Parousia with views ranging from agnosticism all the way to setting the date. In the present time, it appears that only fringe sectarian groups retain any sense of urgency and watchfulness

---

36. Anthea Butler, "In a Season of Reckonings, Forgiveness Is Not Forgetting," Faith & Leadership: A Learning Resource for Christian Leaders and Their Institutions from Leadership Education at Duke Divinity, October 27, 2020; https://faithandleadership.com/season -reckonings-forgiveness-not-forgetting.

about the imminent coming of Christ; but we cannot leave to them all the reflection on God's shepherding of history to its conclusion.

Every generation must refresh its theological conversation and construction as the context shifts, as the assumptions of earlier frameworks may no longer obtain. Reading the works of Martin Luther King Jr., Dan R. Stiver portrays how "King's translation of the kingdom of God as 'the beloved community,' gives not only inspiration but shape and direction to efforts to transform this world."[37] Rather than hoping for resolution in the "sweet by and by," the present call is for Christians to work for justice now. The goal must be "on earth as it is in heaven." God is not summoning God's own to disavow any hope for current transformation. It is this world that we occupy, and it is this world that needs our attention.

In other words, theological imagination must include present circumstances when engaging Scripture. For example, when previous interpreters have engaged the Thessalonian letters, they have placed eschatological expectations at the center rather than the multiethnic nature of the congregation. The latter may be as important in our day as the former. As Jim Wallis strongly advocates, "It is time for churches to emphatically renounce bigotry and become the multiethnic body of Christ that God wants us to be."[38] Robert P. Jones observes that

> No segment of White Christian America has been more complicit in the nation's fraught racial history than white evangelical protestants. And no group of white evangelical Protestants bears more responsibility than Southern Baptists, who comprise the overwhelming majority of white evangelicals, particularly in the states of the former Confederacy.[39]

As the population shifts to being more ethnically diverse, the church lags far behind as it remains racially segregated and ethnically homogenous.[40] By some estimates, as soon as 2030 there will

---

37. Dan R. Stiver, *Life Together in the Way of Jesus Christ: An Introduction to Christian Theology* (Waco, TX: Baylor University Press, 2009), 431.
38. Jim Wallis, *America's Original Sin: Racism, White Privilege, and the Bridge to a New America* (Grand Rapids: Brazos, 2016), xxi.
39. Robert P. Jones, *The End of White Christian America* (New York: Simon & Schuster, 2016), 167.
40. See the insightful work of Soon-Chan Rah, *Many Colors: Cultural Intelligence for a Changing*

no ethnic group in the United States that holds a numeric majority. This is why many right-wing white supremacists yell "you will not replace us," as they see the end of their hegemony.[41] I will address the multiethnic aspect of this early Thessalonica church in this commentary, albeit giving primary focus to the eschatological dimension of this second epistle.

The writer of 2 Thessalonians must thread the way between calming anxious claims and indifference to this fundamental expectation that history remains within God's providence and eternality. The text remains a helpful corrective source, as we are also tempted to fall at either end of this polarity. Remembering that time is not forever elastic spurs us to think about horizons both personal and cosmic. This early primer continues to have a word of hope and grace for us.

World (Chicago: Moody, 2010). Also helpful is *Intercultural Ministry: Hope for a Changing World*, ed. Grace Ji-Sun Kim and Jann Aldredge-Clanton (Valley Forge, PA: Judson, 2017).

41. Robert P. Jones offers an obituary for this epoch in his several important works, e.g., *White Too Long* (New York: Simon & Schuster, 2020).

2 Thessalonians 1:1–12

Preparing for the Coming Judgment of God

Moving into the second epistle, we see a notable shift in tonality. The vision of God's judgment is more central and the fate of the enemies of God is more dire. The author writes with clear instruction about how to live even if the details of the Parousia are opaque. That the thriving of the Thessalonian community remains of concern in the apostolic tradition is palpable, and this second epistle seeks to extend the work of the founding apostolic team.

1:1–2

Greetings of Grace

Once again, the three apostolic names are a part of the salutation. Paul, Silvanus, and Timothy are ostensibly the senders of the epistle, although an unknown author is at work in its crafting. Addressed to the church of the Thessalonians, the greeting notes that it exists "in God our Father and the Lord Jesus Christ." This is a theologically rich observation: A congregation has no source of life but the providing and redeeming character of the triune God who sustains their perseverance as believers. They have no other grounding than the indwelling of the holy presence granting them life, for their spiritual home is found in God. That the Spirit is the source of this indwelling we can infer from other writings in the Pauline tradition. The Spirit makes Christ present to them, the One who binds and is their life together. The existence of the Thessalonian congregation "in God" is what secures them.

My Baptist forebear, Walter Rauschenbusch, who shaped the "Social Gospel" through his writings and ministry in Hell's Kitchen, finds that "living in God" is what enabled his work to continue as he wrote in "The Culture of the Spiritual Life" in 1897.

The greeting of grace and peace, a regular part of the Pauline nomenclature, underscores the spiritual benefaction of the community. It is only because of God's unmerited and overflowing largesse that a congregation could be formed and sustained over against competing religious affections. It is a sheer act of grace, and the peace they enjoy (with some exceptions) points to their life together in God. As in the first epistle, the author wants both to encourage and to teach for their uncertain times. With apocalyptic fervor buzzing in the ethos, they need steady forbearance as they discern how to respond to the grace and peace God offers. This writer wants them to recognize the means through which God is with them: through apostolic encouragement, through one another, and through their own forbearance. As Paul Fiddes and other Baptist scholars observe, it is in the gathered community, through the presence of other Christians, that we discern Christ.[1]

The source of grace and peace is God's merciful bounty. Not only has God as Abba allowed the Son to be of benefit for the whole creation in his death and resurrection,

> The main thing is
>
> to have God;
>
> to live in God;
>
> to have God live in us;
>
> to think God's thoughts;
>
> to love what God loves;
>
> to hate what God hates;
>
> to realize God's presence;
>
> to feel God's holiness
>
> and to be holy;
>
> to feel God's goodness
>
> in every blessing of our life
>
> and even in its tribulations;
>
> to be happy and trustful;
>
> to join in the great purposes of God
>
> and to be lifted to greatness of vision
>
> and faith and hope with God—
>
> that is the blessed life.
>
> Quoted in Dennis L. Johnson, *To Live in God: Daily Reflections with Walter Rauschenbusch* (Valley Forge, PA: Judson Press, 2020), xi.

---

1. Paul S. Fiddes, Brian Haymes, and Richard Kidd, *Baptists and the Communion of Saints: A Theology of Covenanted Disciples* (Waco, TX: Baylor University Press, 2014), 69.

but God has also been attentive to this outpost of new Christian faith in a religiously plural world. Claiming the Thessalonians believers as part of the people of God—Jews and Gentiles alike—points to God's own economy of grace, which is broader than formerly considered. While deeply rooted in the Hebrew Scriptures, the idea of including all the nations had suffered an eclipse as the Jewish people struggled for survival. The diaspora had only compounded issues of identity.[2]

The greeting of grace and peace is the very heart of the gospel. God has made peace with an untoward people through the giving of the Son for their sake. This peace means that persons are no longer counted as estranged from their maker; rather, they have been brought near through the one who inaugurates a new creation (2 Cor. 5:17), bringing humanity and nature to their true purposes. Christ has broken down centuries of barriers, and his continuing work of loving inclusion enlivened their community just as it does our own when we are receptive to those unlike ourselves. This grows harder in an increasingly factionalized culture.

Because we live in a transactional world that scrupulously measures legal requirements, for example, loans, contracts, marital covenants, and other things, the idea of grace remains a challenging concept. That God would offer forgiveness, the chief expression of grace, without demanding recompense, is more than we can easily make sense of, or more demanding, accept. It offends our sense of responsibility, our belief that we can make our own way. Currently, as of this writing, we have a president in the United States of America who is on record saying that he has never felt compelled to ask God's forgiveness for anything. We are so accustomed to "paying" for any service that we resist that which only God can provide—chiefly, forgiveness for our sin. We resist this, for it recalibrates all our senses of

---

2. N. T. Wright spends considerable time thinking about this in his section "The People of God, Freshly Reworked," in *Paul and the Faithfulness of God*, parts 3 and 4 (Minneapolis: Fortress, 2013, 774–94. His perspective on Jesus as "incorporative Messiah" (834) details how Israel's Messiah expansively includes the Gentiles.

worth and indebtedness.[3] We do live in a culture "stripped of grace," in the words of Miroslav Volf.[4]

Volf distinguishes three basic modes in which we conduct our lives: taking, getting, and giving.[5] He writes: "God's gifts oblige us, first, to a posture of receptivity."[6] Only when we receive the grace offered through the death and resurrection of Jesus from God the Giver can we move toward giving ourselves and our possessions away as an expression of our transformation. While none of us can remedy all the world's ills, we can learn to be faithful with what we have received as we care for those God puts in our pathway. If we have the mind of Christ, Paul writes in Philippians 2:4–5, the interests of others displace our own self-absorption. This is the work of grace in our lives.

One of the best known of the Puritan writers is John Bunyan (1628–1688) who authored *Grace Abounding to the Chief of Sinners* and *The Pilgrim's Progress*. It was his sense of the immense grace of God in the cross for sinners that prompted these works. In the

---

Christian gave three leaps for joy, and went on singing—

"Thus far did I come laden with my sin,

Nor could aught ease the grief that I was in,

Till I came hither. What a place is this!

Must here be the beginning of my bliss?

Must here the burden fall off from my back?

Must here the strings that bound it to me crack?

Blest Cross! Blest Sepulchre! Blest rather be

The Man that there was put to shame for me!"

John Bunyan, *The Pilgrim's Progress* (London: Collins, 1953), 53.

---

3. Significant works on forgiveness recently are F. LeRon Shults and Steven J. Sandage, *The Faces of Forgiveness: Searching for Wholeness and Salvation* (Grand Rapids: Baker, 2003); L. Gregory Jones, *Embodying Forgiveness: A Theological Analysis* (Grand Rapids: Eerdmans, 1995); and Miroslav Volf, *Free of Charge: Giving and Forgiving in a Culture Stripped of Grace* (Grand Rapids: Eerdmans, 2005).

4. Volf, *Free of Charge*.

5. Volf, *Free of Charge*, 157.

6. Volf, *Free of Charge*, 42.

second work, his depiction of the pack rolling off the back of Christian, disappearing down the hill into the empty tomb, is a beautiful portrait of the grace that frees the believer from burdens borne.

Bunyan's sense of God's encompassing mercy and the joy that comes from God's reconciling overture reflects the Pauline tradition. For Bunyan, it meant that he could not be unconcerned about the salvation of his family and neighbors and, as the allegory unfolds, we see his urgent efforts to make sure they are on the right pathway. The opportunity to be joined to Christ permeates this second Thessalonian epistle and, as Christian learned, it is the way that leads to eternal life.

Likewise, the recent spiritual memoir of Serene Jones accents the remarkable role of grace in her life. As she recounts her upbringing in Oklahoma that is both painful and prodigious, she becomes all the more persuaded of grace as the grounding reality of life.

> The challenge for us is to open our eyes, ears, hands, minds, and hearts to receive the truth of God's real, *persistent presence*, God's grace. When we open ourselves to it, we are changed by it. The way we perceive the world shifts, like a radically refocused camera lens, and we experience life differently. You see everything around you as suffused with God's love. You see God's grace everywhere, saturating all existence.[7]

It is only because of grace that she can bear the racism in her ancestry and the trauma in her family of origin. Her testimony to its sufficiency offers a constructive word in our fractured time.

1:3–4

Giving Thanks for Faithful Discipleship

The writer begins, as in the first epistle, with thanksgiving for the progress in faith that the Thessalonian Christians are experiencing. Their faith is "growing abundantly" and their love for others in the community is increasing. Grateful for their flourishing, the writer offers thanks to God for their steadfastness as well as boasting of

---

7. Serene Jones, *Call It Grace: Finding Meaning in a Fractured World* (New York: Viking, 2019), xix; author's emphasis.

them to others. I wonder what might transpire in a community if pastoral leadership found more supportive ways to affirm the direction of congregants rather than focusing on reprimand, encouragement rather than condemnation. While not many will gripe to their churches when assembled or confront individuals who have experienced personal failures, pastors are known for their privately dismissive comments with other colleagues when discussing their flocks. It is not possible to lead those we do not love.

No doubt, the apostles would commend one community to another as an inspiration toward virtue for the discrete challenges each faces. In the same way, we draw strength from the witness of other communities of faith. Their faithfulness and creativity reinforce our own persistence in missional purpose. When another congregation provides an innovative and much needed ministry, it inspires other churches to venture toward new horizons of community engagement. The church, in its comprehensive identity as the body of Christ, sustains its unique local expressions.

In the midst of the current pandemic, as most congregations have shifted from in-person gatherings to virtual connections, we learn from their adaptations how to manage different ways of being the embodiment of Christ for one another and for our neighbors. For example, we prepare the bread and wine at home and partake with our families rather than processing to the altar or Communion table together. Pastors preach to empty sanctuaries or into the cameras of their laptops, labor-intensive work, to be sure. Many choirs have fallen silent because of the threat of singing in close proximity to others. Summer mission trips did not occur, and many ministries such as food pantries and those that shelter the homeless have made necessary shifts, such as driving through a church parking lot or devoting mission money to those social service outlets who can make more significant accommodation. Many are suffering in these days, and congregations are seeking means to alleviate all they can. Faithful discipleship also expresses care for the health of others by taking the precautions required, such as wearing a mask and frequent handwashing, small sacrifices for the sake of the more vulnerable. I give thanks for persistent belief that the body of Christ can withstand many onslaughts and, by the Spirit, can remain resilient.

Faithful congregants and their spiritual leaders are sensing an inflection point for gathered communities. Already churches have been facing decline, and many now wonder whether, when they do reconvene, there will be a sufficient critical mass to retain buildings, personnel, and former ways of doing mission. This may prove to be a constructive sifting as questions of Christian identity are in sharper relief. The church is not the building; mission is not meant to be solely for the sake of those who already belong to the fold. Christians are also discovering that caring for the underserved requires collaboration with other persons of good will, persons of other faiths or none.

The Thessalonian Christians were experiencing persecution, enduring affliction for their faith in Jesus Christ as Lord (1:4). The author names this reality as a way of recognizing the truth of their situation in addition to giving it a theological meaning. Their suffering is not an expendable casualty of their faith; it is the hallmark of their faithfulness under siege and their call to a new form of justice. They have entered the paschal mystery, which I will describe more fully at the end of this chapter in further reflections.

As J. Christiaan Beker writes, "When Christians suffer for the sake of justice in the world, they do so not only on the basis of realizable objectives but also in cooperative solidarity with the body of Christ."[8] As Christ has suffered, so will his followers as they contravene the prevailing wisdom of their age. The closer they draw to their Lord, the more like him they will become.

We can see this in the witness of the first martyr, Stephen. He dies with words on his lips similar to those of Jesus as he died: "Lord, do not hold this sin against them" (Acts 7:60). He dies as did his Lord, seeking forgiveness for those who put him to death. He does not seek revenge; rather, he lives out a generosity of spirit that only a Christ-formed identity can embody. We can only speculate what impact his manner of death had on Saul, the persecutor of Jews who believed Jesus to be the Messiah, as he was "consenting to his death" (Acts 8:1).

---

8. J. Christiann Beker, *Suffering and Hope: The Biblical Vision and the Human Predicament* (Grand Rapids: Eerdmans, 1994), 93.

The idea of sharing in Christ's suffering is familiar in the New Testament. In the post-Pauline tradition this emphasis remains as the pastoral instruction is to "Share in suffering as a good soldier of Christ Jesus" (2 Tim. 2:3). Likewise, we hear this encouragement from one of the widely circulated Catholic epistles: "But rejoice in so far as you share Christ's sufferings, that you may also rejoice and be glad when his glory is revealed" (1 Pet. 4:13). Linking present suffering as preparation for sharing in Christ's triumph is common in these texts, and Christians should not expect to be exempt, especially if they offer public witness for their faith.

> **The empire—always and everywhere—has declared that the embrace of vulnerability and loss is not a viable way to be in the world.**
>
> Walter Brueggemann, *Disruptive Grace: Reflections on God, Scripture, and the Church*, ed. Carolyn J. Sharp (Minneapolis: Fortress, 2011), 289.

Blaming the suffering ones for weakness or odd religious commitments is common.

1:5–12
The Coming Righteous Judgment

The writer links the suffering of the Thessalonians with the righteous judgment of God, the one who is making them worthy of belonging to the realm of God (v. 5). Andy Johnson observes that their suffering "is not the general hardships of life but results from acting in ways that make public their allegiance to the sovereignty of Israel's God embodied in the lordship of Jesus."[9] Indeed, it is public faith that draws scorn from secular neighbors, then and now. It does not appear that the Thessalonians are suffering for their sin; rather they are being refined by what they are passing through and thus will be more worthy to participate with Christ in a joint future.[10]

---

9. Andy Johnson, *1 and 2 Thessalonians*, The Two Horizons New Testament Commentary (Grand Rapids: Eerdmans, 2016), 166.
10. Abraham J. Malherbe, *The Letters to the Thessalonians*, Anchor Bible 32B (New York: Doubleday, 2000), 408.

Scholars point to the possible influence of Jewish literature of a slightly earlier period on the perspective of 2 Thessalonians. Attempting to construct a theology of suffering as they seek to find meaning in the extreme suffering of the Jewish people, Psalms of Solomon and 2 Maccabees articulate God's movement toward justice even in the exigencies of persecution.[11] As Gaventa observes, "Instead of being retribution for sins, the sufferings presently undergone by the good have the function of rendering them 'worthy of the Kingdom of God.'"[12] Interpreters have to be careful as they reflect on what purpose can be found in suffering, as much damage has accrued from those who want to rationalize all suffering as somehow God's will. This moves in the direction of fatalism rather than faith in God's just actions.

All is not well in the Thessalonian community, however, as we will see in the next chapters of the letter. It may be that the suffering of the community is a result of some within the community sowing discord through their eschatological enthusiasm, their claim to have secret knowledge others do not have. Confusion surrounding whether the day of the Lord has already arrived or when it might occur is a destabilizing force in the community. How far this word of disappointment about the Parousia had traveled beyond the community is not known, but it may have drawn further antagonism from non-Christian neighbors. The author seeks to address these concerns because they are proving corrosive for the congregation.

The writer states adamantly that God's righteous judgment will repay those who have caused their suffering, an ominous warning that seems to move against a theme of forgiveness. The least we can say is that God is not oblivious to the reckoning of justice. In this context, it appears that grace and peace are for only those who are found faithful. God's own justice is at stake, in the thinking of the writer. Forthrightly he states, "God deems it just to repay with affliction those who afflict you" (v. 6). While mercy is the larger theme of Scripture, God is not oblivious to serious injustice and in the divine calculus allows the punishment for sin to go forward, even

11. Beverly Roberts Gaventa, *First and Second Thessalonians*, Interpretation: A Bible
    Commentary for Teaching and Preaching (Louisville, KY: John Knox Press, 1998), 102–3.
12. Gaventa, *First and Second Thessalonians*, 103.

while sparing the offending one the full recompense of their actions. Sometimes this is merely letting the consequences of sin reveal themselves rather than any direct retribution. Sin has its own built-in punishment, which can rarely remain hidden. It is helpful to note that God is not subject to moral laws of human construction; God is free both to forgive and to let justice take the form of reaping what one has sown. God is also free to allow divine wrath to sear the dross of sin for the sake of healing, also an expression of mercy.

This latter idea has fallen out of favor in more progressive wings of Christianity. We project our "culture of affirmation" onto the divine, believing that only positive reinforcement can produce character and virtue ethics. A recent flap about a line in the hymn "In Christ Alone," speaks to this. The Presbyterian Church (U.S.A.) decided that the lyric "on that cross, as Jesus died, the wrath of God was satisfied" did not comport with its present theological views and decided to drop the hymn when the authors refused to substitute the words, "the love of God was magnified." This ecclesial body was right to eschew an outright penal substitutionary view of atonement: that is, the idea that God cannot forgive until God's wrath is expended on a sacrificial victim. Dating back to medieval times, primarily voiced by Anselm of Canterbury in the eleventh century in his *Cur Deus Homo* (*Why God Became Man*), this view is a gross distortion, as if protecting divine honor is God's primary concern. It is not; redemption is. God's humility in self-giving always outruns God's desire for evening the score with unfaithful covenantal partners.

Yet it is not possible to read the biblical narratives without recourse to the idea of divine wrath. In the New Testament, God's wrath is not about divine emotion but of opposition to all that is evil. The enmity humans bear toward God is overcome by God's triune movement of love. Jesus does not save us from an angry God; rather he is God's own expression of self-giving so that love actually wins.[13] God's love is expressed through the outstretched arms of the Son.

It is hard not to project human rage and wrath on God, as if our experience dictates that of the divine. As Della, Marilynne Robinson's thoughtful character in her recent novel *Jack*, states, "I am

13. See the theological game-changing work by Rob Bell, *Love Wins: A Book about Heaven, Hell, and the Fate of Every Person Who Has Ever Lived* (New York: HarperOne, 2011).

actually full of rage. Wrath. I think I feel a little like God must feel the second before He just gives up and rains brimstone. I've heard people blame Him for that! I don't blame Him. I can imagine the satisfaction."[14] While I can only imagine what rage a woman of color must have experienced in her segregated society in the 1950s, or even now, her notion that God gains satisfaction from pouring out wrath lacks theological nuance. It is important that we continue to look to Jesus as God's sacrament of compassion to assess the idea of wrath.

Many theologians link wrath with their views of atonement. There are many images of atonement found in the New Testament and historical theology: sin-bearing (Col. 2:14); conquest of death (1 Cor. 15:54–55); reconciling overture for friendship (2 Cor. 5:19); an act of satisfaction (Anselm); demonstration of love (Abelard); the demand of justice (Luther and Calvin); modification of law (Socinus); potency of divine action (Schleiermacher); bearing of penalty (Brunner); evidence of victory (Aulén)—to mention only the prominent theories offered by male theologians.[15] This sheer variety speaks of the surplus of meaning (*sensus plenior*) that interpreting the cross entails.

Feminist and womanist theologians,[16] as well as mujerista[17] and female Asian theologians,[18] have articulated their concerns about how many traditional views glorify suffering, promote violence, and encourage abuse, all of which disproportionately affect women. The groundbreaking work of Delores Williams continues to shape conversation about the critique of the Anselmian atonement theology.[19]

---

14. Marilynne Robinson, *Jack* (New York: Farrar, Straus and Giroux, 2020), 65.

15. These descriptions come from H. D. McDonald, *The Atonement of the Death of Christ: In Faith, Revelation, and History* (Grand Rapids: Baker, 1985).

16. Kelly Brown Douglas, *The Black Christ*, The Bishop Henry McNeal Turner Studies in North American Black Religion 9 (Maryknoll, NY: Orbis Books, 1994), accents the life Jesus lived over the death he died. See also Jacquelyn Grant, *White Women's Christ and Black Women's Jesus: Feminist Christology and Woman Response*, American Academy of Religion Series 64 (Atlanta: Scholars Press, 1989). See also Kathryn Tanner, "Incarnation, Cross, and Sacrifice: A Feminist-Inspired Reappraisal," *Anglican Theological Review*, 86, no.1 (Winter 2004): 35–36.

17. The groundbreaking text is Ada María Isasi-Díaz, *En La Lucha* (Minneapolis: Fortress, 2004).

18. Grace Ji-Sun Kim, *Making Peace with the Earth: Action and Advocacy for Climate Justice* (Geneva: World Council of Churches, 2016), moves toward a participatory understanding of the impact of Jesus' atonement, which includes all creation.

19. Delores S. Williams, *Sisters in the Wilderness: The Challenge of Womanist God-Talk* (Maryknoll, NY: Orbis Books, 1993), offers a passionate reading of the Hagar tradition

Two texts in particular, written over a decade apart, explore the questions of redemption that most of these views raise.[20] They critique the legalism of these regnant views, especially the ways in which God is trapped in laws of God's own making, an inexplicable conundrum.[21] While appreciating these critiques, Kathryn Tanner takes a different approach, arguing that the incarnation itself is the primary way to understand atonement. She writes, "The humanity of Christ (and united with Christ our humanity) is purified, healed, and elevated— saved from sin and its effects (anxiety, fear conflict, and death)—as a consequence of the very incarnation through which the life-giving power of God's own nature are brought to bear on human life."[22] Her approach defuses some of the speculation about wrath, surrogate suffering, sacrifice, and other aspects that arise from focusing more on the cross than the Word made flesh.

We do long for the scales of justice to be balanced by God's wisdom, especially as we see the relentless oppression in the "pyramid of domination" that characterizes our world.[23] We do not yet see the prophetic words of the Magnificat where the "mighty are cast down" and the "rich sent away empty" (Luke 1:52–53) realized. Nor have the words of Jesus' first sermon in Nazareth where he proclaims "liberty to the captives" come to pass (Luke 4:18). In the earlier epoch in which the apostolic author writes the Thessalonians, there is a similar impulse to the gospel witness of God overturning structures of oppression. God will bring justice for all—for some it will mean punishment, for others it will mean vindication.

---

and argues that her role as surrogate is akin to Jesus as the ultimate surrogate figure in substitutionary atonement.

20. Joanne Carlson Brown and Carole R. Bohn, eds., *Christianity, Patriarchy, and Abuse: A Feminist Critique* (New York: Pilgrim, 1989), and Rita Nakashima Brock and Rebecca Ann Parker, *Proverbs of Ashes: Violence, Redemptive Suffering, and the Search for What Saves Us* (Boston: Beacon, 2001), offer clarifying critiques of the outcomes of traditional views that accent scapegoating, satisfaction, substitution, and suffering.

21. I find J. Denny Weaver's sustained engagement with Anselm and his defenders as well as his narrative approach to the *Christus Victor* tradition a way forward. See his *The Nonviolent Atonement* (Grand Rapids: Eerdmans, 2001),

22. Tanner, "Incarnation, Cross, and Sacrifice," 41.

23. I first heard an earlier generation feminist theologian, Letty M. Russell, use this language in the 1980s as some of her groundbreaking feminist theology was taking shape. See her constructive work, *Household of Freedom: Authority in Feminist Theology* (Philadelphia: Westminster Press, 1987), 33.

While those who afflict God's people will receive vengeance, the specifics of which are not described until later in the chapter, God's plan for these believers is to "grant rest with us to you who are afflicted" (v. 7). This judgment will occur "when the Lord Jesus is revealed from heaven with his mighty angels in flaming fire" (v. 7). The reader hears the longing of the author, writing in the name and spirit of Paul, to be relieved of his own affliction and at rest (*anesis*).

It is God alone who has the right to repay persons for evil done; yet the urge to avenge ourselves is strong. In the first epistle, Paul enjoins the readers not to repay evil for evil (1 Thess. 5:15); the writer of the second epistle follows in that vein of thinking. Only God's sovereign judgment should prevail, and humans are not to take into their own hands the divine prerogative.[24] Some of God's judgment will occur in this life (v. 5), and some will occur only as God brings to conclusion history as humans know it. It is trustworthy, and God's reckoning will be just, neither winking at evil nor forgetting the cost of fidelity.

This apocalyptic language of heaven, fire, angels, and the Lord Jesus (v. 7) brings the drama of the Parousia into view. The writer cares for the practical needs of the readers "by applying to their situation apocalyptic traditions he considers appropriate."[25] This kind of improvisation is constructive as it responds to the different circumstances and mostly likely to a different audience. In the first epistle, Paul assures the Thessalonians that all believers, whether dead or alive, will share in the joy of the coming of the risen Christ. Here in the second, the writer emphasizes God's justice "in judging the oppressors and on their separation from the Lord."[26]

Revealing Jesus from heaven with flaming angels in his entourage is not intended solely as a comfort to the believers; it is, rather, a specter for those who will suffer judgment from the "one who wreaks vengeance on the church's enemies by banishing them eternally."[27] The writer's vision of the appearing signals the way in which the

---

24. Miroslav Volf has written at length about this temptation in his significant work *The End of Memory: Remembering Rightly in a Violent World* (Grand Rapids: Eerdmans, 2006).
25. Malherbe, *The Letters to the Thessalonians*, 408.
26. Malherbe, *The Letters to the Thessalonians*, 406.
27. Gaventa, *First and Second Thessalonians*, 105.

divine would arrive.[28] Fire regularly accompanies theophanies in Scripture, with angels being the accompanying emissaries to accomplish holy work. How literally we should take this imagery is questionable, and when we press the scenario for precise detail, we tend to fashion a picture that serves a preconceived notion rather than the unexpected revealing that apocalyptic thinking portends. Here the scene seems more to serve the rhetorical purpose of reinforcing eschatological judgment and Jesus' role in that. It is truly a revelation (*apokalypsis*) as Jesus now comes from heaven to finalize his work of redemption. The crucified one who conquered death and ascended to the right hand of God holds the fate of the wicked in his purview, his appropriate authority.

Their fate is to "suffer the punishment of eternal destruction and exclusion from the presence of the Lord and from the glory of his might." (v. 9). Righteous judgment is actually already present, although the evidence of it (v. 5) is not clearly articulated how before the Parousia it is meted out to believers and those who afflict them. God will through Jesus judge those "who do not acknowledge God." Johnson contends that these are persons "who have been exposed to knowledge of God *through the church's life/witness to the good news about Jesus the true Lord*."[29] They have spurned the gospel and brought harm to those who have obeyed its summons, those living as righteous (*pistis*) followers of the Lord Jesus Christ. Of course, this raises the age-old question about the culpability of those not exposed to the knowledge of God. I will take this up in further reflections.

This pronouncement of coming judgment on those who oppose God's own echoes prophetic literature such as Jeremiah 10:25:

> Pour out your anger on nations who do not acknowledge you,
> indeed on people who have not called on your name,
> because they have devoured and consumed Jacob and have laid
>   waste his pasture.

---

28. Isaiah 66:15 offers similar language of how God comes to punish the wicked.
29. Johnson, *1 and 2 Thessalonians*, 171; author's emphasis.

Similarly, Psalm 79:6–7 condemns those who refuse to respond to God's overtures and oppress God's people.

> Pour out your anger on the nations that do not know thee
> and on the kingdoms who do not call on thy name! For they
> have devoured Jacob and laid waste his habitation.

Punishment of "eternal destruction and exclusion from the presence of the Lord" (v. 9) requires explanation. Gordon Fee suggests that this phrase most likely "reflects a Hebraism in which the *nature* of the judgment itself ("destruction") is collapsed into its *ultimate result* (being cut off "from the face of the Lord)."[30] Whether the writer is thinking about eternal conscious torment or not, the separation from God is the real punishment. Malherbe writes, "What is striking, once more, is that Paul does not dwell on the eschatological pains so vividly described in Jewish apocalyptic literature reflected elsewhere in the New Testament, but describes ruin as separation."[31] Hell is not a part of the prediction—it does not figure in Pauline theology—yet destruction is sure. I will explore the challenge of thinking about eternal destruction for the wicked in a further reflection at the end of the chapter.

The primary assurance the writer offers is that the one they have confessed as Lord will come, and his coming will bring glory to the saints and will be "marveled at in all who have believed, because our testimony to you was believed" (v. 10). Rather than a secret unveiling, it appears that the writer wants the readers to think of a public event in which both they and their Savior will be vindicated. That Jesus takes the place of God in this powerful appearing is central to the writer's thinking. The risen One is God's consummating presence, and YHWH gladly shares this authority with the Son. The glory (*doxa*) of Christ is not for him alone; those who entrust their future to him will share in this honor. It will also bring glory to the apostles who first bore witness to the Thessalonians. Their testimony will be proven true, and the trouble (*thlipsis*) that both the apostolic

---

30. Gordon D. Fee, *The First and Second Letters to the Thessalonians*, The New International Commentary on the New Testament (Grand Rapids: Eerdmans, 2009), 258–59.
31. Malherbe, *The Letters to the Thessalonians*, 402.

team and the congregation endured prepares them to be conformed to the image of the Christ, their true destiny. As in the first epistle, the reputation of the apostolic team depends on the perseverance of this Christian community in Thessalonica.

This is a heavy burden to place on leaders. A thriving and faithful community is a testament to their labor, yet unexpected circumstances may thwart ongoing growth. The church I attended while in seminary was a target of arsonists, with the whole sanctuary burned to the ground. Before long the pastor departed, and interim pastors and staff led the congregation during the time of dislocation and rebuilding. When a new pastor came to the church a year later, his style was very different from the former pastor, and his time was very rocky. He came to a traumatized people, and his good gifts of preaching and leadership were not sufficiently appreciated. His own health suffered, with his even losing his voice for an extended time. It would not be fair to place all the responsibility for the church's difficult years on this able leader.

The writer concludes this section with the commitment to continue in prayer for these faithful ones. It is only by the power of God that they may be worthy of God's call and "may fulfil every good resolve and work of faith" (v. 11). Those of us who have journeyed long in our faith, knowing our own spiritual frailties and divided hearts, realize that our calling as Christians requires God's own sustaining power. The closer we draw near to God the more we see the incongruities that beset us. We depend on the prayers of others who add their own love energies to that of the divine as they yearn over us in their intercession, as my teacher Glenn Hinson has stated.[32] We can become "worthy" of God's call only by the power of the one who summons us to follow the way of Jesus. God continues to call (*kalountos*). We cannot fulfil every good resolve and work of faith by sheer dint of effort; rather, we depend on the "divine assistance to remain always with us," as the Benedictine prayer puts it. Grace always upholds effort.

---

32. E. Glenn Hinson, *A Serious Call to a Contemplative Lifestyle*, rev. ed. (Macon, GA: Smyth & Helwys, 1993), 53. See also his helpful text *The Reaffirmation of Prayer* (Nashville: Broadman, 1979).

The writer wants to make sure that this audience is not deceived about the timing of the day of the Lord. The bewilderment and anxiety in the community need not continue. The earlier teaching of the apostolic team now will be recast so that balance can be gained. As McKinnish Bridges notes, "The members of the church in Thessaloniki misunderstood Paul's words. In the energy and enthusiasm for the gospel message they pushed too hard."[33] Their concern about their loved ones who had gone before them ratcheted up their belief in the proximity of Christ's coming.

The inclusion of this second letter illustrates the dynamism of doctrine and warns against reifying a particular stage of development. This is the ongoing concern of hermeneutics, i.e., how to take Scripture seriously without extrapolating teaching inappropriately to a much different context. Especially when apocalyptic language is in play, caution encourages a judicious attentiveness to the difference between first century social location and today. This second epistle evinces another stage of faith in this community.[34] The intertextual reading of the two procures balance.

This chapter ends with the concept that God's actions and human participation will synergistically shape their lives into a "colony of cruciformity," in the apt description of Johnson.[35] Desiring that "the name of our Lord Jesus may be glorified in you, and you in him," the writer again refers to the source of grace, "God and the Lord Jesus Christ" (v. 12). The interdependence of glorification speaks of the humility of the crucified one. That he would lean his own future exaltation on the frail faithfulness of his followers, an exaltation he gladly shares, speaks of limitless grace.

In the next chapter, the writer will move toward particular developments that will precede the day of the Lord. Christ has not yet appeared, and this apostolic writer wisely resists setting a date. The paramount concern is that the believers not be deceived by false

33. Linda McKinnish Bridges, *1 & 2 Thessalonians*, Smyth and Helwys Bible Commentary (Macon, GA: Smyth & Helwys, 2008), 208. The second epistle, in her opinion, calcified Pauline teaching and "made strict doctrinal monuments out of them" (209). Their preoccupation with the return of Christ ultimately distorted the apostolic teaching that sought to comfort the bereft who grieved the death of their loved ones before the Parousia.

34. McKinnish Bridges, *1 & 2 Thessalonians*, 211.

35. Johnson, *1 and 2 Thessalonians*, 178.

rumors and that they be apprised of what is to come. The care for the community is expressed through the methodical analysis of the times in which they live.

While not as tender in tone as the first epistle, the pastoral concern of this second letter is clear. The apostolic writer wants to offer guidance that will strengthen their faith, love, and hope that they might persevere in troubled times. This pastoral task is a part of every epoch, as the people of God need encouragement to continue as disciples of Jesus Christ. Especially during our time of cataclysmic disease, public witness seems diminished as Christians offer their ministry virtually, yet in many cases the reach of churches has increased as online services are more accessible. Wise pastors provide both empathy and encouragement to live well while in a liminal season, and I am grateful for those who have learned new skills in these difficult days.

FURTHER REFLECTIONS
Does God Intend Eternal Destruction for the Wicked?

The writer offers stark words: "They shall suffer the punishment of eternal destruction (*olethron*) and exclusion from the presence of the Lord and from the glory of his might" (2 Thess.1:9). The meaning of "eternal destruction" is contested, but at the least it means "*separation from*" the Lord's presence.[36] "Eternal destruction" is an expression found in the Dead Sea Scrolls: namely in "The War of the Sons of Light against the Sons of Darkness," according to Leon Morris.[37] He does not think the punishment is annihilation of the flesh, as he cannot imagine a disembodied state, but "as the loss of all that is worthwhile, utter ruin."[38] "Eternal" means "age-long," in his perspective, and we cannot determine the length of the age.

The traditional view of the fate of the wicked is eternal conscious torment.

36. Johnson, *1 and 2 Thessalonians*, 173.
37. See Leon Morris, *The First and Second Epistles to the Thessalonians*, New International Commentary on the New Testament (Grand Rapids: Eerdmans, 1959), 205.
38. Morris, *The First and Second Epistles to the Thessalonians*, 205.

Medieval writers, especially Dante, enjoyed graphic descriptions of what went on in hell where punishment was concomitant with the sin committed. For example, when Virgil and Dante enter the third circle of hell, the realm of the gluttonous, they witness the punishment of the naked shades who howl and roll around in the mire, a stinking substance that continually descends on them. One political leader, Ciacco, has the form of a hog, surely a voracious image.[39]

Jürgen Moltmann offers further explication about the durative nature of this destruction. He believes that there is damnation but that it is not eternal. "The Greek word *ainios,* like the Hebrew word *olam*, means time without a fixed end, a long time, but not time that is 'eternal' in the absolute, timeless sense of Greek metaphysics. . . . Only God is 'eternal' in the absolute sense, and 'unending' in the qualitative sense."[40] Thus he does not believe that an unbeliever is given over to ruin for all eternity.

On the other hand, N. T. Wright, takes seriously the meaning of eternal ruin, believing that those who abjectly refuse to worship God by pursuing various idolatries actually cease to be human. They no longer bear the image of God, and "they pass simultaneously not only beyond hope but also beyond pity."[41] They are not enclosed in an eternal torture chamber, a realm within God's good world. Indeed, they are no longer human, as they cannot reflect God's goodness in any way. What keeps them alive is a question for which I do not find a satisfactory answer in his proposal.

A counter-voice, Moltmann poses a perceptive question about the coming judgment: "If Jesus is the judge, can he judge according to any other righteousness than the law which he himself manifested— the law of love for our enemies, and the acceptance of the poor, the sick and sinners?"[42] He concludes "no," but makes room for both a double outcome of judgment for the righteous and the wicked and the ultimate restoration of all things, universal salvation for humans

---

39. *The Divine Comedy of Dante Alighieri*, trans. Charles Eliot Norton (Chicago: Encyclopedia Britannica, 1952), 60–61.

40. Creative and comprehensive, Moltmann's *Coming of God* (Minneapolis: Fortress, 1996), 242, offers a fresh reading of eschatology.

41. N. T. Wright, *Surprised by Hope: Rethinking Heaven, the Resurrection, and the Mission of the Church* (New York: HarperOne, 2008), 182.

42. Moltmann, *Coming of God*, 236.

and all creation.[43] He holds the tension of justice and hope in a constructive paradigm. I contrast these two leading theologians as they set forth clear alternatives about eternal punishment.

Actually, the language of the Pauline tradition is mild compared to some Jewish apocalyptic sources, according to Ben Witherington, "as he does not relish or dwell on descriptions of the damned and their pains, but rather in essence describes their condition and eternal separation from God and God's people."[44] This is in contrast to the fourth-century homiletician John Chrysostom, Archbishop of Constantinople. He interpreted this text as harshly as possible, arguing that keeping hell before Christians was a great deterrent, and those who rejected the gospel surmised that it was less grievous than its true prospects.[45] He said far more about the punishment than the writer of the second Thessalonian epistle offers.

Likewise, Augustine stoked the flames of imagination for the sake of preserving God's right to inflict unending physical torture. Dan Stiver notes that "Augustine even speculated that God might have to resurrect the wicked in bodies that could continue to burn without being burned up in order to continue their torture."[46] This vision of God as cruel executor of punishment flies in the face of the loving mercy, the good faith (chesed) that marks the divine character, especially as revealed in the face of Jesus Christ. As God's own sacrament of compassion, at the cross Christ reconciles wrath and mercy; wrath is submerged in mercy, as Martin Luther said.

When we review these trains of thought about eternal destruction, I am drawn more to a vision of temporal punishment for the sake of eternal restoration. Eternal punishment for a temporal sin hardly seems just, so I lean toward universal salvation as God's true intent, balanced with accountability and appropriate punitive requirement. We can trust the justice of God who makes all things new to deal fairly with faithful and unfaithful human beings.

---

43. Moltmann, Coming of God, 243
44. Ben Witherington III, 1 and 2 Thessalonians: A Socio-Rhetorical Commentary (Grand Rapids: Eerdmans, 2006), 196.
45. See his Homilies on 2 Thessalonians III, in Nicene and Post-Nicene Fathers (Edinburgh: T & T Clark, 1994), 384–85.
46. Dan R. Stiver, Life Together in the Way of Jesus Christ: An Introduction to Christian Theology (Waco, TX: Baylor University Press, 2009), 459, citing City of God, 21.1–4.

Johnson adds a cautionary note against certitude: "While it is a mistake to diminish the seriousness of God's judgment by presuming upon God's love and mercy, a healthy dose of humility and caution ought to govern the attempts of any to consign this or that persons or group to ultimate perdition."[47] This is wise counsel as we probe the mystery of judgment and redemption.

FURTHER REFLECTIONS
How Does One Participate in the Paschal Mystery?

At least two kinds of suffering emerge in Scripture. There is the involuntary suffering that comes from finitude. Even Jesus, Word made flesh, endured this kind. A remarkable text tells us that "Jesus, wearied as he was with his journey, sat down beside the well. It was about the sixth hour" (John 4:6b). Jesus walked the hilly, stony land of his birth, and physical exhaustion and hunger and thirst were part of embodiment. There in Samaria, at about noon, he evidently was spent. I heard Bishop Stephen Neill say in a lecture in Cambridge in 1980 that this was his favorite verse, as it reveals Jesus' solidarity with frail humanity.

Every human knows the challenges of finitude. Our bones break, our skin is not impermeable to cuts and blisters, infection and malignant processes overtake our bodies and, with age, our vision dims, our hearts fail, and our hearing diminishes. Our lives are bounded by time, limits for which we should actually give thanks since they can prompt a sense of urgency about important matters. Bonhoeffer suggested that the original sin was the refusal to live within limits.[48] It is a part of humility and wisdom to recognize this bounded life in time. It will prompt us to number our days and seek hearts of wisdom, as the psalmist writes (Ps. 90:12).

Just this morning I heard from a friend whose cancer has recurred and metastatic process is hastening onward, shortening her life. Her response is to seek to live as fully as possible in whatever amount of

---

47. Johnson, *1 and 2 Thessalonians*, 174.
48. Dietrich Bonhoeffer, *Creation and Fall, Temptation: Two Biblical Studies* (New York: Macmillan, 1959).

time she has left. She wants to hold her family close, do outrageous and fun things together, and enjoy her days with abandon, as her radiation and chemotherapy will allow. She entrusts herself to the care of God, and those who surround her are visible signs of God's accompanying love. She is numbering her days with wisdom, even forging ahead with putting in a swimming pool in the backyard even at this chilly time of year. The family is planning on heating it, and she will get in it!

In addition to involuntary suffering, there is also voluntary suffering that is undertaken in the service of love. Primarily, this is the story of Jesus Christ who endured the exigencies of humanity even to its conclusion on a painful and humiliating Roman cross, with a few friends lingering. The New Testament is replete with narratives of his suffering while alive and in death.[49] Drawing from the Suffering Servant passages, especially Isaiah 52 and 53, the New Testament interprets the ministry and death of Jesus through these images of the unknown suffering one. His life is the paschal mystery truly, and we can participate in this voluntary suffering with him.

While it may seem strange for a Baptist to be writing about paschal mystery, one of the central concepts of Catholic faith, I contend it is the very center of Christian theology, as it is shorthand for the passion, death, descent, resurrection, and ascension of Jesus Christ, that cluster of events we celebrate in the Easter Triduum. Subsequently, Ascension Day marks the fortieth day of Easter, also known as Pascha in the Eastern tradition. We also commemorate the sacrifice of Christ when we gather at the table for Eucharist.

The etymology of "paschal" is linked to "passing over," a fundamental concept in the Hebrew Bible describing God's protection of Israel in Egypt (Exod. 12:13, 21–27). The slaughtered lamb is the paschal sacrifice, and this language is later a description of the death of Jesus (1 Cor. 5:7). To speak of mystery, as the Pauline tradition often does, is to acknowledge that things of God transcend human rationality. Mystery is not something we solve as much as receive as gift, believing that God's ways are truly higher than ours. Part of our calling in Christ is to be "stewards of the mysteries" (1 Cor. 4:1–2). There

---

49. The Lukan tradition accents the suffering of Jesus, e. g., Luke 9:21–22; 24:25–26, 46; Acts 3:18; 17:2–3; 26:22–23. Ranging over the Pauline tradition we find Rom. 5:3; 8:18, 35; 1 Cor. 15:3; 2 Cor. 4:17; Philippians 3:10; and many more.

is no greater mystery than the confession that through the suffering of the Son we are made whole.

Few in recent decades have written as comprehensively and movingly as Hans Urs von Balthasar on the theology the *mysterium paschale* entails. Situating the self-giving of Jesus deeply in the Trinitarian life of God, he writes: "The ultimate presupposition of the Kenosis is the 'selflessness' of the Persons (when considered as pure relationships) in the inner-Trinitarian life of love."[50] He calls for an "authentic *theological* deepening of the particular mysteries of salvation in their incarnationally concrete character . . . without losing to view the Trinitarian background."[51] The fact that one of the Trinity has died in the flesh makes human participation in the life of God more accessible. And God invites those joined to Christ to enter the paschal mystery and live in it.

For Ronald Rolheiser this means that human suffering, death, and transformation can be the mode of our Christian spirituality;[52] as we attend to the way of Jesus, we are incorporated into his life. Our lives mirror the dying and rising of Christ. As Christ Jesus journeyed the downward pathway of humility (Phil. 2:5–11), he learned through his own suffering of the resurrecting power of God. It is the same for us, Rolheiser argues, as we "after undergoing some kind of death, receive new life and new spirit."[53]

This is the story David Brooks, *New York Times* writer, tells of his life. Coming to deeper faith after a failed marriage, a faith he construes through an interesting mix of Jewish and Christian traditions, he puts suffering in a different light:

> The people who have been made larger by suffering are brave enough to let parts of their old self die. Down in the valley, their motivations changed. They've gone from self-centered to other-centered.[54]

50. Hans Urs von Balthasar, trans. Aidan Nichols, O P, *Mysterium Paschale: The Mystery of Easter* (Edinburgh: T & T Clark, 1990), 35.
51. Von Balthasar, *Mysterium Paschale*, 41.
52. Ronald Rolheiser, *The Holy Longing: The Search for a Christian Spirituality* (New York: Doubleday, 1999), 142.
53. Rolheiser, *The Holy Longing*, 145.
54. David Brooks, *The Second Mountain: The Quest for a Moral Life* (New York: Random House, 2019), xiv.

He links part of his own renewal to being "outrageously forgiven."[55] Forgiveness is the chief expression of God's triune self-giving, and it is at the heart of salvation.

Dying to parts of our lives is an act of mature discipleship. We let go of our youth and quit trying to act as if we are still young. We let go of whatever stage of wholeness we have enjoyed that does not last. We let go of the dreams never realized because of our own lack of industry or the blockage that has come through sexism or racism. We let go of our honeymoons because, ultimately, we learn that the ecstasy of early love cannot be sustained and that faithful commitment lasts longer, is more enduring. Finally, there is the death of a certain idea of God and the Church.[56] Rolheiser suggests that after all of these deaths, which we all must pass through, we need to "manage an ascension,"[57] a letting go so that we might receive a new spirit by the power of the Holy Spirit, a Pentecost.

Of this dying and rising process, Anne Lamott remembers that she had to let go of the notion that anyone who believed in God was stupid, ignorant, or uncouth. She would rather die than disappoint her hilarious and brilliant progressive friends. When she was in the throes of addiction and appalling behavior, Jesus visited her, she writes. He came to her in patience and love, and finally she bade him welcome in her life. It was a reluctant conversion, real nonetheless, and a new creation rose from the waters of baptism—but only because she entered the paschal mystery.[58]

FURTHER REFLECTIONS
What Is the Fate of Those Who Have Not Heard?

The study of this perennial question requires much more than a brief treatment. Nevertheless, I will offer some perspective on how responses to the question are shifting, especially as we learn more about the vibrancy of other ways of faith through our encounters

---

55. Brooks, *Second Mountain*, 213.
56. I have drawn these categories of death from Rolheiser, *The Holy Longing*, 148–62.
57. Rolheiser, *The Holy Longing*, 152.
58. Anne Lamott, *Traveling Mercies: Some Thoughts on Faith* (New York: Pantheon, 1999), 49–50.

with their devotees. New theological imagination about the nature of salvation will serve the sensibility of our time.

Christianity, with its missionary orientation, long endeavored to make sure that every living being had opportunity to receive the proclamation of the gospel. The belief that faith comes by hearing (*fides ex auditu*), as stated in Romans 10:17, saturated the minds of the faithful, and they sought to enact what they believed was the commission of Jesus himself. "Go therefore and make disciples of all nations, baptizing them in the name of the Father and of the Son and of the Holy Spirit, teaching them to observe all that I have commanded you; and lo, I am with you always, to the close of the age" (Matt. 28:19–20).

Roman Catholic orders sent some of the first missionaries, and their energetic work led to the baptisms of many around the known world. I think in particular of the extensive service of Jesuits (Society of Jesus), founded in 1540. As their first superior general, Ignatius of Loyola famously told his foot soldiers for the Lord, "Go forth and set the world on fire." By this he meant that their proclamation and educational efforts should shine with the flame of God's love, the heat that would refine and temper sinful aspects of the human condition.[59] He did not mean burn down everything you find in a new context. Single men fanning across the globe formed friendships with primal people and "were very sensitive to issues of cultural adaptation, and spurned attempts to impose European values."[60] Sadly, the enemies of the Jesuits prevailed in Rome, and the "Jesuit cultural compromise fell apart at the end of the seventeenth century."[61] Cultural triumphalism returned, and the important gains of the Jesuit approach lost traction.

In the Second Vatican Council, Catholic theology made a robust pivot with the Declaration on the Relationship of the Church to Non-Christian Religions, known as the *Nostra Aetate*, which means "In Our Time." This document of October 28, 1965, set a new course

59. To learn about the founding of the Jesuit Order, see *Ignatius of Loyola: Spiritual Exercises and Selected Works*, The Classics of Western Spirituality, ed. George E. Ganss, S J (New York: Paulist, 1991), 44.

60. Philip Jenkins, *The Next Christendom: The Coming of Global Christianity* (Oxford: Oxford University Press, 2002), 32.

61. Jenkins, *The Next Christendom*, 32.

for how the church would approach religious others, affirming a common humanity, a universal awareness of a hidden power, and the restless desire for sacred rites. The declaration states strongly that "The Catholic Church rejects nothing of what is true and holy in these religions. It has a high regard for the manner of life and conduct, the precepts and doctrines which, although differing in many ways from its own teaching, nevertheless often reflect a ray of that truth which enlightens all men and women."[62]

The largest impact of the document has been for Jewish-Christian relations, although Pope John Paul II was deeply concerned about Catholic-Muslim rapprochement. The church is still living into this interfaith horizon, and Roman Catholic theologians such as Karl Rahner and Hans Küng have offered creative proposals toward an inclusive vision of salvation.[63]

The modern missionary movement in its Protestant form began in earnest just before the nineteenth century as sailing the globe became more possible. Part of the challenge was that colonizing ambition and evangelizing intent traveled on the same ships, and conversion too often meant becoming like the ones proclaiming, and decimation of cultures ensued. Philip Jenkins reflects on the contemporary assessment of this pursuit: "Most modern Europeans or Americans cringe at the claims their ancestors made about their 'civilizing mission' to the rest of the world."[64] More successful entree resulted from learning the language well and respecting the culture as missionaries realized that they were guests rather than commandants wielding noblesse oblige.

The motivation of these spiritual ancestors was clear. They believed that the eternal destination of nonbelievers rested on their willingness to preach the gospel to every nation or people group on

62. Second Vatican Council, *Nostra Aetate*, October 28, 1965, https://www.bc.edu/content/dam/files/research_sites/cjl/texts/cjrelations/resources/documents/catholic/Nostra_Aetate.htm#:~:text=The%20Catholic%20Church%20rejects%20nothing,enlightens%20all%20men%20and%20women, accessed April 4, 2022.
63. See Karl Rahner, *Foundations of Christian Faith: An Introduction to the Idea of Christianity* (New York: Seabury, 1978), especially as he probes the present of Jesus in non-Christian religions, 315 ff., and Hans Küng, *Theology for the Third Millennium: An Ecumenical View* (New York: Doubleday, 1988), 209ff, as he constructs a theology of world religions. He concludes that each religion has a partial grasp of the truth.
64. Jenkins, *The Next Christendom*, 38.

earth. They felt it would be a dereliction of duty to leave their salvific fortunes in the hands of God. After all, they believed that the Great Commission gave them marching orders until the end of the age. Thus, the 1800s are referred to as the "great century" as far as missionary successes were recorded.

This movement continued into the next century, the so-called Christian century. Jenkins notes that by the "1950s, the United States was supplying two-thirds of the 43,000 Protestant missionaries active around the world."[65] This movement flourished even if mixed motivation was at work for converts. Once again, Jenkins offers insight: "Christianity was inextricably bound up with the all-conquering imperial nations, and thus with an image of success and modernity. This appealed to local elites, who could begin the conversion of their societies from the top down."[66]

Today we are more aware that we live in a religiously plural world, and we interrogate some of our earlier practices of seeking to convert persons who pursue a different way of faith. Our earlier certitude is giving way to a more theologically perceptive interfaith engagement. As the eclipse of Christendom has transpired, new assessments of the great world religions are occurring. There are equally venerable traditions, some established long before Christianity. Adherents of Buddhism, Hinduism, or Confucianism, for example, wonder why Christians would insist that they forsake the practice, imbedded in their culture, that has guided them for centuries. The exclusivist theology that maintains that verbal profession of faith in the Lord Jesus Christ is the only way of salvation has been eroding for many decades.

A spectrum of options exists in our time.[67] I will simply list these with a brief explanation to help orient the reader to the variety of perspectives about the necessity of hearing the gospel proclaimed.

1. *Church exclusivism* comes from an earlier time. Cyprian offered the formula "No salvation outside the church" (*extra ecclesiam nulla*

---

65. Jenkins, *The Next Christendom*, 35.
66. Jenkins, *The Next Christendom*, 42–43.
67. I have drawn these from *Faith Comes by Hearing: A Response to Inclusivism*, ed. Christopher W. Morgan and Robert A. Peterson (Downers Grove, IL: InterVarsity Press, 2008), 26.

salus) in the third century. It became the traditional position of the Roman Catholic Church until Vatican II.

2. *Gospel exclusivism,* deeply concerned about personal response to the "good news" (*euangelion*), believes one must hear the gospel and trust Christ to be saved.

3. *Special revelation exclusivism* suggests that the Holy Spirit may on occasion reveal the truth of God's salvific purpose through extraordinary means like a dream, vision, or mysterious messenger. Advocates of this position point to the conversion of Saul.

4. *Agnosticism* is the contention that we cannot know the answer to the question of those who have not heard the preaching of the gospel. Speculation about the efficacy of general revelation is not compelling for this position.

5. *General revelation inclusivism* is a perspective that holds that God does offer enough in nature and a sense of providential working in history to save. Besides, it would call the divine nature into question if God offered only enough in general revelation to condemn but not enough to save.

6. *World religions inclusivism* says that other ways of faith can be a means of salvation, especially since God is at work in them. A key proponent of this view is Karl Rahner, who coined the awkward term "anonymous Christian."

7. *Postmortem evangelism* is a position that says God will deny no one opportunity to be confronted with the gospel of Jesus. Some argue that the "descent" passages in 1 Peter 3:18–20 and 4:6 suggest this view.

8. *Universalism* points to the idea that biblical revelation strongly maintains that it is God's purpose to save everyone and that ultimately God's "yes" is stronger than a human "no." Thus, everyone will ultimately be saved because of God's original intent and that only God has power to condemn.

9. *Pluralism* grants equal status to varied ways of faith, and the views of salvation these religions offer are significantly different. By embracing their discrete vision of redemption, believers will participate fully.

These very real options loom and, for many Christians, the move toward more inclusive or even a pluralistic perspective helps them make sense of divine justice, the accidents of history and geography, and the extent of grace.

While a committed Christian who believes that God in Christ has encompassing significance for all, I have moved over the years from a strict gospel exclusivism toward a recognition of a modified universalism that takes seriously the claims of other ways of faith even as I argue for the enduring import of the incarnation. As Mark Heim contends, different religions pursue different religious ends. So interpretations of salvation must not be imposed from the Christian perspective on other ways of faith. Christianity can maintain its particularistic witness without anathematizing all others.[68]

---

68. S. Mark Heim, *Salvations: Truth and Difference in Religion* (Maryknoll, NY: Orbis Books, 1995).

2 Thessalonians 2:1–17
Considering the Two Comings

The author moves briskly into the chief concern of this second epistle, the coming of the Lord Jesus Christ and how the Thessalonians
will participate in the expected Parousia. This forthright beginning
of chapter two is meant to comfort and instruct. Begging them not
to be "shaken in mind or excited, either by spirit or by word," he
abjures deception and pursues clarity, especially surrounding the
swirling topic of the Lord's return.

They had gotten it wrong, apparently. Linda McKinnish Bridges
perceptively observes, "The members of the church in Thessaloniki
misunderstood Paul's words. . . . They did not get the point, at least
not the major one. The New Testament lovingly and unashamedly
records their gross *faux pas*."[1] Abraham Malherbe shares this perspective, arguing that in this chapter "Paul (the writer) first intro-
duces the doctrinal error and its possible sources, which he feared
might pose a threat to the emotional stability of the Thessalonians
(vv. 1–2)."[2] This second epistle from an apostolic source within the
Pauline tradition helps the community regain its bearings.

Evidently letters are circulating that purport to come from Paul,
with the writer warning them to be wary of such, which is ironic given
that 2 Thessalonians is such a work itself. The writer of this epistle
wants to claim the field in terms of proper instruction and dissuade
the members of the community from being duped by false reporting

---

1. Linda McKinnish Bridges, *1 & 2 Thessalonians*, Smyth & Helwys Bible Commentary
   (Macon, GA: Smyth & Helwys, 2008), 208.
2. Abraham J. Malherbe, *The Letters to the Thessalonians*, Anchor Bible 32B (New York:
   Doubleday, 2000), 414.

about the day of the Lord. Hence, he will talk about "two comings," that of a sinister, blaspheming figure and then the revealing of the Christ, unto whom honor and glory belong. While the apocalyptic language is dense and hard to decipher, its pastoral intent is clear, and the theological imagination of the writer offers new perspective.

2:1–12

Two Comings

Whereas in the first chapter the apostle offers comfort through thanksgiving and reassurance, now he does so "in the form of a warning."[3] Fiercely protective of this community, the writer does not so much offer a roadmap for the future as encouragement for the present.[4] They can ultimately expect key events to presage the two comings, and he seeks to prepare them for both. Reading his context adroitly, the writer draws from a common symbol system both political and cosmic to sketch out an eschatological framework.

2:1–2 The Coming of Christ

The exhortation of chapter 2 begins with strong words about the importance of what will follow. Beseeching these fellow Christians, he launches into his exhortation, laying out "in nonchronological fashion, a scheme in which future and present events alternate."[5] First the author speaks of "the coming [Parousia] of our Lord Jesus Christ and our assembling to meet him" (v. 1). This echoes what is written in the previous chapter as well as in 1 Thessalonians 4:13–18. He assures the readers that they will be caught up to be with him, celebrating his arrival and giving honor to him publicly. "Being caught up" together reflects what we read in 1 Thessalonians 4:17, which speaks of how those still alive and those departed through death will be with Christ when his arrival occurs. They will have

---

3. Malherbe, *The Letters to the Thessalonians*, 414.
4. Andy Johnson, *1 and 2 Thessalonians,* The Two Horizons New Testament Commentary (Grand Rapids: Eerdmans, 2016), 181.
5. Malherbe, *The Letters to the Thessalonians*, 414.

the comfort of being with others who have persevered in their faith, believing that Christ will come and gather them to himself. This has not happened yet (2:2), so they can, with further guidance, extinguish the flames of agitation the topic has fanned in the community. That some are making this claim about the return of Christ has brought not only dissension but also danger into the community. As we shall see in the next chapter, the lure of idleness encroaches when believers think that the imminent end is near or has arrived.

Second, the writer delineates the media whereby confusing messages may have come, "either by spirit, or by word, or by letter" (v. 2). In every age, there are those who believe that they have the final word from God about how human history will end. While helpful warnings to live as Christ commands are constructive for every generation in Christian history as preparation for the return "on that day," those seeking to control their flocks, to influence the wider Christian populace and, too often, to yield to their desire for monetary gain, stretch beyond thoughtful humility on such a hidden topic. Books that purport to lay out the final events at the end of the age do sell! Tim LaHaye (with Jerry Jenkins) has made a bundle on the Left Behind series. I have always found it interesting that in 1970, Hal Lindsey, author of *The Late, Great Planet Earth*, was simultaneously investing in vast real estate holdings while avowing an imminent return just a few years out, in the 1980s. He followed a dispensationalist view of Scripture, which will be the focus of a further reflection at the end of the chapter.

Readers then and now must parse this apostolic language with care. It is hard to imagine that the writer is claiming that they could be shaken and troubled, "either by spirit, or by word, or by letter"" which could deceive them; yet we know that throughout the history of the Church, persons have been willing to claim that they are speaking "through the Spirit" to justify their perspectives. Clearly, the writer is warning against such claims, as well as other pronouncements or writings that claim the realization of the day of the Lord. While we can trust that the Spirit seeks to guide into all truth, human capacity to discern what is truly prompted by the interior dwelling of God is flawed. Important to discernment is the collaborative work of a community; for there with many voices wisdom can be generated beyond individual proclivities. I will give more attention to the process of communal discernment in one of the further reflections.

2:3–12 *The Coming of the "Man of Lawlessness"*

That they not be deceived is the pastoral concern of the writer, and thus he speaks of what must transpire. There will be a great rebellion, and the first of the comings will occur—the revealing of the "man of lawlessness, the son of perdition" (v. 3). The description of this figure is grotesque as he grasps for power that does not belong to him. He usurps the very place of God, which is by God's own design the place that now rightly belongs to the risen One. While the language of the antichrist is not used in this epistle as we find it in 1 and 2 John, the description of the vile deception he will foment is eerily similar. It is important theological architecture to speak of evil in such concrete terms, for even if this personification is metaphorical, it warns against real danger from forces that oppose God.

The writer reminds them that he taught about this figure earlier, but it is not mentioned in the first epistle. Once again, the coherence of the two epistles is questionable, and the writer of the second may be dissembling or, at least, hedging his own opinion. Wanting to call them toward fidelity, the writer may say more than is possible to know, even under the inspiration of the Spirit. It is important for believers to realize the degree to which we "see through a glass darkly" and to not presume that the formation of Scripture is exempt from other human ways of knowing. This, of course, may smack of a dismissive view of Scripture to those who hold inerrantist/infallible views; however, it does speak of how God honors human cognition in seeking to listen to the impress of the Spirit. God does not suspend rationality when speaking to creatures after the divine likeness; if anything, God is supra-rational in ways that are not our own yet does not obliterate or suspend the intellectual properties God has instantiated in human beings. Though inspired, the writer of the second epistle has limits to what he can predict.[6]

---

6. I continue to refer to the writer of this epistle as "he" only because it is more probable in that era that a man would offer this pseudonymous work as one functioning in apostolic tradition.

Who is the "man of lawlessness?" An ominous figure to be sure, in the words of Beverly Roberts Gaventa,[7] this one is against God in every way. Rather than submitting to God's authority, this diabolical character seeks to overturn every rightful claim to authority that God alone holds, now shared with the Son in his obedient self-giving. Destined for destruction, this opposing force, personified in this text, sounds like the blasphemy that Antiochus Epiphanes, a most contemptible person, professed when considering himself greater than any god (Daniel 11:36) as he led a campaign against Jerusalem, leading to its sacking. Other figures from the Hebrew Bible come to mind: the King of Tyre whom Ezekiel excoriates for saying, "I am a god, I sit in the seat of the gods . . ." (Ezek. 28:2) and the supposed claim of the King of Babylon (Isa. 14:13–14) to "raise my throne above the stars of God . . . making myself like the Most High." Each presumes an entitlement that encroaches on what is solely in God's province and rule. Does the writer have someone else in mind than these troubling characters in the First Testament?

We recall that among the sayings of Jesus is the prophecy of the desecration of the temple: "So when you see the desolating sacrilege spoken of by the prophet Daniel, standing in the holy place (let the reader understand), then let those who are in Judea flee to the mountains"(Matt. 24:15–16).[8] The somber threat is clearly a part of the Son's teaching, and this tradition endures in early Christianity.

Both testaments and other early writings speak of individuals who represent a system of evil. This figure portends a final clash with God's forces for good, a great rebellion (*apostasia*). Some scholars suggest that the Sibylline Oracles describe this evil one as revived Roman emperor Nero coming from Babylon.[9] Others point to the reign of Caligula who tried to set up an image of himself in the temple's Holy of Holies in Jerusalem, as recorded by Josephus.[10] While this former emperor did not succeed in this overweening attempt,

7. Beverly Roberts Gaventa, *First and Second Thessalonians*, Interpretation: A Bible Commentary for Teaching and Preaching (Louisville, KY: Westminster John Knox Press, 1998), 111.
8. See other Synoptic parallels in Mark 13:5–13, 21–23 and Luke 21:18–19.
9. These oracles are presumably later than the writing of 2 Thessalonians and cannot be directly connected, yet there is certainly a similar theme of self-exaltation by a usurping power. I draw this allusion from Malherbe, *The Letters to the Thessalonians*, 420.
10. *The Works of Flavius Josephus*, vol. 4, *Antiquities of the Jews*, 18.8 (Grand Rapids: Baker, 1974), 47.

his desire for adulation as a god was remembered among both Jews and Greeks. We see this same impulse through our historical prism in dictatorships across the globe as "strong men" think there are no checks on their powers. This second epistle offers timeless instruction on how those opposed to and usurping the province of God alone will ultimately fare.

Does the author have the behavior of a contemporary leader who exalts himself (*hyperairō*) in mind as he seeks to warn the congregation of what may be coming in due season? Whether or not Paul had told them of the coming of this desecrating personage when he was with them, the writer of the second epistle wants the congregation to know they are not powerless in this scenario. There is something that restrains (v. 6) so that the revealing (*apokalyptō*) of this insurgent power of evil can be utterly transparent for what it truly is, and they can be sure of ultimate triumph for God's own. The corrupting, decimating power of lawlessness is "already at work," a mystery that cannot utterly hold sway (v. 7) even though terrible calamity comes through his power. This evil one cannot escape being fully known, as the mask of deception will be pulled down, revealing the one whom the Lord Jesus will confront in great might (v. 8).

In addition to the "lawless one," another force or figure features in this text, the controller, the one who will curtail this onslaught. The restraining force will be active "until he who now restrains it will do so until he is out of the way" (v. 7). Is it God that keeps the unbridled ambition of the evil one in check, or is it the Roman Empire or the emperor himself? Could it be an "angel of God" as Daniel 12:1–4 suggests? When the writer declares, "you know what is restraining him now," we are without clear guidance. Not having a well-defined word on this in the first epistle, the author of the second improvises as best he can. God works through many media, and using varied individuals, governing bodies, and social movements as instruments of God's purposes. That God works through flawed human structures is an expression of divine humility as well as God's gift of human dignity. It is usually only in retrospect that we perceive the divine hand at work, and even then, we cannot be utterly sure that the narrative we are constructing sufficiently makes room for the mystery of God's own providential action.

The plot the writer offers is simple. Lawlessness is at work in the world; the restraining force keeps it in check to a certain degree; at a future point the restraining force will be set aside, and "full scale rebellion will break out, and the lawless one will himself appear and challenge the rule of God."[11] When that happens, the Lord Jesus will move swiftly to destroy him. While there is no timetable offered for this sequence, the writer wants to assure the Thessalonians that historical events will not outstrip the power of God as revealed in Christ.

The writer speaks of the activity of the lawless one who will make his presence known "with pretended signs and wonders" (v. 9). He will also pursue "wicked deception for those who are to perish" (v. 10). Charlatans are dependent on some sort of "signs and wonders" to cement their claims to special knowledge and power, and replete is the history of such dissolute attempts to claim this spiritual alchemy. Scripture is clear that spiritual powers exist, even though there is little reflection on them. Think of those who performed similar miraculous events in Egypt (Exod. 7:11–12) or the story of the prophetic activity of the slave girl (Acts 16:16–40). How to consider these expressions of powers is complex and most likely beyond the scope of this theological commentary.[12]

Every epoch has hastened to identify this lawless figure, believing that if he could be named there would be a greater understanding of the suffering those of that time were passing through. Not surprising, many have viewed their own historical horizon as the end times for they cannot imagine anything worse than their own experience. We understand the tendency to privilege our own time—the only one we really know—as somehow the apex of human pathos. During the current pandemic, we hear this tone often, and people are not reticent to consider their circumstances in apocalyptic terms. This is understandable, as suffering is an ingredient in every epoch.

While it has been a mainstay to try to identify the malignant lawless one, his identity eludes us. This figure is often conflated with

---

11. Gaventa, *First and Second Thessalonians*, 114.
12. I would recommend the work of Walter Wink to sift how powers are at work in this world. See especially his *Engaging the Powers: Discernment and Resistance in a World of Domination* (Minneapolis: Fortress, 1992).

the antichrist. At one point, Martin Luther suggested that his nemesis John Eck was a likely candidate. Naming various popes (the purview of Protestants, of course), Luther (the view of Catholics, of course), political regimes such as the Roman Empire or Nazi Germany, political leaders like Hitler or Stalin, Putin or Trump, as the "man of lawlessness" has kept the imagery in front of varied sectors of Christian believers. While none of these characters has signaled the day of the Lord, they nevertheless are figures of consequence as they stride through their discrete epochs with destabilizing force. There is a sense in which they become the personification of evil, and people feel it urgent to curtail their power and the damage they broker in their self-exaltation. Abuse of power is always an indicator of "lawlessness," and many suffer under its overreach.

I ask thee, ignorant Antichrist, dost thou think that with thy naked words thou canst prevail against the armor of Scripture? . . . Whether this bull is by Eck or by the pope, it is the sum of all impiety, blasphemy, ignorance, hypocrisy, lying—in a word, it is Satan and his Antichrist.

Martin Luther, an excerpt from "Against the Execrable Bull of the Antichrist." See Roland Bainton, *Here I Stand: A Life of Martin Luther* (Peabody: Hendrickson Classic, 1950), 155–57.

Once revealed, the fate of the lawless one is clear: "the Lord Jesus will slay him with the breath of his mouth and destroy him by his appearing and his coming" (v. 8b). The coming of Christ will put to an end this supposed rival, who is empowered by the activity of Satan. With "pretended signs and wonders," the lawless one deceives many (vv. 9–10), particularly those who "refused to love the truth and so be saved." These will perish because they could not discern good from evil, the chief blasphemy against God.

Part of the popular fascination with this lawless figure is that people can point to heinous activities in every age. Whether it be genocidal decimation of a people, unscrupulous hoarding of wealth, obliteration of environmental resources, or other forms of ruthless power, these pursuits have self-aggrandizing motives and outcomes. As I write, a headline pops up on my screen: "Billionaires are getting even richer despite the ongoing pandemic." Prospering off the suffering of others is an expression of the mystery of lawlessness. Disregard for the unemployed, the family without health care, the immigrant treated as less than human at the border of the United States, the sexual minority, and the enduring caste system in our land expresses the intent of lawlessness.[13]

The might of the Lord Jesus is on display in this passage. Any contest is over when he appears (*epiphaneia*). His coming (Parousia) will destroy his enemy and the enemy of God's people. Echoing Isaiah 11:4, "and with the breath of his lips he shall slay the wicked," the writer assures the reader of the superior power of Jesus. His word will accomplish its purpose, and its power will be evident to all.

This section of chapter 2 ends with these troubling words: "Therefore God sends upon them a strong delusion, to make them believe what is false, so that all may be condemned who did not believe the truth but had pleasure in unrighteousness" (vv. 11–12). Albeit troubling, it is not unprecedented, and Romans 1:24–32 and Mark 4:11–12 offer similar observations. It is at home in an apocalyptic worldview, where special knowledge is revealed to the few but hidden from the many. The writer ostensibly then shifts blame for the perfidy of those deceived onto God. This reaches back toward a much more primitive understanding that somehow everything—good or bad—comes from God. We read in Exodus 4:21 and 9:12 and subsequent texts about God "hardening the heart" of Pharaoh.[14] We also read of God sending an evil spirit on King Saul (1 Sam. 16:23, et al.).[15] Walter Brueggemann notes that YHWH is seen as the primal cause of both good and bad, the single cause of all that happens in the world.[16] These texts are more nuanced than a superficial reading allows, and we would err if we thought divine prerogative dictated human response, rendering any sense of culpability moot. While human perverseness is responsible

---

13. See the remarkable work of Willie James Jennings, *The Christian Imagination: Theology and the Origins of Race* (New Haven: Yale, 2010), 9, who speaks of the "diseased social imagination" that led to the subjugation of persons of color.
14. In Exodus 9:34 Pharaoh is the one who hardened his heart, sinning again by his perverseness. Yet in the following verse it appears that his heart is hardened by a power external to him.
15. See my treatment of King Saul in *Joining the Dance: A Theology of the Spirit* (Valley Forge: Judson, 2003), 41.
16. Walter Brueggemann, *Theology of the Old Testament: Testimony, Dispute, Advocacy* (Minneapolis: Fortress, 1997), 354.

for a hard heart, this expression of free will somehow fits into God's own foreknowing, God's sovereignty in human history. On the question of whether God deludes people, a terrifying thought, Gaventa observes, "Not only will those who are perishing not permit God to be God, but they will also not believe the truth. Because they *will* believe lies, God sends them a lie."[17]

Of this brief section Johnson writes: "There is a consensus among commentators that this passage is one of the, if not the single, most difficult and obscure in the Pauline corpus."[18] This suggests that we should tread carefully without claims of certitude. Helpful is Jeffrey Weima's assessment: "The apostle's first and foremost intention is not to *predict* but to *pastor*."[19] Gaventa suggests that an appropriate name for this passage could be "The Defeat of Delusion."[20] By this she means that we should be willing to join Augustine in conceding about this passage in the *City of God*, "I frankly confess I do not know what he means."[21] Yet we may in faith draw the conclusion that God is all about truth and does not delude people for any divine purpose. To suggest otherwise is to consider a sweeping malevolence in God that Scripture or thoughtful theological reflection cannot sustain. While we must always confess that mystery surrounds Holy being, we trust what God has revealed to us in Jesus Christ.

2:13–15

Chosen for Salvation

Thanksgiving for these believers returns as a focus, much as in the first chapter (1:3–4). Introducing exhortation through the rhetoric of giving thanks always for them, the writer confirms their significance to God as well as to his own apostolic witness. These first fruits (*aparchē*) of the gospel labor in Thessalonica are beloved of

17. Gaventa, *First and Second Thessalonians*, 115.
18. Johnson, *1 and 2 Thessalonians*, 181.
19. Jeffrey Weima, "The Slaying of Satan's Superman and the Sure Salvation of the Saints: Paul's Apocalyptic Words of Comfort (2 Thessalonians 2:1–17)," *Calvin Theological Journal*, 41 (2006): 73; author's emphasis. I learned of this article as I was consulting with Johnson's commentary.
20. Gaventa, *First and Second Thessalonians*, 108.
21. Gaventa, *First and Second Thessalonians*, 108.

God and give testimony to faithful apostolic proclamation in their midst. Their perseverance in faith, love, and hope marks them as a part of God's own elect people.

The writer moves to assure the readers further by reminding them of their chosenness. As he gives thanks for them, he underscores what God has long planned for their salvation. Chosen from the beginning as first converts, they have been the objects of the sanctifying work of the Holy Spirit, God's own agent for a metamorphosis of glory (2 Cor. 3:17–18).

The transformation of their lives is God's holy purpose; their lives will bear the imprint of God's own gospel and its liberating power to save. The ultimate goal is to "obtain the glory of our Lord Jesus Christ." Once again, the motif of participation enters the discourse. This is how they themselves "become the gospel," in the words of Michael J. Gorman.[22] The glory of Jesus invites participation, and he never wants to be untethered from those he has incorporated into his body. Joining the body of Christ means completion of calling, justification, and finally sharing in glorification (Rom. 8:30). This order of salvation (*ordo salutis*) points to the comprehensive project of redemption.

> **The Spirit is the mark of those who belong to Christ.**
>
> D. E. H. Whiteley, *The Theology of St. Paul* (Oxford: Basil Blackwell, 1972), 126.

The apostle's exhortation is clear: "stand firm and hold to the traditions which you were taught by us, either by word of mouth or by letter" (v. 15). Invoking the identity of the original apostolic team, of Paul, Silvanus, and Timothy, the writer reminds them that the instruments of their calling were these early missionaries who proclaimed this good news of redemption. A sense of ownership comes from the writer as he speaks of how God "called you through our gospel" (v. 14). The "traditions" most likely refer to the original witness of Christ crucified and risen, given in proclamation prior to any written epistle. The centrality of this teaching in all of the Pauline tradition (*paradosis*) is the heart of the gospel. Continuity in what he has "handed on" places him squarely within the original apostolic

---

22. Michael J. Gorman, *Becoming the Gospel: Paul, Participation, and Mission* (Grand Rapids: Eerdmans, 2015), 102.

tradition (1 Cor.15:3-8). He claims no hidden teaching and emphasizes that this tradition is well known among the members of this community.[23]

This is pastoral language, laced with compassion and theological teaching. Not only does God claim them, but so do those who have given themselves to founding this community. Malherbe offers significant perspective: "Believers who are aware of the mystery of lawlessness already at work and who know of the wickedness and deception still to come, may be comforted as they are reminded that they have been chosen by God and are at the center of his saving purpose."[24]

Perhaps there is no more precious a concept than being one who is chosen. Whether in team sports, friendship, marriage, or vocation, the knowledge that we are desired to play our distinctive role gives confidence and adds joy to our quotidian, our mundane reality. In hard circumstances, this is sustaining.

Even the true name of the individual is known only to God. There are references to the fact that the designation Child of God, is the only name that is necessary. This gnosis of the individual is an amazing example of the mystical element present in the slave's religious experience. The slave's answer to the use of terms of personal designation that are degrading is to be found in his private knowledge that his name is known to the God of the entire universe.

Howard Thurman, *Deep River and the Negro Spiritual Speaks of Life and Death* (Richmond: Friends United Press, 1975), 45.

God gives our lives inestimable value by choosing us to participate in God's saving work in the world. God not only desires to make us God's own, but the divine also invites our partnership in God's redemptive enterprise. Election is often linked negatively with favoritism, a kind of predetermined claiming of some and allowing reprobation to be the fate of others. I will explore this in further reflections.

---

23. Malherbe, *The Letters to the Thessalonians*, 440.
24. Malherbe, *The Letters to the Thessalonians*, 438.

2:16–17

The Gift of Comfort and Hope through Grace

The writer ends this chapter with a prayer of encouragement. It sounds like a benediction; however, that is yet to come at the end of chapter 3. Stating what God can do—love, give encouragement, and offer good hope by grace—the author invites "Jesus Christ himself and God our Father" to perform these very works. It is striking that Jesus is mentioned before God, as Malherbe observes,[25] and it seems to serve the purpose of underscoring his authority yet to be fully revealed. The theme of exalting the Son is a constant in the Pauline tradition, and this writer knows of its significance.

Calling on God to "comfort your hearts and establish them in every good work and word," this closing section of chapter 2 echoes what Paul originally asked of Timothy as he visited the congregation (1 Thess. 3:2–3). The heart is the center of the human affection, the place where one encounters God when opened to the divine presence. Actually, heart encompasses the whole person and is the center of will and purpose. The phrase "every good work and word" is comprehensive nomenclature speaking of all human activity, and the writer is offering a theological perspective. We cannot do what God desires without the divine assistance. Our speech and actions, if they be good, are upheld by God's power and encouragement. This prayer is deeply assuring as it stresses the actions of God and Christ for the sake of these who are undergoing such penetrating trauma. Desiring their comfort, the writer enters their situation with love and blessing.

FURTHER REFLECTIONS
What Is Dispensationalist Theology and Why Did It Gain Popularity?

One approach to eschatology is provided by the dispensationalist structure, an apocalyptic understanding of history, which has been

---

25. Malherbe, *The Letters to the Thessalonians*, 441.

wildly popular for more than a century. Dispensationalism arose from the work of John Nelson Darby (1800–1882), an Anglican minister who left the Church of Ireland to help found the movement that came to be known as the Plymouth Brethren. It came to the United States in the 1870s as the modernist movement was gaining popularity; and its literal approach to reading Scripture seemed a proper counterweight to modernism's critical methodology.

Dividing the teaching of the Bible into "dispensations," or "economies," dispensationalism's interpretive method said God acts in each period of time from "common principles but with varying mandates."[26] This historical periodization delineating progressive revelation usually follows a seven dispensations structure: innocence, conscience, human government, promise, law, grace, and kingdom. Prophecy holds a prominent role with significant concern devoted to the summing up of the age, especially what will be the fate of the church in the expected tribulation. It is a supersessionist view of Scripture, a diminishing of the First Testament, with God handing on to the church what the Jews had failed to realize. Because they rejected God's Messiah, Israel is basically set aside, only to be sorted out after the church concludes its work and is raptured. The heart of dispensationalism holds that Christ will return before establishing a thousand-year reign of peace and righteousness on the earth, which is the premillennial view.

Darby's ideas became popular through the *Scofield Reference Bible* in the early twentieth century. The notes for this Bible were steeped in dispensational thinking and this publication gained rapid interest as persons found its methodology compelling. Published in 1909, it was revised as recently as 1967, which shows its continuing hold on the imagination of a fundamentalist sector of Christianity. Historian Mark Noll suggests that this interest in eschatology and security for the Church "may also have been a defensive reaction to an implicit realization that American culture was slipping away from evangelical Protestant control."[27] If that was true at the turn of the last century, it is even more evident today. The lack

---

26. Mark A. Noll, *A History of Christianity in the United States and Canada* (Grand Rapids: Eerdmans, 1992), 376.
27. Noll, *A History of Christianity*, 377.

of care in this scheme for anyone other than the Church displays a cavalier attitude toward religious neighbors.

Several aspects of dispensationalism continue to shape the hopes of its enthusiasts.[28] One is the belief that Jesus can return at any minute. This "imminence" doctrine urges high alert and dismisses concerns about urgent contemporary issues such as climate change. The rapture figures prominently as well, a secret to all except the faithful. The Church's expectation to be "caught up with Jesus" at his return grants special privilege to the "bride of Christ" as Christians escape the tribulation. This period of seven years of divine judgment, a futuristic reading of passages in the books of Daniel and Revelation, will culminate with the Battle of Armageddon and the glorious public return of Jesus Christ. Most problematic is the discontinuity between the covenantal theology of the Old and New Testaments, although apocalyptic expectations continue. The dispensationalist hermeneutic is profoundly disingenuous, as it pieces together scraps of Scripture according to a timeline that is not found in the Bible.

> the Hebrew seers announce
>   in time
> the return of Judah to her
>   prime;
> Some Christians deemed it
>   then at hand
> Here was an object. Up and on.
> With seed and tillage helped
>   renew—
> Help reinstate the Holy Land.
>
> Larry Edward Wegener, quoting Herman Melville, in *A Concordance to Herman Melville's Clarel* (Glassboro, NJ: Melville Society, 1979).

Many Zionist Christians retain this premillennial dispensational teaching in their approach to the modern state of Israel. They believe that the founding of the nation in 1948 was a fulfillment of prophecy. This has led many to an uncritical support for Israel, "lest one be found working against the purposes of God."[29] The return of Christ is linked to the fulfillment of the hopes of the Jewish people for their own homeland. Herman Melville voiced this longing in 1876 in his epic poem *Clarel: A Poem and Pilgrimage in the Holy Land*.

This "land tradition" is strong in the biblical narrative, and

---

28. For a listing of leaders who held to dispensationalism, see *The Blackwell Encyclopedia of Modern Christian Thought*, ed. Alister E. McGrath (Oxford: Blackwell, 1993), 108.
29. McGrath, ed., *The Blackwell Encyclopedia of Modern Christian Thought*, 110.

according to dispensationalism, Israel will be the site of the long-awaited reign of God as the Messiah returns to set up his kingdom. Regrettably, the long game among such thinkers is the conversion of the Jews, with Christian Zionism actually having a self-serving motivation. The fundamental belief is that "God will bless those who are good to God's historic people." The mixing of faith and politics is palpable, with Israel enjoying the robust support of Christians of this ilk.

Dispensationalism continues to attract those who want an interpretive system and scheme that helps make sense of history and the future. It has shaped popular notions of the end times and influences the apocalyptic expectations of conservative Christians.[30] Yet a dispensational reading of Scripture is highly problematic and claims more "insider" knowledge, highly literalistic interpretation, and a great chasm between heaven and earth. Using Thessalonians for this purpose actually presupposes a dispensational framework.

FURTHER REFLECTIONS
How to Think Christologically of Election

The idea of election remains an enduring and troubling question in Christian theology. It provokes questions about the favoring of Jacob over Esau;[31] preferential treatment of Israel over against her enemies, especially in the story of the Exodus; why Scripture speaks of "vessels of wrath made for destruction" and "vessels of mercy prepared beforehand for glory"; and, ultimately, about God's justice.[32]

An organizing theme for the Hebrew Bible, the chosenness of Israel is clear. As Brueggemann observes, the "specificity of Israel's chosenness evokes not embarrassment or need for explanation in Israel's own self-understanding. Israel accepts and relishes

---

30. See Timothy P. Weber, *Living in the Shadow of the Second Coming: American Premillennialism 1875–1982* (Grand Rapids: Zondervan, 1983). I find Susan R. Garrett's *No Ordinary Angel: Celestial Spirits and Christian Claims about Jesus* (New Haven, CT: Yale University Press, 2008), 106, helpful as she assesses the Left Behind series with is dispensational slant.
31. Mal. 1:2–3; Rom. 9:13.
32. Rom. 9:220–25.

its specialness."[33] I have heard rabbis suggest that God sought to run a test case with Israel to see if God could forge a relationship of intimacy with a people that then could include all the nations. The evidence that this experiment did not easily work as intended is the biblical saga of rebellion and restoration. More faithful to a covenant of election than was God's chosen partner, Israel, the Holy One continued to improvise new opportunities for fidelity for this "recalcitrant partner," in the words of Brueggemann.[34]

Not only does Scripture wrestle with this concept, but the challenges of thinking about chosenness have endured in Christian theology. A brief review of key theological architects may prompt further questions as well as point to major shifts in the doctrine of election. Surely the notion of predestination, which usually accompanies election, raises questions about divine sovereignty and human freedom. When treated as an abstract idea in the eternal counsel of God before the creation rather than what God has done in Jesus, the conundrum seems insurmountable.

Augustine offered an early proposal on unconditional election as he probed John 15:16.

> "Ye have not chosen me," He says, "but I have chosen you." Grace such as that is ineffable. For what were we so long as Christ had not yet chosen us, and we were therefore still destitute of love. . . . What were we then, but sinful and lost? We had not yet come to believe on Him, in order to lead to His choosing us; for if it were those who already believe that He chose, then was He chosen Himself, prior to His choosing. But how could He say, "Yet have not chosen me," saving only because His mercy anticipated us?[35]

Augustine had puzzled over why some were "being saved" and others were not. It could only be because God had determined this in God's own foreknowledge, not by any merit of those being chosen. His assessment of predestination regarded God as more interested

33. Brueggemann, *Old Testament Theology*, 416.
34. Brueggemann, *Old Testament Theology*, 434.
35. Augustine of Hippo, "Lectures or Tractates on the Gospel According to St. John," *St. Augustin: Homilies on the Gospel of John, Homilies on the First Epistle of John, Soliloquies*, ed. Philip Schaff, trans. John Gibb and James Innes, vol. 7 (Edinburgh: T & T Clark, 1991), 353.

in power than in love, ultimately. Dan Stiver notes that "Augustine allowed more scope for freedom early in his career, but in his life he saw that this freedom was meticulously controlled by God behind the scenes."[36] If one was wicked, it was because God willed it. Those whom God chooses will respond to God's election, and those not chosen will act out their fate accordingly. Augustine's little book, *On the Gift of Perseverance,* seeks to balance God's seeming malevolent decision with grace for those of God's choosing. Besides, what human should question God or have too much curiosity about things beyond our knowing?

Students of theology know the story of the hapless learner who proffered the question to his teacher, Augustine: "What was God doing before God created the heavens and the earth?" His memorable rejoinder was "creating hell for people who ask such questions." Augustinian monk Luther went a little further than his forebear and said God was creating sticks with which to beat the insolent who asked such questions.

In the return to the sources (*ad fontes*) movement of the Protestant Reformation, Calvin returned to the earlier thinking of Augustine and went even further in his declaration of "double predestination" (*decretum absolutum*), a dreadful and horrible decree, in Calvin's own words.[37] He believed that it was an inescapable teaching of Scripture that before the foundation of the world God divided all people into two classes: the elect and the reprobate. This was God's decision, with human performance already adjudicated by God's dread majesty (*horribilis Dei maiestas*).[38] Even though the fall into sin was through God's decree, he believed that sin is voluntary. Through lengthy citation of Scripture and engagement with interlocutors in the manner of disputations, Calvin shaped a theological system that has cast a long shadow in our thinking about God and human freedom.[39] Granted, his followers went even fur-

---

36. Dan R. Stiver, *Life Together in the Way of Jesus Christ: An Introduction to Christian Theology* (Waco, TX: Baylor University Press, 2009), 121. See especially Augustine's "On the Predestination of the Saints."

37. John Calvin, *Institutes of the Christian Religion* 3.22.7; ed. John T. McNeill, trans. Ford Lewis Battles, Library of Christian Classics (Philadelphia: Westminster, 1960), 955–56.

38. Calvin, *Institutes* 3.20.17, 874–75.

39. For further thinking about Calvin's assessment of his theological project, see Richard A.

ther in cementing his thinking into a logic tight framework. Thinking that God has no limits, these interpreters, along with Calvin,
sacrifice human responsibility to divine prerogative.

The freedom of the grace of God is the inflection point for
influential twentieth-century theologian Karl Barth, who makes a
well-known theological turn when engaging this idea of Calvin.[40]
He struggled with departing from this theologian from whom he
had gained so much; nevertheless, he reconstructs Calvin's doctrine of double predestination through his own view of Christ who
is both elect (the one who stands in for all humanity) and reprobate (the one who bears the punishment in our place). For Barth,
Jesus Christ is the electing God and elected human. The incarnation is the natural expression of God's desire for relationship with
humanity:

> In so far as God not only is love, but loves, in the acts of love
> which determines His whole being God elects. And in so far as
> this act of love is an election, it is at the same time and as such
> the act of His freedom. There can be no subsequent knowl-
> edge of God, whether from His revelation or from his work as
> disclosed in that revelation, which is not as such knowledge
> of this election.[41]

Through God's gracious gift of the Son, all humanity is elect in
Christ. This is an incorporative Christology that sets the human trajectory on a different course because of God's merciful decision to
be for us in Christ Jesus. Because Christ has assumed humanity as
word made flesh, all humanity is graced through this action.

Barth writes also of the Son as the Reprobate One, the judge who
is judged in our place, an oft-repeated description. Taking the penalty of our sin on himself, the Son bears God's temporal rejection for
the sake of eternal possibility for all. In this moving section, Barth
speaks of those who deserve rejection but who find new promise

Muller, *The Unaccommodated Calvin: Studies in the Foundation of a Theological Tradition*
(Oxford: Oxford, 2000), 105.

40. As R. Michael Allen, *Karl Barth's Church Dogmatics: An Introduction and Reader* (London:
    T & T Clark, 2012), 71, writes: "Of all his many contributions to theology, Karl Barth is
    undoubtedly most widely known for his revisions to the doctrine of election."

41. Karl Barth, *Church Dogmatics* II/2, *The Doctrine of God*, ed. G. W. Bromiley and T. F.
    Torrance (Edinburgh: T & T Clark, 1957), 76–77.

in the work of Christ. Indeed, every "individual" in himself and such would be rejected if it were not that his own election is incorporated in that of Jesus Christ, if it were not that Jesus Christ was elected for the very purpose of taking his rejection on Himself, and therefore removing it from him. This is what Jesus Christ willed to do and has done for him in the consummation of His own (and therefore the proper and primary) election.[42]

By grace, those elected in Christ have "gained the status and right of . . . a child and friend of God."[43] This is God's purpose for all, and this eternal decision is accomplished through God's own incarnational work. Not being "willing that any should perish" as another early Christian writer proclaims (2 Pet. 3:9), God always moves in the direction of redemption, while maintaining God's own realm of justice.

If we take a more Barthian approach, some of our concerns about election cease. Rather than favoritism or divine compulsion, we see the donative rather than dominative power of God. We learn the extent of God in giving the Son, and we have a better understanding of why God is only too glad to share the divine authority with the one who bears the name above all names. The way in which the Thessalonian correspondence makes the lordship of Jesus Christ central to its message demonstrates both the humility of the Abba and the enervating power of the Spirit.

FURTHER REFLECTIONS
Reading Scripture for Communal Discernment

In this commentary I have drawn attention to varied individuals who have stoked apocalyptic frenzy because they believed God had revealed the plan of the end times to them alone. These leaders have drawn devotees who trusted their teaching only to end up deluded. Could a deliberate practice of communal discernment have waylaid their eschatological scheme? It is possible for a whole

---

42. Barth, *Church Dogmatics* II/2, *The Doctrine of God*, 351.
43. Barth, *Church Dogmatics* II/2, *The Doctrine of God*, 351.

community to go off the rails, but the safeguards of multiple perspectives can be constructive.

What theological and practical principles should guide this process? At the outset of this discussion, we must place the Spirit at the very center of discerning the guidance of Scripture when we face critical decisions. Kilian McDonnell speaks of the Holy Spirit "as a way of knowing."[44] We trust that a richer understanding of the Spirit's function will lead the church to know and embody truth in dynamic trajectories.[45] Spiritual discernment is a practice we hone over time but one which remains fraught with uncertainty, even danger, for it can be either "prophetically subversive or grossly self-deceptive."[46]

A fruitful collection of essays, *The Art of Reading Scripture*, suggests ways in which the Spirit beseeches the congregation as faithful readers of the Bible.[47] The Scripture Project, a colloquy composed primarily of teachers in theological schools (leavened by a couple of congregational ministers), set out to assess what denotes faithful reading of scriptural texts, an exercise that led them far beyond the usual critical methodologies espoused in theological education. The outcome of their work was the production of nine theses to guide reading of the Bible in community. I want to appropriate the final thesis for the purposes of this further theological reflection.

We live in the tension between the "already" and the "not yet" of the kingdom of God; consequently, Scripture calls the church to ongoing discernment, to continually fresh rereadings of the text in light in light of the Holy Spirit's ongoing work in the world.

Ellen F. Davis and Richard B. Hays, eds., *The Art of Reading Scripture* (Grand Rapids: Eerdmans, 2003).

---

44. Kilian McDonnell, *The Other Hand of God: The Holy Spirit as the Universal Touch and Goal* (Collegeville, MN: Liturgical Press, 2003), 216.
45. Parts of this section are drawn from my chapter "Breathing, Bearing, Beseeching, and Building: Reading Scripture with the Spirit," in *The Lord and Giver of Life: Perspectives on Constructive Pneumatology*, ed. David H. Jensen (Louisville, KY: Westminster John Knox Press, 2008), 51.
46. Frank Rogers Jr., "Discernment," in *Practicing Our Faith: A Way of Life for a Searching People*, ed. Dorothy C. Bass (San Francisco: Josey-Bass, 1997), 113.
47. Davis and Hays, *The Art of Reading Scripture*.

In the New Testament, spiritual discernment is directly connected to faith in Jesus Christ. No one who curses Jesus is led of the Spirit, and no one can say "Jesus is Lord" except under the influence of the Holy Spirit (1 Cor. 12:2–3). Paul speaks of the "distinguishing" (*diakrisis*) of spirits as a gift of the Holy Spirit (1 Cor. 2:10). Christopher Morse wisely perceives that faith in the Holy Spirit is a "refusal to deify human subjectivity."[48]

No spiritual practice is more needed in our communities of faith today than discernment. Luke Timothy Johnson names the challenge of this procedure. It is a theological process that "enables humans to perceive their characteristically ambiguous experience as revelatory and to articulate such experiences in a narrative of faith."[49] Many venerable methods—from Ignatian to Quaker— as well as contemporary process such as "Appreciative Inquiry" and "Worshipful Work" have proven useful.[50] The method is less important than the commitment to seek the "mind of Christ" in planning, budgeting, sorting ethical issues, and revising missional focus.

Many congregations resist the work of communal discernment, as it is messy and labor intensive. Five things get in the way of successful engagement in this process: (1) impatience with a process that requires careful, forthright, time-consuming listening and reflection; (2) an assumption that this is the province of religious professionals; (3) lack of trust that the Holy Spirit really will guide the congregation; (4) patterns of Scripture reading shackled to deadly literalism; and (5) a persistent expectation that we will reach a perfect conclusion, unsullied by human opinion and sociocultural context.

A cruciform hermeneutic is essential for reading Scripture aright and then following its guidance for decisions at hand. If we do not read the Bible as Christians through the lens of Christ crucified and raised, we are missing its primary message, through which all else

---

48. Christopher Morse, *Not Every Spirit: A Dogmatics of Christian Disbelief* (Valley Forge, PA: Trinity Press International, 1991), 181.

49. Luke Timothy Johnson, *Scripture and Discernment: Decision Making in the Church* (Nashville: Abingdon, 1996), 109.

50. See Sue Annis Hammond, *Thin Book of Appreciative Inquiry,* 2nd ed. (Plano: Thin Book, 1996); and Charles M. Olsen, *Transforming Church Boards into Communities of Spiritual Leaders* (Bethesda: Alban Institute, 1995).

becomes clear. John Webster argued persuasively for this kind of reading "as an instance of the fundamental pattern of all Christian existence, which is dying and rising with Jesus Christ through the purging and quickening power of the Holy Spirit."[51] Reading in this way is both "mortification and vivification: to read Scripture is to be slain and made alive."[52] Richard B. Hays writes of the promise this kind of reading portends: "The Resurrection purges the death-bound illusions that previously held us captive and sets us free to perceive the real world of God's life-giving resurrection power."[53]

The witness of the Spirit to dying and rising with Christ is the center of gravity for biblical narratives in the Christian tradition and should inform our discernment practices. Apostolic preaching in early Christianity was a demonstration of reading the whole of Scripture in light of this surpassing event in salvation history. This suggests that discernment requires the willingness to let certain things die: for example, prestige, outdated programs, buildings that do not collaborate with mission, specialized staff positions no longer viable, to name only a few.

The Spirit invites human consent in discernment. Spirit-led consensus is generative, allowing members of the Christian community to decenter themselves for the sake of extending the grace of Christ. While discernment is never complete, when the Church can say, "it has seemed good to the Holy Spirit and to us" (Acts 15:28), then it has discerned the guidance of God.

51. John Webster, *Holy Scripture: A Dogmatic Sketch* (Cambridge: Cambridge University Press, 2003), 87.
52. Webster, *Holy Scripture*, 88.
53. Richard B. Hays, "Reading Scripture in Light of the Resurrection," in Davis and Hays, eds., *The Art of Reading Scripture*, 235–36.

2 Thessalonians 3:1–18

Concluding Apostolic Teaching and Prayer

How one concludes a letter is as important as how one begins it. Both are intended to strengthen credibility and enhance relationship. Usually a closing underscores what has already been stated and makes a further offer on behalf of the recipient. As a seminary president, I wrote many appeal letters to the school's donors, and the most effective letters focused on the interests of the recipients, both praising their investment as well as inviting further support for what honored their values. This letter follows that form, as it both declares need and assures of God's strength to see them through the turbulence of their situation. Thanksgiving is the sustaining theme.

Apostolic letters were intended to be heard, not read, "written as they are in and for oral settings and an environment where perhaps only ten percent of the audience could read or write."[1] Letters in the Pauline tradition are surrogates for the presence of the apostle who would have further instructed the new converts through proclamation and teaching if he had been able to remain with them. It is not surprising, therefore, that there is repetition and circling back through earlier arguments so as to make key points lodge in their minds. Stanley K. Stowers notes the importance of epistolary material: "Something about the nature of early Christianity made it a movement of letter writers. We possess more than nine thousand letters written by Christians in antiquity."[2] We can easily point to

---

1. Ben Witherington III, *1 and 2 Thessalonians: A Socio-Rhetorical Commentary* (Grand Rapids: Eerdmans, 2006), xiii.
2. Stanley K. Stowers, *Letter Writing in Greco-Roman Antiquity* (Philadelphia: Fortress, 1986), 15.

Paul's model of correspondence as being a founding agent that others emulated, in tone if not in long-windedness.[3]

The writer of this brief letter offers final words that call the congregation and the apostolic team to common cause. Peril remains for both, as faithful witness to the risen One draws ready opposition. Those who take seriously cultivating a communal life in the way of Jesus Christ will be at odds in a culture saturated with idolatry, promiscuity, and imperial aspirations. That is as true now as then, which is why the Thessalonian epistles find resonance with today's church. The call for a community to have boundaries remains critical.

We hear again the tenor of the voice of Paul through this pseudonymous writer who seeks the flourishing of the congregation amidst uncertain times. Moving from the predictions about the day of the Lord in the prior chapter, the apostle returns to very practical advice, enveloped in prayer on behalf of the church.

3:1–5

The Desire for Prayerful Interdependence of Apostles and Congregation

The request for prayer begins the chapter, as the apostolic writer feels the need for the congregation's spiritual undergirding of the ongoing mission of forming new congregations. The author's desire that "the word of the Lord may speed on and triumph, as it did among you" (v. 1) both speaks of the Thessalonian perseverance and the confidence that it will also have benefit elsewhere. The Pauline tradition always demonstrates concern that the preaching of the gospel may extend beyond its present recipients, the goal being no less than the evangelization of the Roman Empire. Yet the writer, as a part of the apostolic mission, knows that the work of the gospel flies on the wings of prayers, those who support the apostolic team and their own. Without prayer, the energy for gospel work is depleted. Prayer puts persons in touch with the Holy Spirit, and the Spirit guides true

---

3. See Witherington's comparison of the length of Paul's letters to those of Cicero and Seneca, two other famous letter writers of his era (*1 and 2 Thessalonians*, 260).

prayer, "for we do not know how to pray as we ought" (Rom. 8:26). It is also the Spirit's presence that empowers missional pursuits.

Anywhere the gospel makes inroads, there will be wicked and evil detractors (v. 2) who will seek to extinguish this word of hope, for they are faithless and resist this miraculous story of Christ's resurrection, forgiveness, and ultimate restoration when he appears. Either scandalous or foolish in their minds, the gospel does not appeal to them and thus the apostolic prayer is to be delivered from them. The writer has already told them of the outcome of their rebellion (2:11–12).[4]

It is a mark of humility to request the prayers of others if it arises out of deep sensing of spiritual need rather than a perfunctory request. I recall that when Pope Francis was elected in March 2013, his reflexive greeting to all he encountered was "pray for me." An esteemed leader from South America, he knew that his challenges were great and there would be many to oppose a non-European papal leader, the first since the eighth century. Additionally, he is the first pope from the Southern Hemisphere, the first Jesuit to hold the office, bringing strong pastoral experience from his leadership in Argentina. In humility, he also knew that the prayers of others could strengthen and uphold his new calling. This request connected him with those who looked to him for a spiritual exemplar and may have done more to humanize his papacy than most anything else, perhaps even more than his ugly brown shoes rather than the resplendent red ones of his predecessor, as he desired not to be the "Prada Pope." He also prefers to live simply, forsaking the papal apartment for two rooms in the hotel used by clergy visiting the Vatican.

We sense the same kind of call to the interdependence of apostolic leaders and members of the Thessalonian congregation in these opening words of the final chapter of the second epistle. The writer knows that God will deliver them from those who oppose them, those without faith. This is because God is faithful, offering strength and protection from the chief doer and other doers of evil (v. 3). The form of God's faithful care comes in the shape of the other believers who participate in the common mission with them, as the writers

---

4. Scandalous and foolish are descriptors of how Jews and Greeks respond to the kerygma.

have professed throughout this correspondence. Praying for others is a central practice, binding persons and communities together and proving transformative in its power through the Holy Spirit. While it is hard to trace direct outcomes from intercession for others, it is a discipline of love that entrusts both enemies and friends to the care of God. It transforms the one who prays into a more compassionate and engaged member of the body of Christ, and it demonstrates trust in God to use human praying in God's own providential purposes. Thinking that we may influence outcomes through our intercession remains a hopeful posture.

With strong affirmation the writer underscores his confidence about their destiny in God as they "are doing and will do the things which we command" (v. 4). This encompasses a significant tableau of expectations—how to prepare for the "comings," how to live productively, how to manage ethical requirements, and how to form a community honoring to God—as spelled out in the two epistles. Living in this way is a high calling and will not be achieved without God's undergirding grace.

As a summative encouragement, the writer offers this abiding blessing: "May the Lord direct your hearts to the love of God and to the steadfastness of Christ" (v. 5). In sparse words, this guidance distills what the community should be about in trying times. Directing one's heart to the love of God suggests a total orientation of life in order to set one's affection on the One who invites such reciprocal love. When persons realize that they can participate in the dynamism of the overflowing love of the Trinity, they begin to display God's self-giving relations toward others. Indeed, it is through relationship that identity is determined.

On the chapel door of the seminary I served as president is an ancient Trinitarian shield that displays the movement within God's own life. It hearkens back to the six century Athanasian Creed that perceives that while each member of the Trinity is fully God (*deus*), each member is also not the other (*non est*). This means for example that while the Spirit is fully God, the Spirit is not (*non est*) the Son, and the Son is not the Father (*pater*) nor the Spirit. Differentiation and unity comprise the life of God, and the dynamic interchange of relations is ongoing. One day while taking my theology class out to view the door, a student asked: "Where am I in this?" It was truly a perceptive question she offered. I said you are in the space between the varied Trinitarian movements as the Spirit draws you into the life of Christ to the glory of the Abba. After all, the Greek word *chōrein* can mean "to make space for," as humans are invited into the relational movement (*perichōrēsis*) of the divine life to find their true home and true selves there.

One can begin participating in this dynamism by recognizing that one's heart also must initially be transformed by being attuned to the steadfastness of Christ. The reader can track what is in the thinking of the writer concerning Christ's own steadfastness, the One who gave himself for the sake of the unrighteous so that they might become an expression of his own righteousness. This close kinship between Christ and his followers is ever before the community, and that Christ chooses to make divine presence known within the community nourishes them.

Transformed identity moves one toward Christlike action. I recall the witness of a doctoral student from the Kachin State, the northern most state in Myanmar, abutting China to the north and the Shan State to the south. It is a place where conflict continues, with the Kachin Independent Army (KIA) maintaining resistance to the Myanmar military forces. It is also a place of rampant poppy growth and heroin addiction, where pastors regularly confront the deaths of parishioners because of this scourge. This student, a loving pastor and shepherd to his traumatized community as they are a persecuted Christian minority, invited his church members to pray for their enemies. Other pastors thought he had sold out to the federal forces; some KIA soldiers in his church thought he had taken a weak way forward in the midst of regular skirmishes where lives were being lost. This pastor simply believed that this was the instruction given by Jesus, and he wanted to follow it. While it did not forestall all the violence, the members of his congregation began to see their opponents in a more human way. The Myanmar army was also comprised of young fearful men, they concluded, who functioned at the behest of rapacious generals who desired only to vanquish more insurgent resistance to their hegemony. This pastor's leadership led to considered conversation about pacifism, just war, and nonviolent approaches to peace. In my judgment, he exhibits a heart attuned to the steadfastness of Christ.

It is the faith *of* Christ more than our faith *in* Christ that permits steadfastness. In recent years it has been a scholarly concern to point this out. The dissertation of Richard Hays on Galatians 3 helped open this conversation,[5] displacing the common interpretation that Martin Luther helped foster. "Faith in Jesus" became a nearly universal translation following the Reformer, and only in the late twentieth century has this been revisited. It now appears that "the faith of Christ" (*pistis tou Christou*) is primary; the believer's faith in Christ is subsidiary and dependent on that of Christ. Romans 3:22, 26; Galatians 2:16; and Philippians 3:9 offer a similar semantic structure, yet without any sustained Pauline commentary, meaning that we cannot presume certainty. We do know without any reservation, however, that Christ is the essential focus of the gospel; it is in his faith that the believer puts trust. His steadfastness is sure over against the wavering commitments humans make. Once again, there is reciprocal action as the believer is called to respond to what preveniently (God's proffer of Christ through Christ) has been accomplished. What is at stake is how much weight to put on the human side of salvation, a perennial issue in thinking of God's holistic redemption.

In the conservative tradition that nurtured my early faith, great emphasis was given to a "moment of decision" that defines one's eternal destiny. God had provided a means of salvation, but it was up to the believer to claim that through "voluntary faith." Any notion of the larger work of grace that undergirded such a decision was subordinated to the will of the one being converted. Emotion and volition were the critical ingredients. The sincerity of the profession of faith seemed almost to outweigh Christ and his benefits. A compounding problem was a lack of attention to the process of sanctification, where effort trumped grace even if there was not a clear understanding of its process. It is no wonder our Southern Baptist churches

---

5. Richard B. Hays, *The Faith of Jesus Christ: An Investigation of the Narrative Substructure of Galatians 3:11–4:11*, SBL Dissertation Series 56 (Chico, CA: Scholars, 1983).

loved to sing those venerable old gospel hymns like, "We'll Work 'til Jesus Comes" and "To the Work."[6]

Human effort downplayed the centrality of grace in this calculus, although spiritual labor was seen as a constructive element in sanctification, a perspective never sufficiently explored. The work of the Holy Spirit in this metamorphosis of glory was downplayed, as it was all about Jesus.[7]

In 3:5, according to Andy Johnson, the writer "seems to be using a word play to contrast Christ's own faithfulness with the lack of that quality in those who are opposing the message about this Lord and his faithfulness."[8] The One who has proven himself trustworthy and faithful in the face of the extremities of testing can empower them to persevere. It is Christ's own perseverance that grounds their own.

> O land of rest, for thee I sigh!
> When will the moment come
> When I shall lay my armor by
> And dwell in peace at home?
> (Refrain)
> To Jesus Christ I fled for rest;
> He bade me cease to roam,
> And lean for comfort on His
>   breast
> Till He conducts me home.
> (Refrain)
> I sought at once my Savior's side,
> No more my steps to roam:
> With Him I'll brave death's
>   chilling tide,
> And reach my heav'nly home.
> (Refrain)
> Refrain:
> We'll work till Jesus comes,
> We'll work till Jesus comes,
> We'll work till Jesus comes,
> And we'll be gathered home.
>
> Elizabeth Mills and William Miller, "We'll Work 'til Jesus Comes," *Baptist Hymnal* (Nashville: Convention Press, 1956).

3:6–13

Warning against Idleness and Exhortation to Persevere in Well-Doing

The writer echoes the first epistle (1 Thess. 5:14) in warning against idleness. Indeed, the members of the community should stay away from idlers, as they will prove detrimental to perseverance in faith.

6. Each can be found in *Baptist Hymnal* (Nashville: Convention Press, 1956).

7. See my treatment of this work of the Holy Spirit in this metamorphosis of glory in *Joining the Dance: A Theology of the Spirit* (Valley Forge, PA: Judson, 2003), 106.

8. Andy Johnson, *1 and 2 Thessalonians*, The Two Horizons New Testament Commentary (Grand Rapids: Eerdmans, 2016), 209.

They are exhibiting "a pattern of life at odds" with what the apostolic team had taught.[9] Their refusal to participate fully in the community's needs is a grave threat and will be sure to sow dissension. Idleness is not productive; rather, it presents a drain on the larger community, causing others to carry a disproportionate load. Evidently there are those who rationalize this kind of behavior, and the writer reserves "the harshest form of moral exhortation ... for members of the church who conducted themselves in a disorderly manner by not earning their own living."[10]

Congregants in our time know that the burden of resourcing their church often falls on a faithful few. While financial officers are usually circumspect in keeping records private (often even from the pastor!), it does not go unnoticed that rarely is there equal sacrifice in stewardship. When this awareness ultimately seeps into the congregation, there is consternation and a sense of imbalance. Of course, while givers rarely judge those without resources to offer, they do resent those who display selfishness rather than generosity toward the agreed-on mission of the church. This has an eroding effect in the community, and the apostolic writer wisely seeks to circumvent this in his own epoch.

Persons tend to conform to the company they keep. If those in one's close circle are given to a hard-partying life or a laissez-faire approach to sexuality, it is likely that each person will participate accordingly. Human desire for belonging can lead to a violation of conscience, yet the untoward behavior continues as it is easier to fit in than to withdraw from a social network. Many younger adults sought to follow the norms of the sitcom *Friends* because the sense of community was strong, never mind the lax moral standards of the group. For a decade (1994–2004) devotees were drawn into the narrative of these friends, seduced no doubt through the opening song, "I'll Be There for You." The series had a powerful shaping influence on generations, perhaps more than we can assess. Had pastors warned against consuming this media, they would have been thought of as puritanical prudes even if their theological perspective

9. Johnson, *1 and 2 Thessalonians*, 216.
10. Abraham J. Malherbe, *The Letters to the Thessalonians*, Anchor Bible 32B (New York: Doubleday, 2000), 448.

may have been well grounded. It is not easy to be countercultural, and most simply conform.

The counsel of the writer of 2 Thessalonians is to stay away from those who would compromise ethical behavior, in particular the idle. The idle (*ataktos*) can only create mischief; they demonstrate disorderly and undisciplined activity as they lack focus. They flout "accepted standards of social behavior within a community."[11] They become a burden to the community, something that the first apostolic team never allowed (1 Thess. 2:9). From the outset, Paul and Silvanus modeled the kind of industry and investment in the common good that now seems lacking, and this writer instructs the idlers to correct the damage that is already ensuing by returning to work, their rightful responsibility.

My father told the three Marshall kids this cautionary tale, most likely handed down from his father:

> There was a man who was so lazy that his neighbors decided that they had enough of his mooching ways and that there was nothing left to do but to haul him away to the cemetery for burial. So they put him in the back of a cart and began the journey down the road. Along the way, they encountered a farmer pulling a wagon load of corn. The driver of the cart saw an opportunity for the laggard to take care of himself, as some of the corn was being offered by the farmer. "Do you want some of the corn?" the driver asked the lazy man. The man stirred slightly and asked, "Is it shucked?" The farmer replied "No." The lazy man lay back down in the cart and there was nothing to do but continue on to the cemetery.

We got the point that there would be no laziness tolerated in our household.

Christians are to pursue self-differentiation from their culture, an objective that is best upheld by a faithful community. In this text, the community is suffering because of disorderly idleness, a major distraction in a minority group of people committed to a redemptive purpose. The dereliction of responsibility is cascading beyond the community to a public that views its internal problems with

11. Johnson, *1 and 2 Thessalonians*, 214.

> Richard Mouw believes that there "are boundaries around Christians' openness to being changed by others. Our willingness to be changed by our encounters with other people cannot be a completely open-ended, 'anything goes' commitment."
>
> Richard J. Mouw, *Uncommon Decency: Christian Civility in an Uncivil World*, rev. ed. (Downers Grove, IL: IVP, 2010), 127–28.

disdain, compromising any claim by the church of being a disciplined community.

Are we right to conclude that any idleness is a shirking of responsibility? In Benedictine life, there is a category called "holy leisure," in addition to work and prayer. It is a period of time in the rhythm of monastic life that allows a sort of re-collection of one's soul. This spiritual tradition recognizes that it is not laziness or selfishness to "come away" for a season of reflection, rest, and renewal. As the Benedictine tradition teaches, "No schedule is to be so tight that there is no room for reflection on whether what is being done is worth doing at all." Holy leisure can take the form of contemplation amid other periods of prayer and work (*ora et labora*), or it can be a full stop when soul weariness rather than body weariness presents. It is a different discipline that does not require utter cessation of work or lessening one's commitment to a larger community. It is the sort of brief Sabbath Jesus managed to work into his days.

What the Thessalonian congregation is facing is not a disciplined holy leisure, but a segment of the community who is refusing to work and thus is dependent on the community to provide for their needs. The exhortation of the first epistle is lost on these, as they have refused to keep "working with their own hands" (1 Thess. 4:11) and have become a pernicious influence on the morale of those who continue their industry. They are resisting the expectations of the church's communal life, and subsequently the whole body is suffering.

The writer appeals to the "highest ethical ideals already extant in this Greek city."[12] We know from the first epistle that it was the express desire and effort of the apostolic team not to be a burden to

12. Johnson, *1 and 2 Thessalonians*, 214.

the community, exhibiting the best of Platonic Greek ideals,[13] and they had modeled the kind of work ethic that invited others to similar diligence. Now their example is being diminished by these who will not work.

Interpreters informed of the social milieu in which the Thessalonians participated direct us to think about the patronage system of the first century when examining this text. Peter Oakes describes patronage as "a social relationship central to behavior . . . a non-market relationship between socially unequal people in which dissimilar benefits are exchanged. The most characteristic exchange involves the patron providing access to resources unavailable to the client, and the client providing honor to the patron."[14] Often a client established a relationship with a patron so as to be free of the day-to-day work of sustaining livelihood, "so as to be an advocate and aid for the patron in various ways."[15] This Thessalonian Christian community was immersed in this economic system, and evidently some within the church maintained these patron/client relationships while participating in the life of the community, thereby degrading its ethos.[16] It is possible some even maintained this arrangement with other members of the community, a particularly complicated affiliation, and the charge that some are living disorderly idle lives is lodged against presumably a few in the church who are engaging in the patronage system.

> Honorable behavior was to take precedence over that which is merely convenient, pleasurable, or expedient.
>
> Ben Witherington III, *1 and 2 Thessalonians: A Socio-Rhetorical Commentary* (Grand Rapids: Eerdmans, 2006), 247.

In the name of Paul, the writer reminds them to imitate the good example set by the apostolic team, who was by no means idle when with them (v. 7). Working diligently, "with toil and labor we worked night and day" (v. 8) remains the testament of the early church planters. While they could have requested support for their mission as apostles,

---

13. Johnson, *1 and 2 Thessalonians*, 214.
14. Peter Oakes, "Urban Structure and Patronage," *Understanding the Social World of the New Testament*, ed. Dietmar Neufeld and Richard E. DeMaris (London: Routledge, 2010), 178.
15. Witherington, *1 and 2 Thessalonians*, 247.
16. Helpful is Bruce Winter's analysis in *Seek the Welfare of the City: Christians as Benefactors and Citizens* (Grand Rapids: Eerdmans, 1994).

they chose to conduct themselves in a way worthy of emulation (v. 9). This is a continued refrain in Paul's approach to his apostolic vocation, and subsequent writers in the Pauline tradition also honor it. It becomes a key dimension of what is handed on (*paradosis*). As Linda McKinnish Bridges aptly perceives, "The members of the group need to be reminded of the responsibilities that each member brings to the success of the group. This group needs to function well in order to succeed economically as well as spiritually."[17]

In the next verse, we hear one of the most oft-quoted verses of the Bible: "If anyone will not work, let him not eat." Cited by John Smith in the colony of Jamestown in the early 1600s as well as by John Winthrop, a Puritan preacher, this text has remained an aphorism meant to instruct against sloth and shirking of communal responsibility. Even Vladimir Lenin used this text to undergird his principles of socialism. The phrase appears in his 1917 work *The State and Revolution*, which argues for every individual's being a productive unit. "If anyone will not work, let him not eat" (v. 10). A long tradition lies behind this verse. For example, Genesis 3:19 states to Adam and Eve, "By the sweat of your brow you shall eat bread." An early Christian writing also echoes the Genesis edict and the exhortation of 2 Thessalonians 3:10.

In the early Christian manual, the *Didache* we find, [N]o Christian shall live idle in idleness. But if anyone will not do so [i.e., work] that person is making Christ into a cheap trade; watch out for such people" (12:4–5).

This is Beverly Roberts Gaventa's translation, *First and Second Thessalonians*, Interpretation: A Bible Commentary for Teaching and Preaching (Louisville, KY: John Knox Press, 1998), 130.

Many have summoned this text as witness against those who are dependent on a social safety net because of poverty, disability, or other circumstances that prevent full entry into the work force. Politicians have frequently made hay against "welfare moms" while ignoring all the contextual realities that render them unable to provide for their families—racism, sexism, geographical location, and structural economic disempowerment that shapes generations in

17. Linda McKinnish Bridges, *1 & 2 Thessalonians*, Smyth & Helwys Bible Commentary (Macon, GA: Smith & Helwys, 2008), 255.

poverty. Blaming the victim is a blood sport for many in our fractured and partisan political arena. Our lack of capacity to see from
the perspective of others diminishes compassionate responses. It
is not surprising that empathy (or lack thereof) may be the most
used word of 2020 in assessing the deficits in the social contract
operative in our society. The lack of empathy is strangling too many
approaches to a more just society, and our failure to cultivate this
virtue is deeply damaging.

Church folk in our time often make this text about eating being
the necessary corollary of working a default position, failing to
understand all the factors that are in motion when a family simply
cannot work to fully provide for itself. Especially in the epoch of pandemic, the lost jobs and compounding responsibility of educational
instruction at home make it impossible to find balance on the high
wire of competing needs. Federal support of struggling families has
been meager; conflicting political and theological views stymie the
provision of sufficient help for these who wonder where money for
the rent or the next meal is coming from, many out of work actually
not eating, as the verse says. As families scour food pantries, waiting in long lines in church parking lots or other relief organizations,
our Congress trundles on with self-interested bickering. These representatives and senators do not face similar struggles for survival, as
their estimated median wealth is over one million dollars. They have
put political ambition ahead of the common good of those they supposedly serve. Not since the Great Depression have there been so
many suffering in our midst. Federal relief for families with children
have lifted some out of poverty, and some have found more gainful
employment; yet the pandemic has upended much of the economic
system. Those who are able to find work often find positions at far
less pay and status than before the pandemic. People are anxious
about survival, and the great majority are quite willing to work to
give buoyancy to life for themselves and others they love, yet many
sectors of work—food services, taxi drivers, professional musicians,
to mention only a few—have greatly reduced available positions.
Their prospects for imminent recovery are not promising, however,
as the gridlock in the nation's capital prevents delivering the urgent
assistance needed. In the period of waiting for relief, homelessness,

debt, and food insecurity escalate. Many feel forsaken by agencies entrusted with providing assistance, and they are running out of places to turn, as all the systems are strained.

Recently I visited an African American congregation where I witnessed a form of compassion sorely needed. Socially distanced in the assembly, we heard the minister's summons to give to the stewardship campaign with this caveat: "Please don't give money you need for rent; don't give money you need for medication; don't give money you need for food or transportation. God knows you have these needs and wants you to take care of them." This pastor knew that forced layoffs had shifted the profile of stewardship for these faithful ones, and he did not want them to participate in a deadly legalism of tithing that might put them at further risk. I greatly respect his perspective for its realism and his faith that God would sustain his congregation without jeopardizing the most vulnerable. This is great faith, indeed.

Similarly, in a predominantly white congregation I have attended virtually in this season, there is an awareness that not all in the community have fared as well as others as their household incomes have moved from two salaries to one, as women have been forced to leave the workforce in order to oversee the online education their children are receiving as well as the ongoing household oversight. Because women usually make less than men, the painful decision for many families has been for women to suspend their vocations, which diminishes resources and constricts financial margins. This congregation has taken a more constructive approach to the stewardship campaign in naming this material difference economically. Thankfully, others in the congregation not similarly affected have increased their giving, and their church's mission is flourishing because of this empathic response.

The apostolic writer then calls out "busybodies," a less-than-flattering name. In this section, which Malherbe calls "discipline of the disorderly," the author argues that rather than being "busy" with orderly pursuits, the so-called busybodies (*periergazomenous*) are simply stirring up trouble by meddling in others' affairs rather than tending to their own. Malherbe suggests that the author "uses a well-known term of opprobrium that was applied by his contemporaries to people who thought of themselves as representing higher values."[18] Too good for work, they thought? Criticizing others who continued their trade with attentiveness? Acting in obsequious ways with patrons? The busybodies were stirring up dissension.

Beverly Roberts Gaventa offers insightful perspective on the particular language used: "The Greek of verse 11 employs a delightful play on words that does not translate well into colloquial English. Literally the Greek refers to those who are 'not working but working around.'"[19] These troublers are not building up the community, and the writer commands (*parangellomen*) them to "do their work quietly and to earn their own living" (v. 12). Sternly ordering them to not be idle, but to practice their craft without causing a stir, the writer wants to curtail disruptive behavior. Gaventa surmises that "apocalyptic frenzy has triumphed over responsible behavior."[20] Exhorting them in the name of the Lord Jesus Christ is the strongest authority to summon, and the writer does not hesitate to do so. It is the same language with which the writer began this section (v. 6).

I remember a time when I was perhaps "working around" others in my own congregation. It came to my attention that a member of the finance committee was not contributing to the church. I learned of it because I was the chair of the fall stewardship campaign. I (perhaps unwisely) confronted the man about this situation, and he and his wife were furious with my appeal to help lead the congregation in giving. I thought I was sparing the pastor the pain of speaking about this matter to this officer of the church and that I was assuredly being of help. The acrimony that transpired between this couple and me prompted me to question whether I was being a busybody or a conscientious leader. These are not easy situations, and things can easily go awry. And rarely is the truth on only one side.

None should be "weary in well-doing," for perseverance will hold deep reward.[21] This seems an almost super-human expectation, yet members of the community are granted spiritual resources to continue. "Compassion fatigue" is a contemporary description of the toll well-doing can exact. Particularly vulnerable are those in helping

---

18. Malherbe, *The Letters to the Thessalonians*, 453.
19. Gaventa, *First and Second Thessalonians*, 128–29
20. Gaventa, *First and Second Thessalonians*, 129.
21. See also Gal. 6:9.

professions such as teaching, social work, and health care. The high rates of burn-out demonstrate how taxing this intensive work is. During the pandemic we are learning anew of the cost of serving a public ravaged by a virus that shows little signs of cessation, whose death toll daily grows exponentially. Teachers, social workers, and health care personnel sustain heroic efforts at keeping the educational process for students ongoing, at securing resources for devastated families, and at tending the critically ill and dying (often cut off from family members); these servants of humanity are surely weary. Little by little we are growing in recognition of the cost of this labor.

So how does one not grow weary in the ongoing work of love that is wrapped in well-doing? Some holy leisure can help, as those trained in monastic rhythms know. All can be made better by leaning into the power and supply of the Holy Spirit, the sustaining source of the spiritual life. The patterns of Jesus bore witness to his dependence on prayer, retreat, fellowship, and rest. Not pursuing a frenetic pace—walking everywhere creates a more deliberate tempo—he measured his days with both urgency and patience. He found time to celebrate, to care for his friends, and to do the hard and suffering salvific work that was his calling as the anointed one. His later apostolic disciple who writes this epistle also knows the challenge of continuous well-doing and offers encouragement. If, as some scholars think, Paul is no longer alive at this point,[22] keeping his teaching before the congregation required herculean effort from the next generation. Conventions shift as communities are reconfigured, and maintaining a founding vision amidst new challenges requires pastoral wisdom.

3:14–15
How to Relate to the Obstinate

Building on the admonitions offered in vv. 6–13, the apostolic writer instructs the community on how to deal with the obstinate, those who refuse to do what is explicitly stated in this letter. A process

22. Marcus J. Borg and John Dominic Crossan, *The First Paul: Reclaiming the Radical Visionary behind the Church's Conservative Icon* (New York: HarperOne, 2009), 222.

of ostracizing the offending one is for the purpose of restoration, necessary though painful. Excluding that one so that "he may be ashamed" is not to be a continuous state (v. 14). It is to be hoped that it is a disciplinary interval that moves toward restoration.

The Rule of St. Benedict has guided monastic communities for over 1,500 years in such a process of discipline. In a chapter called "On Excommunication for Faults" we read,

> If a brother is found to be obstinate, or disobedient, or proud, or murmuring, or habitually transgressing the Holy Rule in any point and contemptuous of the orders of his seniors, the latter shall admonish him secretly a first and second time, as Our Lord commands. If he fails to amend, let him be given a public rebuke in front of the whole community. But if even then he does not reform, let him be placed under excommunication, provided that he understands the seriousness of that penalty; if he is perverse, however, let him undergo corporal punishment.[23]

A thorough process in dealing with a wayward brother or sister ensures that both finding fault and forgiveness are practiced in the community for its ongoing health. While the word "excommunication" is used in the *Rule,* it does not hold the sense of being banished indefinitely from the community or the faith. Every measure is taken for restoration, a methodical practice, not a pronouncement of anathema. While members of a monastic community may voluntarily leave if they discern a different sense of calling, it is not the desire of a monastic house to leave the one undergoing punishment without a pathway to full reintegration into the community. It is never meant to be harsh, but it is clear in its expectation of accountability. The community has a critical role in calling persons to live well. Without it, we cannot flourish.

---

23. *The Rule of Saint Benedictine,* trans. Leonard Doyle (Collegeville, MN: Liturgical Press, 2001), 74–75. Many readers flinch when corporal punishment is prescribed; however, this was a more common practice in earlier times. The *Rule* instructs what other measures are appropriate given the degree of fault. Some are as simple as kneeling in front of the choir when late to prayer; others require separation at mealtime or being excluded from the choir, the oratory. Other members of the community must resist association with the excommunicated until the Abbot believes that the delinquent one has made "humble satisfaction" for his error. That he not "be overwhelmed by excessive grief," is the goal of this process, a lesson drawn from Paul in 2 Cor. 2:7.

If we refuse to learn from the community and to cooperate with it, he [Benedict] implies, we have no right to its support and should be suspended from participation in it. Once we have separated ourselves from the community by withdrawing our hearts, then the community must withdraw from us in order to soften them. . . . Benedict is teaching very clearly that to disturb the human community is serious. It makes us outcasts to our own kind.

Joan Chittister, OSB, *The Rule of St. Benedict: Insights for the Ages* (New York: Crossroad, 1992), 95, 97.

I recall witnessing this discipline of exclusion at a Benedictine community I frequently visit, taking these sojourns as an opportunity to participate in prayer and their practice of hospitality. Over several months I noticed that one of the monks was not able to participate in the monastic choir. He came to the times of daily office but sat at a distance toward the back of the basilica. He was not allowed to process with the others, was denied his rotation as an organist, and was observably isolated from the community's work. I suspect that he took his meals in a separated context, also, as the *Rule* prescribes. I never asked any of the monks about his situation because I wanted to respect the boundaries of their community, believing that this discipline was an internal matter. Ultimately, he reappeared on the organ bench and was fully integrated into the services. I detected a joyfulness in his playing, a greater amplitude of the community's fine organ, as a sign of restoration. When he became ill a couple of years later and eventually died, he received all the care his community could offer as they sat vigil with him, two monks at a time in his final hours, and then buried him in the monastic cemetery as a restored confrere, brother in faith. I witnessed in part the full trajectory of exclusion from and reclamation to the community.

There are several New Testament texts that deal with the kind of exclusion noted in 3:14.[24] In 1 Corinthians 5:3–5, Paul presses for harsh discipline, "destruction of the flesh," for the member of the church who has been living with his father's wife. Second Corinthians 2:5–11 also urges a process of punishment and forgiveness for one who has caused harm to come to Paul. The offender need not endure excessive trauma; it is in the community's best interest to find a way to comfort him. As Malherbe writes, "It is as a brother that the individual

24. In the Gospel tradition, see Matt. 18:15–18 and Luke 17:3.

errs and as a brother that he continues to be admonished."[25] This sense of enduring bond makes punishment bearable for those who must inflict it and those who must endure it. Discipline can inflict great harm if not offered with discretion and compassion. Standing with the offending one enables that one not to be regarded as enemy, but as one who has a common spiritual destiny.

"Admonish them," he says, "as brethren," do not insult them as enemies. He who admonishes his brother, does it not publicly. He does not make an open show of the insult, but he does it privately and with much address, and grieving, as hurt, and weeping and lamenting. Let us bestow therefore with the disposition of a brother, let us admonish with the good will of a brother, not as if we grieved at giving, but as if we grieved for his transgressing the commandment.

Chrysostom, *Homilies on Galatians, Ephesians, Philippians, Colossians, Thessalonians, Timothy, Titus, and Philemon,* in Nicene and Post-Nicene Fathers, vol. 13, ed. Philip Schaff (Edinburgh: T & T Clark, 1994), 395.

What procedure the apostolic writer has in mind with his injunction is not clear, but he cares chiefly for the integrity of the boundaries of the Christian community and the restoration of the offending ones. He proposes additional instruction, which I render in a more inclusive way: "Do not look on them as enemies, but warn them as believers" (v. 15). By this the writer assumes that the community needs to live in bonds of trust and enduring faith. Overtly this suggests that an imminent return of Christ is not in his thinking; rather ensuring the sanctity of the community that prepares for the day of the Lord however distant in the future is his priority. Only a bounded and secure community can live in anticipation and make present commitments evident to neighbors that are observing their way of life.

3:16–18

Apostolic Benediction

Some ecclesial traditions regard the benediction as an insignificant way to conclude a service of worship, as sort of a pastoral goodbye,

---

25. Malherbe, *The Letters to the Thessalonians,* 459.

"see you next week," or an opportunity to re-preach the sermon. We know how well that goes! Yet when we reflect further, we understand how important this "good word" actually is. Among Baptists in Myanmar, one cannot pronounce the benediction without having been ordained. Only those set aside with this formal recognition can lift their arms in blessing and send forth their congregation duly empowered. Rather than the sermon being the high point of the liturgy, it is the benediction. Congregants look forward to this pastoral blessing, and when it is well-crafted and familiar, it can be sustaining and, more likely, remembered.

I remember a pastor regularly using Philippians 4:4–7 as his benediction. These words sent us forth with renewed confidence and hope.

> Rejoice in the Lord always; again, I will say, Rejoice. Let all men [author's interpretation: persons] know your forbearance. The Lord is at hand. Have no anxiety about anything, but in everything by prayer and supplication with thanksgiving let your requests be made known to God. And the peace of God, which passes all understanding, will keep your hearts and your minds in Christ Jesus.

As I was experiencing anxiety in the fundamentalist takeover of the first seminary I served, the phrase "be anxious for nothing" was a reminder to place greater trust in God. The repetition of a familiar benediction provides reassurance to a congregation. The members depart feeling both blessed and strengthened. While every participant in a congregation has the power to bless others through word and deed, the ecclesial symbolism of the shepherd of the flock offering a benediction is enduring. Clergy need to use this liturgical opportunity to its fullest, as these examples illustrate.

Think of the memorable benediction of William Sloane Coffin:

> May God give you the grace never to sell yourself short;
> Grace to risk something big for something good; and
> Grace to remember that the world is now too dangerous
>   for anything but the truth and
> too small for anything but love.

Two of my favorite pastors, female copastors in Nashville, Tennessee, currently use this benediction:

> In our coming and in our going,
> May we be attentive to the world around us,
> May our hearts be open,
> May our minds be wise,
> May our lives be filled with hope;
> May our spirits be filled with love,
> Beloved friends, may all be blessed;
> May you be blessed,
> Amen.[26]

A pastoral couple in North Carolina fashioned this blending of OT and NT texts, weaving the Aaronic blessing from Numbers 6:22–27, Micah 6:8, and the Great Commandment:

Now, may the Lord bless you and keep you.
May God's face shine upon you; may God be gracious to you.
May God give you grace to love with all your heart,
That you may do justice;
To love with all your soul,
That you may show kindness;
To love with all your mind,
That you may walk humbly with your God.
Friends, go from this place to love the Lord your God with all
    your might,
And love your neighbor as yourself.
Go in peace, to follow Christ. Amen.[27]

Their congregations depart with a graceful sending forth. Benedictions matter.

---

26. This comes from Rev. April Baker and Rev. Dr. Amy Mears, Glendale Baptist Church, Nashville, Tennessee.
27. This benediction is originally from Rev. Dr. Russ Dean and Rev. Amy Jacks Dean, Park Road Church in Charlotte; its present adaptation as included is from Rev. Dr. Paul Simpson Duke and Rev. Dr. Stacey Simpson Duke, First Baptist Church, Ann Arbor, Michigan.

The writer of 2 Thessalonians offers a tender concluding word, his benediction, to the community who had gathered, no doubt, to hear the letter read aloud in the assembly. We can imagine the excitement of the community as they received this further validation and instruction for their developing church. In the spirit of Paul, he asks the Lord of peace to give them "peace at all times in all ways" (v. 16). The same prayer he offered at the beginning of the epistle (1:2) is now a summative consecration. The prayer is in the form of the priestly blessing in Numbers 6:26, "May the LORD . . . give you peace." Peace has been a theme throughout both epistles; recall 1 Thessalonians 5:13, "be at peace among yourselves," and now in the preceding section of the current chapter the call to admonish a wayward member for the goal of peace in the community. As Wendell Berry writes, "The relentlessness of tragedy is redeemed by the persistence of grace."[28] The community's exercise of grace toward those they desire to restore will produce peace.

The conflicts that have arisen in the community—and the writer knows that there will be more—need not displace what God desires to grant them, which is God's own peace. A constant in the Pauline tradition, peace from God "passes all understanding" (Phil. 4:7). Peace is a part of every greeting Paul writes to the churches. While similar to the common greeting other Greek-speaking letter writers employed, the apostle offers his own distinctive stamp.

Gordon Fee unpacks this Pauline locution. "The traditional greeting in the Hellenistic world was *chairein* . . . meaning simply 'Greetings!' . . . In Paul's hands this now becomes *charis* (grace), to which he adds the traditional Jewish greeting *shalom* (peace, in the sense of 'wholeness' or well-being).'"[29] Mentioned first at the beginning of the epistles, grace is what makes peace possible. True disciples know that God's forgiveness is unmerited and that peace amid the cacophony of competing demands from a culture hell-bent on destruction can come only from God.

Verse 16 has a liturgical quality with its repetition and alliteration. "The Lord be with you all" underscores the source of peace.

28. Wendell Berry, *What Are People For?* (New York: North Point Press, 1990), 64–70.
29. Gordon Fee, *Paul's Letter to the Philippians*, The New International Commentary on the New Testament (Grand Rapids: Eerdmans, 1995), 70.

Whether the writer is referring to Jesus as Lord in this context is not clear, but we may assume so since one of the forthright teachings of both epistles is the authority that God has granted to the risen Christ, the designation "Lord" most often referring to him. We cannot overestimate the significance of this for Jewish believers who grew up with the Shema, "Hear O Israel, the Lord is our God, the Lord is one." Taken from Deuteronomy 6:4, this most famous of all Jewish prayers accents the monotheism that sustains their tradition as it is repeated morning and evening. That the Pauline tradition deliberately uses the divine name Adonai from the Hebrew Scripture in referring to Jesus (and then to the Holy Spirit in 2 Cor. 3:17) speaks of significant theological development toward Trinitarian doctrine without compromising the oneness of God.

The prayer is on behalf of the whole community, as a good benediction should be. The apostolic writer longs for them to be at peace among themselves, for this is how their faithful witness can go forward. With this prayer, Johnson believes that the author "calls upon the cruciform Lord to be present among them engendering peaceful relationships as they try to deal with the potentially divisive issue of those among them living in disorderly idleness."[30] Holy living contributes to peace and is the response to Christ who draws them into his body.

The text shifts from this benediction to a closing that identifies the writer. "I, Paul, write this greeting with my own hand. This is the mark in every letter of mine; it is the way I write" (v. 17). I have been contending throughout my treatment of 2 Thessalonians that a pseudonymous writer has produced this text. Clearly within the Pauline tradition, maybe even a colleague of Paul, the writer offers perspective on the teaching of the first epistle, while adding a distinctive further word. The different nomenclature, tonality, and tensions with the first epistle argue, in my judgment, for a different writer, this concluding word notwithstanding. No two Pauline benedictions are alike, however, as the distinctive circumstances of the writing give shape to them.[31]

---

30. Johnson, *1 and 2 Thessalonians*, 222.
31. Witherington, *1 and 2 Thessalonians*, 262.

What may be a case of special pleading, "it is the way I write," refers to the distinctive mark that supposedly authenticates its apostolic origin. Gaventa observes "nowhere else do we find such insistence."[32] While Paul sometimes closes a letter with his signature, the majority do not contain such a signature.[33] Perhaps a controversy about disputed apostolic letters circulating summons this assertion, a question raised in examining 2:2 when the writer said not to be shaken by a letter purporting to come from us, the apostolic team who first visited Thessalonica.

The letter comes to an end with these words: "The grace of our Lord Jesus Christ be with you all" (v. 18). It is the same benediction that concludes the first epistle (1 Thess. 5:28), with exception of "all" being added. American Southerners have long joked about the use of "you all," claiming that their language mirrors the apostolic language. Regrettably, this colloquialism has endured even when it was not racially inclusive. "You all," or more frequently its contraction "y'all," was an in-group kind of speech that gave privilege to those deemed worthy of embrace through class and race. I am not hanging all the blame for racism on whites in the southern part of the United States, even though it was the primary locus of slavery; others have surely maintained their prejudice also. Thankfully, a reckoning is occurring in our time about racial disparities. I will give more attention to this in a further reflection.

Intended to be read as a part of worship, this epistolary closing echoes the thread of peace that laces the two epistles together. Whether expecting an imminent return or preparing for a duration of common life in a community of faith, peace will allow members of the congregation to live in hope. The uncertainty of their times is no stranger to us as we consider how to live in our own time wisely.

Generations have been attracted to the great saga The Lord of the Rings. More popular than ever because of film renderings, we know well the following lament. As J. R. R. Tolkien memorably wrote in the voice of Frodo, "I wish the ring had never come to me. I wish

---

32. Gaventa, First and Second Thessalonians, 133.
33. See 1 Cor. 16:21 and Gal. 6:11 where he signs off with, "See with what large letters I am writing to you with my own hand." And see the endings of Romans, 2 Corinthians, Galatians, Philippians, 1 Thessalonians, and Philemon, among the undisputed letters of Paul, where Paul's name is not mentioned.

none of this had happened." Gandalf answered, "So do all who live to see such times. But that is not for them to decide. All you have to decide is what to do with the time that is given you."[34] We do not decide the time in which we live, and ours is a threatening time. Discord and disease accompany humanity, with every epoch facing the challenge of living wisely, even though the future remains unclear. This is the urgent call of the church: how to understand our time and live in it with faith, love, and hope.

The Thessalonian correspondence seeks to offer comfort in a time when apocalyptic expectations were causing great disruption for a young church. Threatened by the oppression of Rome, persecuted by antagonists toward the proclaimed gospel, challenged by the idolatrous sophistry of the first century, and scorned by the philosophical schools of the Hellenized Mediterranean world, the good news of the resurrection of Jesus Christ and forgiveness in his name continued to move forward. Exhorting the community to not grow weary in well-doing, the author seeks to guide them to mature discipleship. Thankfully, we have these epistles from early Christianity that point to a way of life that embodies God's redemptive purpose. Not only do these letters tell us of the founding apostolic mission in Thessalonica, they also continue to provide insight into ways a community can make an impact that kindles hope both internally and externally.

FURTHER REFLECTIONS
A Time of Racial Reckoning

The church at Thessalonica comprised a diverse community, which may have been its most distinguishing marker. Differences in social class, ethnicity, and religious tradition were not able to pull the community apart, as its ongoing life attests as recipients of these epistles. A bold experiment in diversity, the congregation sought to withstand the conflicts that arose from this variety of persons, and they were able to do so because the body of Christ is sustained by the breath of the Holy Spirit, a mediating presence granting hope.

For over four hundred years, however, the body of Christ in its

34. J. R. R. Tolkien, *The Lord of the Rings: The Fellowship of the Ring*, directed by Peter Jackson (Burbank, CA: Warner Bros. Entertainment, 2001), DVD.

American embodiment has been torn apart by the travesty of chattel slavery and has yet to be fully healed. Forcibly removed from their homeland, enduring the hellish middle passage, undergoing the lash that treated them as less than human, African American brothers and sisters in Christ have been subjected to atrocities, regrettably at the hands of white Christians. The myth that justified slaveholding had a centuries-long reach, and White Christians maintained that the practice would enable them to convert slaves to Christianity. A lingering stain on White Christianity, this subjugation of fellow humans is far from over. Biblical exegesis, theological construction, and ecclesial politics have all participated in the perpetuation of white supremacy.

In recent years, White persons of good will are finally awakening to police brutality, mass incarceration, neighborhood redlining, and ongoing educational disparities.[35] The deaths of Trayvon Martin in Sanford, Florida; Michael Brown in Ferguson, Missouri; Ahmaud Arbery in Brunswick, Georgia; George Floyd in Minneapolis, Minnesota; and Breonna Taylor in Louisville, Kentucky, to name only a few who have been in the news, demonstrate the unspeakable atrocities white persons inflict on persons of color. Kneeling on the neck, shooting in the back, dragging out of a car, culpable law enforcement officers have wreaked sustained violence on many people of color. The leniency which the officers have received is none other than a further perpetuation of racism. It is no wonder that so many Black communities are outraged, protesting, and seeking reparations. I am cheered that White persons are joining in these expressions of resistance as they become more cognizant of their own privilege and seek solidarity by naming their complicity in structures of oppression. While some White persons take a cavalier attitude and say, "why don't you just get over it, that was a long time ago" or "I did not participate in the institution of slavery, so why blame me?," more thoughtful ones see the many layers of structural racism that continue to make a less than even playing field. Thankfully, some

---

35. James H. Cone, *The Cross and the Lynching Tree* (Maryknoll, NY: Orbis Books, 2011), 163, writes, "The lynching of black America is taking place in the criminal justice system where nearly one-third of black men between the ages of eighteen and twenty-eight are in prisons, jails, on parole, or waiting for their day in court." See also Willie James Jennings, *After Whiteness: An Education in Belonging* (Grand Rapids: Eerdmans, 2020).

White people are beginning to educate themselves rather than expect that persons of color will do that for them.

The Black Lives Matter (BLM) movement has fueled new energy for reform of racial inequity. For too many years, Black lives have been treated as expendable, as they were during the long history of slavery. Wide-ranging and loosely organized, the BLM crusade seeks to redress the casual efforts of majority culture to dismantle racism. Its public advocacy is beginning to shape thinking, seeping into the political realm as an urgent and horizonal issue of human rights. Some communities paint streets with language emblematic of the movement, some fly banners, and some continue to host public rallies that communicate their concerns to policing entities. Like the earlier civil rights movement, this expression of resistance to structural racism will not disappear soon, and our nations needs the continuous prodding it provides. Sadly, self-interest moves persons toward greater equity, and White persons will ineluctably acknowledge that America's future will be solidly multicultural, yet more tremors of opposition to the reality will occur.[36]

Too often it has been left to Black scholars, poets, and essayists to write about racial matters. And they have done so magnificently. The works of Zora Neale Hurston, Howard Thurman, James Baldwin, bell hooks, Maya Angelou, Langston Hughes, Alex Haley, Alice Walker, Toni Morrison, and Ta-Nehisi Coates, to name only those with whom I am most familiar, open a vista on the Black experience that most White Americans ignore or remain willfully ignorant of. The challenge has been that whites and Blacks have almost lived in a parallel universe in certain areas of our country, and the educational curriculum has never given full attention to the contributions of these writings. Even in predominantly black schools, whiteness has prevailed in those studied, as the norm has been white self-determining masculinity.

---

36. Harold Bloom's much debated book, *The Closing of the American Mind: How Higher Education Has Failed Democracy and Impoverished the Souls of Today's Students* (New York: Simon and Schuster, 1987), includes no scholars of color in his taxonomy of what should be read by the college student. His critique of how Cornell handled the wave of incoming Black students in the 1970s and going forward is a testament to viewing Blacks through a white lens, thus disparaging the academic promise of Black students.

Commenting on the reality of racism in theological education as well as other forms of education, Willie James Jennings writes,

> The slave legacy of Western education, especially theological education, is lodged deeply in our educational imaginations. It set our work of formation inside a pedagogy of the plantation. Plantations throughout the colonial world were always about more than just cultivating crops and preparing goods and services to be exported throughout the known world. Plantations were also about cultivating leadership and establishing a social order necessary for promoting commerce and civilization.[37]

Other ethnic groups come into play in a time of racial reckoning; however, Asian, Latinx, and other minorities have not suffered the same extremity of discrimination of those who endured slavery. Our nation has demonstrated schizophrenia toward immigrants, some seen as more desirable than others. Persons of color were made to feel more like "conditional citizens" when our former president Donald Trump wanted more European immigrants, but not more from countries he denigrates. By stoking the fears among whites about immigrants replacing them, taking their jobs, he alerted them to the fact that indeed, whites are becoming a demographic minority. Hate crimes are on the rise because of these fears.

Our time of racial reckoning has focused primarily on the educational, economic, and health care disparities Black Americans daily face. When we glibly move past the pain of African Americans by saying "all lives matter," we have not paid sufficient attention to the particularity of their suffering nor their role in reshaping the social landscape. Removing emblems that exalt those who advocated the institution of slavery is only a cosmetic beginning; many more economic measures are required.

A recent article in *The Atlantic* by Clint Smith, "Teaching Should Be Political," which chronicles the academic year (2018–2019) of first year teacher LaQuisha Hall, illumines the challenges of teaching the specifics of racism. Smith notes her developing understanding of the task of teaching: "The work of teaching, for her and for

37. Jennings, *After Whiteness*, 82–83.

her teenage students, was most meaningful when it was a part of a larger commitment to addressing the realities of the historically oppressed and underresourced communities they were growing up in."[38] She helps her students understand, as did James Baldwin's essay "A Talk to Teachers," how the lives of students were compromised by "those streets, those houses, those dangers, those agonies by which they are surrounded, are criminal."[39]

While we may be thankful for this inflection point in our nation's history, we also know that policy changes are necessary to move forward the prospects for Black people to flourish alongside fellow citizens. I can hope that access to education, wealth creation, and physical wellness become a part of the reparations owed to Black Americans.

God loves the diversity of human beings, and Christian communities will reflect that reality as we live into the vision of the reign of God taught by Jesus. The church at Thessalonica began this journey and remains a testimony to including both slaves and free in its community, becoming one in the body of Christ.

---

38. Clint Smith, "Teaching Should Be Political: How to Talk about Race in the Classroom," *The Atlantic*, December 2020, https://www.theatlantic.com/magazine/archive/2020/12/bringing-politics-into-the-classroom/616934/.
39. Cited in Smith, "Teaching Should Be Political."

Postscript: The Enduring Theological Legacy of Paul from the Thessalonian Correspondence

Engaging these brief epistles over the months of writing has opened new vistas of understanding of the nascent Church. While I have long admired and, at times, wrestled with Paul, I believe I have underestimated his sheer theological genius. His construction of a Christian worldview is breathtaking in its sweep of Israel's history, textual mastery, and cultural sensitivity in the first century of the Greco-Roman world.

It would be impossible to think about Christianity apart from Paul. It is not surprising that just over a century ago he was venerated as "the second founder of Christianity."[1]

Actually this title is not overdrawn. Without his rethinking of Israel's prior relationship with God and its expansive vision of inclusion, he could not have found a way to think of Gentiles as a part of God's redemptive determination. Nor could he have re-visioned the messianic promise in the crucified one without deep engagement with the Old Testament and early believers in Jerusalem and Antioch. As the Church's first theologian, his epistles remain foundational for the architecture of Christian theology.

He was as zealous for the mission of Christianity as he was zealous earlier for its extinction, and his conflict with other early Christian leaders as well as the Jewish kinsfolk with whom he disputed the status of Jesus Christ made for significant enduring theological discourse.

---

1. William Wrede, *Paul*, trans. Edward Lummis (London: Philip Green, 1907), 180.

> One of the chief reasons why we will have so many of his letters is that his
> teaching was quickly challenged by varying opponents from both within and
> without the churches he established; it was characteristic of Paul that he did
> not hesitate to respond vigorously to such challenges.
>
> "Introduction," in *The Cambridge Companion to St. Paul,* ed. James D. G. Dunn (Cambridge: Cambridge
> University, 2003), 1.

His literary output was prodigious, responding to the particular
needs or controversies within discrete communities, and there were
those eager to use his name and keep him alive for further generations. He desired a theological conversation with the recipients of
his correspondence. As Bruce Malina and John Pilch note, "Reading
is primarily a social act. Readers and writers always participate in a
social system that provides the clues for filling in implicit information or for reading between the lines."[2] We have seen this in the Thessalonian epistles, especially the first one that is undisputedly from
Paul. He wanted to continue the conversation he had begun when
he and the other missioners arrived in Thessalonica from Philippi.
With too brief a stay by his own admission, he sought to keep the
lines of communication open.

It would not be possible to think of the evangelization of the
Roman Empire, the emergence of the New Testament canon, the
formation of early creeds, the Protestant Reformation, the Wes-
leyan movement, the revolutionary thinking of Karl Barth, the fruitful labor of womanist and feminist scholars in their thinking about
women in ministry, and the new insights on Jewish-Christian relationships apart from the groundbreaking work of the best-known
apostle. His letters have shaped Christians from the early origins
of the faith and continue to do so. His long shadow casts its influence in sacramental theology, church polity, and mission strategy,
not to mention the key areas of Christology, Pneumatology, and
Ecclesiology.

While the Thessalonian correspondence does not flesh out a fully
orbed Pauline Christology, it does give enough of a summary of his

2. Bruce J. Malina and John J. Pilch, *Social Science Commentary on the Letters of Paul*
   (Minneapolis: Fortress, 2006), 2.

preaching in the first epistle (1 Thess. 1:9–10) that enables us to see how Paul's monotheism can absorb the identity of the Son as full participant in God's own mission. Emerging Trinitarian construction moves toward ascribing the fullness of deity for the risen One, and the role of the Spirit is crucial in both Thessalonian Epistles. While the creedal tradition would not codify Trinitarian doctrine until the fourth century, we can see the impact of Pauline thinking of the shared identity of Son and Sending One (Father) that took form in his early writing, a gift to the larger church. The distinctive role of the Spirit emerges as Paul continues to reflect on the ways God is present to humanity.

The apostle Paul is the one who speaks more definitively about what the return of Christ means for those who have placed their hopes in him as he brings all of creation (with humanity) to its concluding acts, and the Thessalonian letters remain focal for this early teaching.

Even though he does not give the detail of the seer of the Apocalypse in his treatment of cosmic eschatology, Paul clearly believes that creation will share in the hopes of being made new as a fitting place for God to dwell in the midst of God's people. Indeed, the images of Parousia, particularly in 1 Thessalonians, do not portend departure as much as presence when Christ returns to meet his own. The earthly exaltation of Christ is the consummating event of the redemptive arc of life, death, resurrection, and return.

The emphasis on prayer in these epistles is paramount. The Spirit is the facilitator of prayer, as we have seen.

For Paul, prayer is prompted by the Spirit and is offered in the Spirit, for "we do not know how to pray as we ought" (Rom. 8:26). True prayer begins with the Spirit who always intercedes for us "with sighs too deep for words." Searching our hearts, cleansing our motives, the Spirit prays according to the will of God.

When I was a professor, I occasionally taught a course with the ambitious title: "Prayer in Christian Tradition." I remember a student who was a relatively new Christian asking me how to begin to pray. I suggested that he begin to listen to the prayer already being prayed within him by the Spirit. Gradually he would be able to give words to the sighs of the Spirit who voiced his deepest longings.

It required the discipline of silence and deep listening, which are important aspects of prayer. The Spirit's desire to make habitation within us is a comforting thought, and our lives in prayer are not solitary pursuits unaided by God's own presence. We pray in the Spirit who guides our intercession, praise, and confession as we are drawn into God's own inner communion.

The Spirit is also the provider of joy. In 1 Thessalonians, Paul speaks of the members of the unseasoned congregation as receiving "the word in much affliction, with joy (*charas*) inspired by the Holy Spirit" (1:6). Only through the Spirit could they bear the trauma of recalibrating all of their social relationships, their mode of worship, and their suspect standing in the larger community. The Spirit granted joy to these early Christians, hardly a superficial giddiness. Etymologically, grace (*charis*) and joy (*chara*) are closely linked, and together they sustain faithful living.

Joy displaces anxiety and creates a more integrated sense of well-being. Joy allows us to sense the promise of the future as we live "on the brink of everything," in the words of Parker Palmer.[3] Joy arises when we decenter ourselves in praise and service and we find wholeness through relating to God and others. Hardship cannot defeat joy, as it is an enduring gift of the Holy Spirit.

Our study of 1 and 2 Thessalonians has provided a window into early Christian thinking about community, culture, the coming of Christ, and perseverance amid suffering. We have seen how Paul and one writing in his name sought to nurture faithful witness in the early generations of those committed to following the way of the risen Christ. The apostolic witness called them to live in community marked by moral character, public accountability, and mutual support and abiding fellowship. Prayer and service even amid crises were the signs of hope, instilled by the Holy Spirit. These marks of fidelity remain indispensable in our time, as well, and the enduring theological legacy of Paul persists as a reliable guide. Thanks be to our triune God.

---

3. Parker Palmer, *On the Brink of Everything: Grace, Gravity and Getting Old* (Oakland, CA: Berrett-Koehler Publishers, 2018).

Select Annotated Bibliography

Bauckham, Richard, ed. *God Will Be All in All: The Eschatology of Jürgen Moltmann*. Minneapolis: Fortress, 2001. Key interpreters of Moltmann's vision of final things, along with additional articles by Moltmann, offer analyses of this foremost theologian's distinctive contribution to the consummation of all things.

Borg, Marcus J., John Dominic Crossan. *The First Paul: Reclaiming the Radical Visionary behind the Church's Conservative Icon*. New York: HarperCollins, 2009. The renowned and popularizing New Testament scholars use the best of critical scholarship to expose the church's conspiracy to silence the radicality of the apostle Paul.

Bridges, Linda McKinnish. *1 & 2 Thessalonians*. Smyth & Helwys Bible Commentary. Macon, GA: Smyth & Helwys, 2008. McKinnish Bridges offers the creative contention that the Thessalonian correspondence is directed to an all-male artisan community, a marketplace setting for this early congregation.

Felder, Cain Hope, ed. *Stony the Road We Trod: African American Biblical Interpretation*. Minneapolis: Fortress, 1991. Consummate interpreter of the New Testament, Felder has assembled premier Black biblical scholars who probe hermeneutical moves for resisting oppression and creating social change.

Gaventa, Beverly Roberts. *First and Second Thessalonians*. Interpretation: A Bible Commentary for Teaching and

Preaching. Louisville, KY: John Knox Press, 1998. This accessible commentary displays adroit use of Greek and constructive approaches for the teaching and preaching ministries of the church.

Gaventa, Beverly Roberts. *Our Mother Saint Paul*. Louisville, KY: Westminster John Knox Press, 2007. Gaventa explores Paul's use of maternal imagery as a key to his apostolic task. Writing in apocalyptic tenor, the apostle uses these metaphors for guidance and comfort.

Johnson, Andy. *1 and 2 Thessalonians*. The Two Horizons New Testament Commentary. Grand Rapids: Eerdmans, 2016. Written from a Nazarene/Holiness perspective, Johnson offers a constructive vision of the theological import of these epistles.

Rowe, C. Kavin. *World Upside Down: Reading Acts in the Graeco-Roman Age*. Oxford: Oxford, 2010. This reading of Acts, drawing from historical and sociopolitical analysis in addition to biblical and theological insights, offers an illuminative view of the challenges of the Pauline mission.

Seitz, Christopher. *The Elder Testament: Canon, Theology, Trinity*. Waco, TX: Baylor University Press, 2018. Seitz offers a vision of canonical unity of the Old Testament, giving special attention to those texts used by the church in its Trinitarian reading.

Witherington, Ben, III. *1 and 2 Thessalonians: A Socio-Rhetorical Commentary*. Grand Rapids: Eerdmans, 2006. This commentary is most helpful in situating Thessalonians in the rhetorical world of the first century. Deeply acquainted with ancient sources, it provides a fresh reading.

Wright, N. T. *Paul and the Faithfulness of God*. Parts 1 and 2. Minneapolis: Fortress, 2013. Wright's magisterial study situates Paul clearly at the intersection of his Jewish, Greek, and Roman context. In his deeply learned view, Paul is the world's first and greatest Christian theologian.

Index of Ancient Sources

Index of Subjects

Abelard, 139
Abraham, 68
abundance. *See* generosity; grace
abuse
  avoiding, 17
  of power, 165
  traditional views and, 139
  See also sexual abuse; *specific topics,*
    e.g., slavery
accountability, 61, 87, 93, 148, 197,
  213
Achaia, 30
action/actions
  Christlike, 185
  divine, 89, 105, 139, 163
  embodied, 73
  harmful human, 33
  Paul's cruciform, 48
  publicly visible, 31
Acts, book of, 2–5
admiration ("holy envy"), 58n16
admonishment, 198–99
Adonai, the name, 203
affirmation, 6, 44, 83, 86–87, 138, 184.
    See also encouragement
African Americans. *See* Black
    Americans
After Virtue (MacIntyre), 54n9
agency, divine and human, 82
agnosticism, 126, 156
alarmist opinions/perspectives, 19, 59, 83
"all lives matter," 208
"always," 81

America. *See* North America; South
    America; United States
American identity, 9
anathema, 39, 157, 197
Angelou, Maya, 207
angels, 62, 141–42, 163
  the archangel's call, 78, 80
anger (divine wrath). *See* wrath/divine
    wrath
Anglicans, 171
"anonymous Christian," 156
Anselm of Canterbury, 138–39
antichrist, 161, 164–65. *See also* "man of
    lawlessness"
Antiochus Epiphanes, 87, 162
anti-Semitism, 27, 39
anxiety, 10–12, 16–17, 49, 96, 120, 125,
  128, 140, 145, 193
  "be anxious for nothing," 200
  joy as displacing, 213
  North American, 10–11
  Paul's, 5, 53, 57
apocalypse/apocalypticism, 15, 17,
  28n6, 59n19, 62, 87–88, 102,
  120, 123–26, 130, 141–43, 148,
  164, 166–67, 177, 195, 205, 212
  apocalyptic language, 59, 76, 78–79,
    83, 141, 145, 159
  See also dispensationalism
apostles, 76
  apostolic witness, xvi, 1–2, 34, 107,
    167, 213
  apostolic work, 36

CPSIA information can be obtained
at www.ICGtesting.com
Printed in the USA
JSHW042258270722
28350JS00001B/10